Francis William Upham

Star of our Lord

Christ Jesus, King of all Worlds, both of Time or Space

Francis William Upham

Star of our Lord
Christ Jesus, King of all Worlds, both of Time or Space

ISBN/EAN: 9783337184209

Printed in Europe, USA, Canada, Australia, Japan

Cover: Foto ©ninafisch / pixelio.de

More available books at **www.hansebooks.com**

STAR OF OUR LORD:

CHRIST JESUS, KING OF ALL WORLDS, BOTH OF TIME OR SPACE.

WITH

Thoughts on Inspiration,

AND THE

Astronomic Doubt as to Christianity.

By FRANCIS W. UPHAM.

AUTHOR OF "THE WISE MEN: WHO THEY WERE; HOW THEY CAME TO JERUSALEM."

The root and the offspring of David, the Bright and Morning Star. Rev. xxii, 16.

NEW YORK:

PHILLIPS & HUNT.

CINCINNATI:

HITCHCOCK & WALDEN.

CONTENTS.

———♦♦♦———

INTRODUCTION.

THOUGHTS ON THE BIBLE.

POWER of the Heart to control the Intellect—Unbelief not of intellectual origin :—in its last analysis, the dislike of the Heart to the Word of God, because of its holiness—That Holiness, convincing evidence of the Divine origin of the Bible—This proof of its Divine origin not confined to the learned only, but open to all —Sir Walter Scott's witness to the One Book—Heine's reproof of those critics who have tried to utter the mystery of the power of the Hebrew Bible.

Unbelief tends to unsettle the Intellect—Example of this in the Fellows of the Royal Society of London —Their Denial of God, and their Denial of Man—Dangerous consequences of such doing away with veneration for the Deity, and respect for Humanity—Some of those recent discoveries which infidel scientists would wrest against the Scripture, in some degree, anticipated, and only intelligible, through its Revelations of scientific truths.

The present forms of scientific Atheism evanescent, like the forms of Atheism that have come before, and others that are sure to come hereafter—Of chief interest as one of many warnings' of an approaching

THE STAR OF OUR LORD.

CHAPTER I.

THE FIRST HISTORIC CYCLE OF TIME.

CHAPTER II.

WAS A STAR FORETOLD?

CHAPTER III.

THE STAR OF OUR LORD ONE OF THE STARS OF HEAVEN.

CHAPTER IV.

THE MIRACLE OF THE GUIDING.

CHAPTER V.

MIRACLE OF THE GUIDING STAR: CONTINUED.

CHAPTER VI.

THE RELATION OF THE UNIVERSE TO CHRIST.

CHAPTER VII.

THE ASTRONOMICAL DOUBT AS TO CHRISTIANITY.

Statement of the Astronomic Doubt—Reaching all, it has more to do with modern Unbelief than all the other intellectual elements in it. Confession of its power by Webster—Reply to it, in five sections—That the Earth is too small to have been the scene of the Advent: answer to this, Sec. I, II—That the Knowledge of those Wonders of Grace of which, according to the Scriptures, the Earth has been the scene, must have been meant for all the intelligent universe: answer to this, in the Revelation that in some Hereafter all the Worlds will be put under that New Race of Man born of the Will of God, Sec. III—Inmost power of this Doubt: answer to this, in connection with what has been said, in Chapter VI, of the mysterious presence of the Word of God in all Nature and all Life...............................

NOTE.—So far as this Doubt arises from what seems to it the insufficiency of the Christian System, it is a sufficient reply to it to show what that System is, so far as here brought out for that purpose. Its truth is not here in question; and the argument is addressed to believers in the Bible. As to reasons for which, see The Wise Men, 187, 188.

CHAPTER VIII.

THE WORSHIP OF CHRIST BY THE MAGI.

Glance at the self-evidencing character of the history of their Pilgrimage—Two of its lesser difficulties con-

CHAPTER IX.

THE LESSON TO MEN OF SCIENCE.

CHAPTER X.

THE HOLY INNOCENTS.

BRETHREN, we are now ere long to part asunder, and the Lord knoweth whether ever I shall live to see your faces again. But whether the Lord hath appointed it or not, I charge you before God and his blessed angels to follow me no further than I have followed Christ. If God should reveal any thing to you by any other instrument of his, be as ready to receive it as ever you were to receive any truth by my ministry; for *I am very confident the Lord hath more truth and light yet to break forth out of his holy Word.*— *John Robinson's Farewell to the Pilgrim Fathers at Leyden, A. D.* 1620.

As it is owned, the whole scheme of Scripture is not yet understood; so, if it ever comes to be understood, before the restitution of all things, and without miraculous interpositions, it must be in the same way as natural knowledge is come at—by the continuance and progress of learning and liberty; and by particular persons attending to, comparing, and pursuing, intimations scattered up and down it, which are overlooked and disregarded by the generality of the world. For this is the way in which all improvements are made; by thoughtful men's tracing on obscure hints, as it were, dropped us by nature accidentally, or which seem to come into our minds by chance. *Nor is it at all incredible, that a book, which has been so long in the possession of mankind, should contain many truths as yet undiscovered.* For all the same phenomena, and the same faculties of investigation, from which such great discoveries in natural knowledge have been made in the present and last age, were equally in the possession of mankind several thousand years before. And, possibly, it might be intended that events as they came to pass should open and ascertain the meaning of several parts of Scripture.—*Butler's Analogy of Natural and Revealed Religion, A. D.* 1736.

IT has been with religion as with the glory of arms and with the splendor of literature. According to a mysterious but indisputable law, it is always from east to west that progress, light, and power have proceeded. Like the light of day, they are born in the East, but it is to arise and to shine more and more in proportion as they advance toward the West.—*M. de Montalembert.*

THOUGHTS ON THE BIBLE.

IS it said, The Mind must decide according to the evidence it has? The mind sees; it reasons, it never decides; and that a man always decides according to the evidence is no more true than that he never does. Out of nothing the jealous heart makes evidence. The angry heart makes nothing of what is evidence. In Unbelief the mind is the instrument of something whose origin and seat of power is in other regions of the soul. It is the Heart—here using the word as when it is written, The fool hath said in his heart, No God—it is the Heart that sways the intellect, alike in the unbelieving disobedience of the believer, and in the open denial of the Bible. In its last analysis, Unbelief is the dislike of the heart to the word of God, because that word sits in judgment on its sins. Were man all mind, all that is said by all the long array of witnesses, whom the prince of this world calls to the stand to swear foolishly or falsely against the Bible, would weigh as nothing against *the proof in its holiness of its divine origin.*

PROOF OF THE BIBLE OPEN TO ALL.

Though some little part of the evidence for the Bible be open only to some few of the learned, very much more of it is entirely within the common reach;

and there is one kind of its evidence, apart from and superior to all the others, that is not hidden away in the Astor Library; it is open to all. It requires no critical learning, no searching of the past. It comes with the book, and it goes with it wherever the book goes. It is the Voice of the Book, the voice of no other. That voice speaks in no earthly tone. It is a voice from the Holy One, saying, "Be ye holy, for I am holy." It is a voice of warning, saying, "Turn ye, for why will ye die?" It is a voice in sadness, saying, "They will not come unto me that they might have life." The soul may not at once hear this divine tone in every part of the book; but hearing it in any part thereof, it hears that, which so hearing nowhere else, and knowing it to be God's own voice, it is sure the book is, as no other book can ever be, God's own Book.

In the loud tumult of passion within, in the din of life's many voices, the soul may not always hear this Divine voice. Scott—whose heart, burning with Scottish love and pride, yet had more sympathy with the murderer, Claverhouse, than with those martyrs slain for the word of God, who kindled a light of glory that shall never fade over Scottish heath, and moor, and glen, and mountain cave, and those waters where women fastened to the stake were drowned* by the rising tide of the Solway—Scott,

---

* "Upon the 11th of May, 1685, Margaret Lauchlane and Margaret Wilson were brought forth for execution. They put the old woman first into the water, and when the water was overflowing her, they asked Margaret Wilson what she thought of her. She said, 'What do I see but Christ wrestling there?'

when near his end, said to his son-in-law, "Read to
me." "What book shall I read?" said Lockhart;
"There is but One," the dying man replied: the ear
of the soul, too much closed in life, opening in death.

Heine—the rarest spirit in the German world of
letters since Göthe; whose untranslatable songs the
boys and women of the Fatherland know by heart,
of a soul so unique that it laughs at critical analysis
as he did at every thing, an atheist who in years of
pain said he made his peace with God, yet in so
strange a mood as to scandalize the Christian as
much as it provoked the infidel, of so mocking a will
as to be cast out of every communion, whom all must
censure, pity, and wonder at, a witness whose witty,
burning scorn of unrealities proves the worth of his
testimony to what is real—Heine said of the criticism
that from the time of the Greek, Longinus, until now,

Margaret Wilson sang Psalm xxv from the seventh verse, read the
eighth chapter of Romans, and then the water covered her."—
Record of the Kirk Session of Pennington, the native parish of
Margaret Wilson, February 25, 1711, twenty-six years after
this martyrdom. It also states: "The Session having certain
knowledge from eye-witnesses of the foresaid sufferings, many
living that have all these fresh in their memory do attest the
same." The Record of the Session of Kirkinner, the native
parish of the elder Margaret, states, April 15, 1711: "That she
was of known integrity and piety from her youth; was in her
own house taken off her knees in prayer and carried to prison;
was sentenced by Sir Robert Grier, of Lagg, to be drowned at
a stake within the flood-mark, just below the town of Wigton."
This perpetuation of testimony by these Churches was at the
request of the General Assembly of the Church of Scotland.
The graves of these martyrs are in the town named. The
elder Margaret was about seventy years old, the younger was
eighteen.

has so often tried to utter the mystery of the power of the Hebrew Bible, "Vain words! vain tests of human judgment! It is God's work, like a tree, like a flower, like the sea, like man himself. It is the Word of God. He that has lost his God can there find him again; and toward him who never knew him, it wafts the spirit and the breath of the Divine word." *

UNBELIEF TENDS TO UNSETTLE THE INTELLECT.

The Soul of Man dreads this known voice of its Maker. The heart calls upon the intellect to discredit it. The intellect hears and obeys, but obeys with a complaining that fills the world,† the wailing

---

* Heine, in his inimitable way, says: "The Jews, who are well versed in valuables, well knew what they were about when, at the burning of the second temple, they left the golden and silver vessels of sacrifice, the candlesticks and lamps, and even the richly-jeweled breastplate of the high-priest behind them, and saved only the Bible. It is a plain old book, modest as nature itself, and as simple, too—like the sun that warms, or the bread that nourishes us. It is indeed justly called Holy Writ."

† In "Childe Harold" this unrest of unbelief broke into the world of poetry in all the grandeur of a storm, its deep tones once subsiding into this exquisite cadence:

> "Yet if, as holiest men have deemed, there be
> A land of souls beyond the sable shore,
> To shame the doctrine of the Sadducee
> And *sophists, madly vain of dubious lore;*
> How sweet it were in concert to adore
> With those who made our mortal labors light!
> To hear each voice we feared to hear no more!"

Now, the unconscious frequent repetitions of the Byronian skepticism, without its stormy sublimity of power, by feeble poets, such as Matthew Arnold and many others, as in these lines, good as the best where all are commonplace—

> "There is no rest at all, afar or near,
> Only a sense of things that moan and go—

of the Intellect of Man coerced to this work. And whenever this coercion by the heart largely succeeds in making it do this work, the Intellect of the World strongly tends to go mad. Of this a passing illustration may now be seen in the vagaries of some few English philosophers and men of science.* A logical

---

have become insufferable, mingled as this whining usually is with the poetaster's insincere confession that he could have been a poet had he been born in some congenial and noble pagan or feudal past: as if Paris were not pagan enough or Mexico mediæval enough; as if this century were not so rich in the heroic as to set little store by heroes, a time of high achievement and of higher aspirations, and thrilling in its heart with the influences of the Spirit of the Lord; confronting great dangers, no doubt, yet with such powers, and hopes, and prophecies, as to prove what was written of old: Say not of former times, they are better than the present, for thou dost not reason rightly concerning the matter !

* For the moment they have almost made out to pass themselves off for British science. A little while ago the "London Spectator" said: "We ask any one who knows English society at all, if we exaggerate when we say there are hundreds of able men in England who refer honestly and confidingly to the authority of science, exactly as men once referred to the authority of the Church, who disbelieve in God, or rather in God's government, because, as they think, Science has dispelled that ancient delusion." As this authority it names "Huxley, Tyndall, and the rest." Somewhat the like may be true as to this country. But this is mistaking for the power of a steam-engine the black cloud and sparks thrown off by the fire that burns within. In both countries the scientists who do the work are Christian men ; as was Faraday, as Morse, as Maury, whose dying blessing to his children was, "The peace of God which passeth all understanding be with you all." Soon after "The Wise Men" was printed Professor Morse wrote to the author—it was then midwinter—to come and see him. The venerable man was in his spacious library, his tall form erect, his eye not dim, nor his natural force abated. A large open Bible was on the library

necessity drives them on from the denial of his Word
to the *denial of God* as the ruler of the world, and
this chastisement of their sin farther drives them on
from this denial of God to *the denial of Man*. These
Fellows of the Royal Institution of London banish
the Omnipresent to an almost inconceivable remote-
ness from the worlds he made, and, so far as man is
concerned, annihilate the Eternal, by saying, in con-
tradiction of laws out of which no mind can think,
however much it may suppose it does, that matter de-
velops all things—life, thought, feeling, and will—out
of itself, by an evolvement without meaning and without end.   Thus—like a railway train supposed to have
its cranks ever turning, wheels ever revolving, by the
self-contained conflict of fire and water ever evolving
force—the world, moving on by itself, passes out of its
Maker's care.   Reason and conscience compel them
to mutter his holy name, and they say nothing can
be known of him ; or they deny him every thing that,
so far as man is concerned, amounts to any thing.
Their God can answer no prayer, can hear none.
He is deaf and dumb.   Man to him is nothing.   He
is nothing to man.   With wit enough to make every
thing, he has not sense enough to take care of any
thing.   As a thoughtless boy blows away a soap-
bubble, he has blown the world from him away.   He
has given the world over to blind chances within itself, and by the world may as well be forgotten.

---

table.   He laid his hand upon it, and speaking with earnestness
and reverence, almost his first words were these : "*I know of
no better employment for my last years than to give them to the
study of this book.*"

These Fellows of the Royal Institution, having rid the world of its worship of Him in whom it lives and moves and has its being, with a remorseless consistency that shows a latent capacity for reasoning, in an equally convincing way, go on to rid man of belief in himself; and denying to our Father in heaven all that is attractive, they deny to his children all that is humane, saying, Man is a beast of a larger brain than the tiger, and when his life's fitful fever is over, sleeps forever in the abyss of annihilation with his kinsman, the baboon.

UNBELIEF HOSTILE TO THE PEACE OF SOCIETY.

Were their power equal to their conceit, these infidels would snatch from sin the hope of salvation, from misery the thought of heaven, from poverty the weapon of prayer ; they would give over the little ones of God to the wicked, whose tender mercies are cruel ; they would relieve wealth of the sense of accountability, destroy the self-control that takes hold on immortality, unchain the tiger in the human breast.

The peace of society is only possible through the adjustment to each other of those divine and human forces in that inner world of thought and feeling, of which the outer world of fact is expression, image, and effect. The widely prevailing negation of the presence and power of God in nature, in life, and in the government of man, makes in both worlds a great void ; then into the vacuum comes the sin-avenging, commissioned storm—as at the close of the last century it came to Bible-denying, Christian-murdering France—and before the wild fury of that equilibrium-restoring tempest, ever go the exalted ravings of philosophic and scientific lunatics.

ANTICIPATIONS OF SCIENTIFIC TRUTH IN SCRIPTURE.

To poison truth is as real a sin as to poison the Croton River; yet these celebrity-loving lecturers seek to wrest against the Scriptures some scientific truths which they did not discover, but which they have interfused with crudities and falsities that transform them into grotesque and malignant errors. The field of the Bible is the spiritual, which the eye sees, the ear hears not; and yet even of some of those *natural* truths, the knowledge of which they suppose to be wholly modern, and whose experimental verification is of recent date, something is shown in the passing glimpses of scientific truth revealed in Holy Scripture.

Thus: the new evidence that races of plants and animals are earth-born products, indigenous in certain circles of the globe, and that new races of plants and animals appeared in some of the past æons of this planet, accords with the revelation, that while the Father of our spirits breathed into man "the breath of lives," there was given to the Earth, by the going forth of his Word, a plant and animal producing power.*   This Power, immanent in the globe through

---

* " And God said, Let the Earth bring forth the living creature after his kind." Gen. i, 24.   In " The Six Days of Creation," Dr. Lewis points to this power.   Once seen, the wonder is every body did not see it before.   First, The power is revealed ; " God said," and his saying is doing.   Second. When God said, " Let there be light," nothing is revealed between the word and its result ; the action of the power seems *immediate.*   It is *mediate*

all the cycles of its duration, in itself being ever the same, those products, of which it is one of the factors, would ever preserve a certain likeness, and it may be a seeming continuity ; and yet, their other factor

---

in the creation of animals ; it empowers the Earth to bring forth living creatures. Between immediate and mediate divine power the Scripture makes not, usually, the distinction we make ; it speaks as when *we* say, " God made us;" but after saying, The animal kingdom is earth-born, goes on to say, (v. 25,) God made the living creatures, taking care the scientific truth shall not hide the moral truth. Third, This law is revealed ; the earth is to bring forth animals producing their kind. Was this power given for once only ? As the result of each of the other goings forth of the divine word is permanent, so it would seem this must be. Yet, as the earth-born living creatures produce their kind, the power given to the Earth is evidently to be put forth at intervals ; and, doubtless, at intervals commensurate with the vastness which Dr. Lewis has proved to be in the time-scale of the world's generation.

That new living things have been formed by chemical art, animalculæ made in the laboratory, has several times been asserted; as also the spontaneous generation of minute living creatures. Up to this hour there is no proof of either ; but, were the latter proved, it would seem to be evidence of the generative power in the Earth as still existing, and stirring in peculiar conditions in a humble way. The doing of the former is not given up ; and if the news were telegraphed, true beyond a doubt, that it had been done in the laboratory at Bowdoin, Middletown, or elsewhere, there would doubtless be a widespread feeling that the Bible religion must end. But this would only be because what there is in the Bible has not been brought out, or rather because he who brought it out has not been listened to while every skeptic had a hearing ; for it would only show that man had reached to the threefold generative power (see II. 20. 24) which the Bible reveals as abiding in the globe ; something, perhaps, no more impossible than that he should have reached to, and gained some control over, the electric power which seems to pervade all nature.

being variable, those products must have ever changed with the great changes in the forming world. Geology has partially traced out some of the workings of this power in the ages before man was made. It still abides in this planet; and when this æon ends in fire, as the Bible reveals it will, "and the elements shall melt with fervent heat," it may be, that, rising to higher effects in the new conditions of the globe, this power will clothe with plant and animal life, surpassing the beauty of all before, the new earth of the sons of God.

Thus : the experimental verification of the unity of certain of the known forces in nature is recent; but the thought that there is only one substance and one force runs clear through old philosophic thinking, and that such is the fact is revealed. The loss of the oriental interpretation of the genesis, when the Church with all the wealth of her ancient records passed over from Asia into Europe, obscured this revelation; and when that great cycle of time and thought, the Ancient World, came to an end, this thought nearly died out from human thinking. Modern science treated as an element every thing it could not decompose, and discountenancing intuition, wisely proceeded by experiment and classified by observation. Beginning at the circumference, it humbly, cautiously, yet swiftly, sounded its experimental way toward the center, and this inductive science now begins to come in sight of these grand old central, intuitive, and religious ideas.* It is

* That modern science would at last prove the old idea—sure from Scripture, and born, it may have been, of oldest revelation—

natural enough that some of its votaries are driven by this glimpse of them almost out of their senses. In the whirl of their wonder, they loosen their hold on the experimental method by which Baconian science wrought its toilsome way into the secret chambers of nature ; they give themselves over to the guiding of the imagination ; they lapse into unscientific ways, and distractedly mix up physics and metaphysics ; they wildly run out true ideas into heathenish speculations ; and, talking of what they know little about, they prate of the religion of science and the science of religion.*

These things are only a little more evidence that Theology, though not unaffected by prevailing opinions

---

became my opinion years ago, and with it a belief in the future harmonizing of much of modern thought with much of the thought in the old world in which the Scripture was given : of which more hereafter. But I did not look for the experimental proof of the one substance in my time, nor do I understand this to be as yet. Baconian science has done great things in discovering some of the hidden forces and resolving them into one ; it has not done the like as to the so-called *elements ;* and to assume their sameness would be to forego the rewards that go with the experimental verification of intuitive ideas. To give the reasons for calling the ideas of one substance and one force intuitive, would be to discuss the nature and range of the intuitive power ; and here it is enough, that the idea of one substance and one force was old, common, and long held. In spite of the fifty elements, and more, that yet hold their places in chemistry, the belief in but one substance has become that of many chemists. In this they agree with the Alchemists, the last workers in the old cycle of thought, who aimed to reach the one substance.

* See the " Chips " and " Lectures on the Science of Religion " by Max Müller—a man with a magical art of popularizing what he does not understand.

and usages, even in error has power to rule the ebb and flow of human thought, as the moon the tides. From out of the poisonous fumes of a sensuous religionism there went forth a little time ago a word of vanity, the all-reconciling, all-explaining, talismanic word, Development. Of course there now goes forth, in the subservient sphere of earth-born scientific gnosticism, the magical, wonder-working, open sesame, Evolution.

EVANESCENCE OF THE PRESENT FORMS OF ATHEISM.

Those forms of philosophic and scientific atheism that do now appear will soon of themselves resolve to nothingness, and in their place will others appear, to pass away. In themselves, these things are more curious than alarming. These are the effervescings and the exhalations of decay. It is the corrupting of the Old World that breeds these things, and across the whole purifying breadth of the waters sends them over here with the opera bouffe and the cholera. There were such things before, and more will come after. The air hath bubbles as the water hath, and these are of them. It is only the spirit of this evanescence that is alarming, and this only as a vanishing warning of what is of lasting and world-wide moment.

THE FAITH-CRISIS THAT NOW IS, AND IS TO COME.*

The Holy Ghost, who came to convince of sin and of righteousness, has purified the eye till it sees in

* Of a faith-crisis the signs are clear. In the Decree of the Vatican Council, (A. D. 1870,) *De Fide Catholicæ*, On Catholic

the three orders equally ordained of God, concurrent
in their function, independent in their sphere, sees
in the Family, in the State, and in the Church, the
Beautiful, the Good, the Just, as they were never seen

Faith, it is declared—"*Late nimis per orbem vagata*, there is
too widely spread through the world the doctrine of rationalism
or naturalism, that labors with all its might to exclude Christ
from the life and morals of nations ; and the true God and his
Christ being denied, *multorum mens*, the minds of many have
fallen into the abyss of pantheism, materialism, and atheism.
Moreover, as this impious doctrine is spreading every-where, it
has unhappily come to pass, *ut plures etiam e catholicæ ecclesiæ
filiis a via veræ pietatis aberrarent*, that not a few even of the
children of the Catholic Church have wandered from the way
of true piety." This seems to be the reason assigned for the
Convocation at Rome of all the Catholic Bishops ; and whatever
be thought of how it met the crisis, the fact has passed into
history, that the only Council of the Catholic Churches for the
last three hundred years was convened in view of Infidelity, or,
more exactly, of Atheism.

In 1860, a Book having in its seven authors a weight of authority, came forth from the ecclesiastical Universities of Oxford
and Cambridge, denying inspiration, prophecy, and miracle.
Those "Essays and Reviews" called forth much zeal in the
Christians in the British Isles, and yet these facts remain : Of
the five living writers of that book, two have since been raised
to the headship of houses of Oxford, and another to the
rank of a bishop ; four thousand of the clergy of the establishment hold similar heresies, though all have signed the articles,
pray out of the Prayer-book, and recite the Creeds ; and such
teaching has since been decided to be permissible under the
ecclesiastical law of the realm.

If there be any Churches whom this conflagration has not
reached, the neighboring houses are on fire, and they may as
well take the warning. Dr. J. F. Hurst, whose "History of
Rationalism" gives the causes and course of this state of things,
in his "Essay on Modern Theology in Holland," says : "The
conflict in Holland is only part of the general warfare. The

before, and the Spirit now impels man to realize what He thus reveals in vision. The eye of the mind sees the vision darkly, for it is darkened by the heart, which resists the divine impulsion. The heart knows not itself, nor the power working to unknown ends. The heart feels that the religion of the Spirit is both destructive and constructive, and it mourns what is passing and fears what is coming to pass. The light shineth in darkness and the darkness comprehendeth it not.

In heathen Rome when the Christians came to the strength of numbers there came a union of Church and State, brought about more by policy than principle, and ever resulting in the struggle of each to subjugate the other. This course of events was foreseen by the apostles, some of its causes were at work while they were living, and its end was foretold by the Lord. The heart now makes a last struggle to prolong this sacerdotal and political misery from which the redemption of the Church "draweth nigh," and foreseeing its failure in this, it prepares open general war against Christ. It has aroused that Culture

---

lines of truth and error extend the whole length of Christendom. In the American Church only the skirmishers have been engaged. The time is yet to come—it will likely reach us before the century closes—when the strife between orthodoxy and skepticism will be as intense, as bitter, and the result as far reaching ,as any page of the history of the Church recalls. But the cause of truth has never permanently lost ground by these conflicts. Let us go on devising, planning, warming with our work, following our enemies to their own chosen battle fields, cherishing the broadest sympathy with every partner in arms of whatever name, each believingly and cheerfully striving for a victory that shall cover every acre of the ground."

which, found only in Christendon owes much of its strength to Christianity, to withstand in all possible ways the onward world-wide movement of the Holy Ghost. Some of this culture is sensitive to his influence, and it sometimes seems to itself fighting Christianity while warring with what is anti-Christian ; and yet much of all the culture of Christendom, whether churchly or worldly, is aristocratic, sin-cherishing, and in spirit is bitterly hostile to the Spirit of the Lord. In the selfishness of its self-love, this patrician culture secretly betrays or openly wars against the religion of Him whose blessing, seeking out neither the strength of riches nor the splendors of power, neither Rothschild nor Bonaparte, falls on the poor in spirit ; the religion of labor, of self-denial, of purity, of truth ; that manger-born religion which preaches the equality of all souls before God, whence follows equality before the law ; the religion of Him who earned his daily bread till he was about thirty years of age by one of the handicrafts of Roman slaves ; the religion of Him who said, " My father worketh hitherto and I work ; " the religion of Him who, striking the chains from serf and slave, calls the people into being, calls into being the laity,* fulfilling that

---

* See Dr. Stevens' " Essay on the Priesthood of the People " in the " Methodist Quarterly Review," January, 1873. Few subjects are now of equal moment, whether regard be had to its religious or to its political importance ; and few such subjects have been treated with like breadth and clearness of thought, or so fairly brought within the comprehension of all. Any form of Christianity false to the teachings of the New Testament, and to the belief of the early Christians as to this doctrine, must in the end prove so hostile to all civil liberty that one

divine purpose to the beginning whereof St. Peter witnessed, saying " to the strangers scattered throughout
Pontus, Galatia, Cappadocia, Asia, and Bithynia, Ye
are a royal priesthood ;" and St. John, saying to the
seven Churches in Asia, " Unto Him that hath made
us kings and priests unto God be glory and dominion
forever."

MISTAKE AS TO THE CAUSES OF THIS CRISIS.

There are some who think that Christianity driven
by this assault gives up aggressive war, which would
be its confessed defeat, and its abandonment of all
claim to a divine origin.   This mistake is the reversal
of the fact, the opposite of the truth.   *The Nazarene
delivers this battle.*   His religion stands not still ; it
has no tears for the beauty of the pagan past ; it wills
the unchristianized present shall not stay ; it wages
war with the exclusiveness or spirit of *caste* that
hardly can be exorcised from a Family, a State, or the
Church ; it has good-will to man, but cannot look
upon his iniquities with the least allowance ; and of
the approaching conflict, whatever the end designed
in the eternal councils be, that conflict is no evidence
of the weakness, it is the sign of the growing power
of Christianity.   For much of the culture of Christendom now begins to see the Christian religion is
not a device to hold the working classes quiet while
the rich and the great enjoy the hard earnings of
misery, and keep as their own the gold which repre-

or the other must perish ; and it would be well that this paper
should be read by every one in our Republic, which, though it
has no foes to fear without, has many foes within.

sents labor and suffering ; begins to see the Christian religion is not a sensuous luxury for pampered and dreaming intellects, the æsthetic sabbath delectation of fashion rivaling the opera, the gilding of social pageantry, the fine touch that harmonizes the vanities of life with the solemnities of death ; knows the hour cometh, and now is, when the Father will have no patterning after those withdrawn splendors of Samaria or of Jerusalem ; hears the voice of one not clad in colored garments, his leathern girdle binding round his loins the robe of the desert, hears what sensuous religionists will not hear though it warn them of the " wrath to come, " hears the barbarian voice of the uncultured Baptist sternly cry in the wilderness of the world, " Prepare ye the way of the Lord ;" sees the Star, as in the vision of the apostate Seer, blazing terror ; knows all farther trust in any priestly compromising with sin is gone forever ; feels driven to choose between God and Mammon ; must submit to the holy and equal laws of the Nazarene or utterly reject him ; and *therefore*, making up its mind to go on in its own name, it looks to the heavens, saying,* there is nothing

---

* These are words from the Westminster Review: " When once the ambition to know the unknowable is awakened, Titan will strive upward. Better the Olympian lightning hurl him back, than that he make his way within the misty chambers where it is bred, and find there no Indra, no Thunder-bearer, no Providing Father. Still higher up there soars a glittering peak, far up ! Never may it be his destiny to surmount it. Titan would survey from thence a desolate and spiritless universe. Never may it be given him to scale the footsteps of the throne itself and behold it vacant."

there, and denies the Lord Jesus, saying, We will not have this man to reign over us ; bewildered and beguiled by the old temptation, ever new, "Ye shall not die, ye shall be as gods."

WITHOUT CHRIST, RELIGION AND CIVILIZATION NO LONGER POSSIBLE.

For Christendom to renounce Christ would be the end of all religion.   The patriarchs had the promise of "things not seen," the guiding of a vision whose light brightened into the presence of the Lord, and that childlike feeling of nearness to God which gives to the patriarchs an inexpressible charm, through Christ continueth forever ; but the patriarchal religion belongs to a world that has passed away. The colder Deism preached by Mohammed may be traced to the primeval religion, it became the creed of nations and races, it has nurtured heroes, scholars, and devotees, it has done grand things and lasted long, it still teaches the Koran to the heathen of Africa, but within its circle of great triumphs it is waning to nothingness ; and its history, while it proves the power of Deism as a religion, proves it has no place in the future.

Christendom is from Christ ; and for Christendom to renounce Christianity would be the destruction of the whole frame-work of society.   Christ is every thing for man, or for man there is nothing.   Apart from the revealing of the Father by the Son, it is no longer possible to believe in God ; apart from God, it is not possible to believe in Man.   These two truths survive in the heart of man, or there perish together.

Therefore, the only alternative for life and light in Christ is atheism and barbarism. This is the meaning of the conflict which is to be as to Christianity, and which is now in so much of the thought of our time, often in unsuspected forms, and comes to light in almost every thing—in law-making, in science, in poetry, in the march of armies. Even now the sky is darkening and glowing with the mingled gloom and light of the cloud of this battle. History records not the like. The changes to come in its progress none can foreknow, nor the way or time of its end.

THE WRITTEN WORD THE CENTER OF THIS CONFLICT.

What is Christianity? who are Christians? what in the Christianity among us is of man's selfish device, and what of God? what the positions that must be held in this war?—as to these questions the approaching conflict will bring out a difference of opinion among Christians that will set a man at variance against his father and the daughter against her mother. A man's foes shall be they of his own household, and he that findeth his life shall lose it, and he that loseth his life for Christ's sake shall find it; but the position which must be held or all be lost, the central position, is determined already by the lines of assault upon Christianity; for, begin where they may, whether within what is called the Church or without it, run where they will, they all at last converge to the Bible, and there they all unite. In this unity of direction in so many lines of thought and feeling there is something not of the human will;

this concentration of so many forces at one point is proof of what many deny, that there is in the human world an evil Being at work who is not human.

THE HEART NOT AT ONE WITH ITSELF IN THIS WAR.

The prayer of the Psalmist, "Unite my heart to fear thy name," holds in its small compass more of soul-wisdom than some large books of metaphysics. In the heart the moral feelings are set over against the passions: these gather strength from the seen, those from the unseen; these from the perishable, those from the everlasting; they strive together as to the Bible, and few there be, or none, who can say from the heart at all times, "Thy word is pure, therefore thy servant loveth it." Yet the conscience is so responsive to the word of God that it cannot wholly perish so long as that word is honored; nor can that word be wholly dishonored while the moral nature remains. And more than this, the Living Word and the Written word are so related that no man can hold to the one and despise the other. Not by chance, then, does the prince of this world lead forth a line of attack upon the written word, a parallel line against the moral nature of man, and a third against Christ himself.

The lower nature in man looks with favor upon the denial of Christ, but infidelity will not have it all its own way when the higher nature sees this will be its own destruction. Yet only by this destruction can the prince of this world make the soul like unto his own, and in many ways he seeks this end: as by teaching that what is natural is right, but treating the conscience, which is as natural to a man as his passions, and was meant to be their rule and guide, as a matter of education, a conventional thing, a superstition, a hinderance to freedom and manhood; calling only the sensual natural, and so making the gratification of the appetites and passions their only law; or else saying that men are equally right in following after sin or holiness, their preference for either being a matter of taste or temperament, and their true course to do what they like, even as do the happier brutes—the difference between right and wrong being a difference in name and not in fact;* and thus many perish through the pride of a false knowledge fatally conjoined with lusts of the flesh. Yet when it becomes clear that infidelity would make a world with nothing in it divine or human, would degrade all men and all women to the immoral state of those dangerous classes in great cities whose lusts, cruelties, and crimes act out the gospel of unbelief, there is reason to hope that man will not crucify his immortal longings though full of doubt and pain, will accept neither chimpanzee nor gorilla for his parent, will not choose blind fate for his God, will remember the peace and joy of home, the mother's holy prayer, and human nature recoil from this immediate, unclean damna-

---

* " Nature as we know her is no saint. She comes eating, and drinking, and sinning. If we will be strong with her strength, we must not harbor such disconsolate consciences, borrowed, too, from the consciences of other nations. *Good and bad are but names*, very readily transferable to that or this. All the universe over there is but one thing; this old two face creator-creature, mind-matter, right-wrong, of which any proposition may be affirmed or denied."—*Ralph Waldo Emerson.*

tion. But in the inscrutable councils of the human will, if the choice be atheism, what then? Of the world's last day and hour no man may know ; but this is known: from heaven suddenly the Lord will come, "in like manner as he was seen by men of Galilee to go into heaven," and this coming will be in a time of luxurious civilization.* If, then, the world's choice be atheism, doubtless, the world will not be suffered to pass into barbarism, as left to itself it must. At the height of its unbelief it will hear the archangel call the last judgment of the Son of man.

THE TRUTH THERE IS IN THE BIBLE.

All those who think of giving up the Bible, before they make up their mind to this would do well to find out more of what there is in the Bible. All that volume is no more known than all the volume of nature. Something in each a little child may read, and man knows no more of much there is in each than the babe that shall be born to-morrow. The Bible contains the answers to questions no man has answered, and no man living can answer ; and to find out all there is in it is impossible. No one soul can inbreathe all its lifegiving. Nor can any one time, for the Bible is the book for all time. In it there is reserve of wisdom from which man cannot foreknow what will come. Each successive generation only feels a little more of its unsearchable infinity of power.

In the Bible there is the Divine Breath whereby,

---

* Luke xvii. 26, 27, 30.

in the beginning, man "became a living soul." *
That Divine Breath so passed from the soul, that
what man calls life, the Scripture calls death.   Christ
quickeneth this death.   By "the Spirit of Christ
which was in them," prophets prophesied ; † words
of the Old Testament are so ascribed to Christ that
a reader of the later Scripture only, could not but
think they were spoken by our Lord when he dwelt
among us in the form of man ; ‡ and when he drew
his last breath on the cross, he so repeated the
opening of one of the Psalms as to make the whole
of that Psalm his dying voice.‖   Our Lord said, " I
am the Life : § because I live ye shall live also ; " ¶
and he said, " The words that I speak, they are spirit
and they are life."**   There is, therefore, in the
Bible more than that Divine Inbreathing through
which the Adam became a living soul ; for "the first
man was of the earth, the second man is the Lord
from heaven." ††   If any man be in Him he is "a
new creation," ‡‡ quickened into the "image"‖‖ of
Him who hath "brought life to light in the Gospel."§§   Unto such the Apostle Peter said, " Ye are
born of incorruptible seed by the word of God, which
liveth and abideth forever, and this is the word which
by the Gospel is preached unto you."

UNLOYALTY OF CHRISTIANS TO THE WORD OF GOD.

It has been, with some reason, said :—" The truth
of the Gospel history is now (A. D. 1864) more

---

* Gen. ii, 7.   † 1 Peter i. 11.   § Heb. x, 5–9.   ‖ Matt. xxvii, 46 ;
Psa. xxii.   § John xi, 25.   ¶ John xiv, 19.   ** John vi, 63.   †† 1 Cor.
xv, 47.   ‡‡ 2 Cor. v, 17.   ‖‖ 1 Cor. xv, 49.   §§ 2 Tim. i, 10.

widely doubted in Europe than at any time since the
conversion of Constantine," (A. D. 323). If so this be,
the chief cause is, that so many of those who call
themselves Christians depreciate the pure word of
God. They are many who make tradition concurrent, additional, and superior authority to that of the
Bible.* By traditions they bind the consciences of

* "Our Roman Catholic brethren, and some even among
ourselves, if I understand them rightly, regard the doctrinal
statements of the Church as forms of doctrine immediately
communicated to the apostles by our Lord and the Holy Spirit,
independent of Scripture, and traditionally preserved through
the successors of the apostles. The Nicene Creed, for example,
is a collection of some of these divine sayings, possessing its own
authority, independent of the Scriptures. To depart, accordingly, at all from the language of the formularies, they regard
as deviating from divine truth itself; nay, *even more than to depart from the expressions of Scripture.* Such was not the
view of Athanasius. Speaking of the term Homoousian in that
creed "—of one *substance* with the Father—" he says distinctly,
the meaning was gathered *out of Scripture.*"—*The Scholastic
Philosophy*, by R. D. Hampden, Bishop of Hereford, Professor
of Divinity in the University of Oxford. P. xxxi. London, 1848.

In the "Replies" to "The Essays," sanctioned by Wilber-
force, Bishop of Oxford, 1862, one writer assumes "the continuous existence of a certain creed from the beginning;" and
if by this were meant an interpretation of Scripture reaching far
back, and of effect like that in the case of a book in a language
no longer spoken, which guides or controls the judgment as to
the meaning of its words, it would be sound sense and indisputable fact; but this writer goes on to say a creed "upon belief in which that book was founded "—meaning the New Testament, and contradicting Athanasius and the early fathers;
and he says that certain men, believing certain things, wrote
them in a book, "which is the embodiment of the words of infallible men." Essentially this is the doctrine of the Essays,
and of Strauss also; for, as to the element of infallibility, these
would grant that in the writings of men honestly writing what

men, and give to doctrines not taught, to ceremonial rites, and to observances of times and seasons no-where enjoined by Scripture, the like authority as if there taught or there enjoined.   Thus they compel those who in any way countenance them to concede to them the sanction of, Thus saith the Lord ; and thus they make of none effect the difference between the word of God and words of men.   Essentially, this is a denial that there is any word of God ; and it opens the door to Naturalism, which saith all is of man, or to Pantheism, which saith all that is of man is divine.   From this setting up of traditions of men in the high place of commandments of God, it has come to pass that Naturalism and Pantheism are, as the Council of the Vatican affirmed, widely spread abroad ; and these errors will not cease so long as what is not in Holy Scripture is upheld and taught as of equal authority with what is.

As some think more of Councils and the early

---

they knew, or even thought to be true, there would be less or more of infallible truth.   These two factions in the English establishment disparage the Scriptures, one of them in favor of scholasticism, the other of sacerdotalism.   The one would de-liver up the Church to the philosopher, the other to the priest ; and between the two the word of God is crucified.

This disparaging of the word of God, by putting in its place traditions of men, marked from the first the Oxford heresy.   In his "Apologia," Dr. Newman says : " Hurrell Froude was a pupil of Keble's, formed by him, and in turn reacting upon him. A friend to whom I owe so much.   He professed openly his *hatred* of the Reformers.   He felt scorn of the maxim, " The Bible, and the Bible only, is the religion of Protestants ; " and he *gloried* in accepting tradition *as a main instrument of religious teaching*."

Fathers, so others think more of Confessions of Faith and the later Fathers, than of Scripture. In all these things there is a claim to inspiration in things of men that cannot be distinguished from that claim to inspiration sometimes made for the Zendavesta, or the Vedas, or the Koran ; for Zoroaster Spitama, for Buddha, for Confucius, for Socrates ; or, to come down to later times, for Anacharsis Clootz, "the orator," and Hegel, the philosopher, "of the human race." Were it, in any case, only a claim that something of divine influence may at times have mercifully blended with thoughts of men, it might have more or less of truth, but the result is treated as of the same effect with Holy Scripture ; that which is less is thus evened with that which is higher and different ; and disparaged is that "sure word" to which St. Peter gave a higher place than to the wonders of glory "he beheld in the holy mount."

To some the Bible is their own system of theology ; that, and nothing more. They read it solely to prove that. Some think more of the Prayer-book than of the Bible. Some put their spiritual director in the place of the Scriptures.* Some, their consciences.

---

* In the Journal of Eugenie de Guerin, a book to which the prize given by the French Academy was awarded, and well known in its English translation, under date of April 28, 1835, a confessor is called, "that friend of the soul, its physician, its master, its light, the man to whom we speak on our knees, calling him like God our Father. Faith makes him truly God and Father." Yet our Lord said, "Call no man your father upon the earth: for one is your Father, which is in heaven. Neither be ye called masters: for one is your Master, even Christ." Matt. xxiii, 9, 10.

They subject its teachings to their own notions of right and wrong, and thus "bring to the clearing of the word of God the very darkness it was intended to illumine." And there is a criticism of the Bible whose lines of erasure run nearly through the whole book.

All these things are *now* of error and sin, and they come of an unbelief in the word of God like that among the Jews, whereof this was written for an everlasting warning, that as yet grows not old : "Then came to Jesus scribes and Pharisees, which were of Jerusalem ; he answered and said unto them, ye have made the commandment of God of none effect by your tradition. Ye hypocrites, well did Esaias prophesy of you, saying, This people draweth nigh unto me with their mouth, and honoreth me with their lips ; but their heart is far from me. In vain they do worship me, teaching for doctrines the commandments of men. Then came his disciples, and said unto him, Knowest thou that the Pharisees were offended ? He answered, *Every plant, which my heavenly Father hath not planted, shall be rooted up.*"

INFIDELITY MORE AN EFFECT OF THIS UNLOYALTY TO THE WORD OF GOD, THAN OF SCIENCE.

The feeling that almost every one has met with, and not in the world only, that the Bible is suited only to a Past that is ever receding and is ever more and more becoming an old-fashioned relic, is much more owing to this Christian unloyalty to the word of God than to any "oppositions of science." From time to time Science has brought to light new truths,

or what have seemed to be such, and, as first unvailed, they have seemed to contradict truth in
Scripture, and the like may long continue so to be.
What then? Is there any reason to fear from these
things lasting evil? None whatever. If they are
not truths, they will come to naught; if they are, it is
hardly too much to say they will harmonize themselves with Scripture. At some points where the
Scripture has scarcely been thought of at all, or not
well thought of, they will lead to its more earnest
study, and this will be only for good; for the interpretation of the scientific thoughts in Scripture is no
more complete and final now than that of its religious
teaching, as to which the thought of the Church ever
has been as the shining light, "that shineth more
and more unto the perfect day."

Over the whole realm of knowledge the Scripture
lifts its scepter, and the Star of our Lord is as truly
the guiding light of science as of faith. The truths of
men are to be encompassed, they are to be illumined
by the truth in Scripture; and from it they are to learn
what without it they cannot know. For there are
truths that Science sublimely believes; "it labors in
their light and journeys in their hope," but it cannot
prove them; it is ever drawing nearer to them, but
it cannot touch them; these truths the Bible makes
certain. The Bible is to be harmonized with itself
alone; that is, so far as possible, its truth is to be
seen in its unity. Vainly into comparison with it is
brought any thing or every thing else, for it is written,
God hath magnified his word above all his name.
The Bible has outlasted forms of society, systems of

science. It will outlive them all. Thousands of years are gone since it was written, *The grass withereth and the flower fadeth, but the word of our God shall stand forever.* Its everlasting truth is of another duration than pertains to the material worlds whose years are numbered. Behind that Book and with that Book there is superhuman power. It can no more perish in any blaze of man's kindling than could the three in the furnace of fire, with whom, walking, the astonished king beheld, One whose form was "like the Son of God."*

That the Bible teaches only religious truth has been said by some who would like to have it so. It has become the common answer to much of the hostile criticism of the Bible, and yet is either weak or dishonest; for there is no truth that is not religious, and there is no such limit to the range of the power of the Bible as this evasion implies. Nor could it have become so common, were there not a great want of appreciation of the power the Bible has put forth and does put forth. The Bible was the first book ever printed; and when printed by stealth, and read by the people at the risk of life, its social teachings at once began to put an end to those barbaric ages, which some ignorantly call, Ages of Faith. Its social teachings are now changing the face of society; and it is these changes which, to many, make the Bible an unwelcome book.

As deep into the secret of things as go its moral and spiritual teachings, so deep into the secret of

---

* Dan. iii, 25.

things go the scientific, the historical, and the social teachings of the Bible. As known from the revelation delivered unto us from oldest time by the hand of Moses, the *element* Light is the creative agency that makes the habitable world, entering as the constructive constituting force into solid abiding things that seem farthest removed from its more spiritual essence. The like is true of the revealed word of God. As to all worlds of thought and feeling, there is truth in the Bible yet to come out in such fuller measure that it will seem to be NEW TRUTH. Its ever shining is never lessening its power to shine. In this time of doubt and trial we may hope and believe the Spirit will cause more of light to come forth from the Bible ; and the prayer of all true Christian hearts should be, *Open Thou our eyes to behold wondrous things out of thy law.*

THE

STAR OF OUR LORD.

INQUIRY into the Lessons of the Pilgrimage of the Wise Men who worshiped Christ Jesus in Bethlehem, having "seen his Star," leads far into the mysteries of the kingdom of the Lord. It opens with the question, Was the celestial sign which they beheld foretold? for its answer leads on to, and becomes a part of, the answer to the greater question, Was it one of the stars of heaven?

ALL the old prophecies of the Messiah are now obscured with excess of light, as stars are vailed with the brightness of the dawn. Some of these prophecies burn with fire so bright as ever to be visible, but they were meant to gladden the evening before the "morning was." To see them we must sit in the twilight with those who "searched diligently what the spirit of Christ that was in them did signify when it testified beforehand the sufferings of Christ and the glory that should follow;" with those of old, to whom each prophecy was "a light shining in a dark place." Then the firmament of old Scripture will brighten overhead as before the dayspring visited the world, its planets will come out from the obscure, its constellations stand in their order on high.

CHAPTER I.

THE FIRST HISTORIC CYCLE OF TIME.

AT the feeble fountain whence the living water chose its path to either sea, at the river-head, *there* Mythology built her temple ;* dreaming the river-god would not unfold all that should come and go on his shores forever, where broadflowing he mirrored Memphis and the Pyramids, but in the difficult solitude far away, "beside the well-spring deep and lone of Egypt's mighty flood."

All *beginnings* strike the mind as prophetic ; for in them come forth to sight powers before unseen, whose common direction, or first strife, betokens what will come afterward ; and this, it may be, for an exceeding duration. To the mere sense-conception, what is afterward seems the greater ; but the mysterious interest that attaches *to the beginning* returns no more.

---

* The most eastern fount of *the sacred Jordan* flowed out from under a cavern in a steep red limestone cliff at the foot of Mount Hermon. This grotto-fountain sanctuary was consecrated by the Greeks to the sylvan god, Pan—whence the name of the town Paneas, which still survives in the name Banias, the town called in Matt. xvi, 13, Mark viii, 27, Cæsarea Philippi. See Josephus, Antiq., xv, 10, 3 ; Robinson, iii, 404. The god to whom this cavern-fount was consecrated was the same of whom the legend ran, that certain sailors sailing on the sea in the night when Christ was born, heard a loud lamenting that in the darkness cried, "Great Pan is dead !"

In human life there is one beginning at birth, one when the child knows good from evil, one when Satan shows to youth the kingdoms of the world; and so in the life of the Church there are many beginnings.

At one of these beginnings Balaam uttered this, his last oracle, in the day when, from the hill of Moab, he looked out on the people of Israel in the plain of the Jordan, "abiding in tents according to their tribes," as they were about to cross the dividing, mystic river and begin the conquest of Canaan, the type of the soul, under Joshua the captain, who, by name and office, was a type of Jesus Christ:

"BALAAM, the Son of Beor, said, the man whose eyes are open said, which heard the words of God, and knew the knowledge of the Most High, which saw the vision of the Almighty, falling into a trance, but having his eyes open: I shall see him, but not now: I shall behold him, but not nigh. There shall come a Star out of Jacob, and a Scepter shall rise out of Israel, and shall smite the corners of Moab and destroy all the children of Sheth.* And Edom shall be a posses-

---

* This oracle was from outside of the Hebrew world, and yet there is little doubt as to its terms, except the term, "children of Sheth." Possibly this is a proper name. Some render it "children of tumult," which is true enough to the general idea. The term rendered "the city," seems to be the name of one of the capitals of Moab. "Coasts of Chittim" are shores of the Mediterranean, then the unexplored great Sea of the West. Chittim, afterward called Cyprus, the most eastern of its greater islands, could just be seen from some of the hills of Canaan.

sion for his enemies ; and Israel shall do val-
iantly. Out of Jacob shall come he that shall
have dominion, and shall destroy him that re-
maineth of the city. And when he looked on
Amalek, he took up his parable, and said, Amalek
was the first of the nations ; but his latter end
shall be that he perish forever. And he looked
on the Kenites, and took up his parable, and said,
Strong is thy dwelling place, and thou puttest
thy nest in a rock. Nevertheless the Kenite shall
be wasted, until Asshur * shall carry thee away

---

* Asshur is put for the Assyrians, of whom he was the great
ancestor: Gen. x, 11 ; and so Eber, or as it should be, Heber,
is put for the Hebrews: Gen. x, 21, 24, 25 ; xi, 10, 16, 26 ; and,
xiv, 13, "Abram the Hebrew." There the Septuagint has,
"the passer-over," the one who came over the Euphrates, as
Abraham did—and as for that, so did all the people in Palestine. All Shemitic titles have a meaning often traceable only
through the words. From this, no doubt, came this error ;
for the Targums (as to which see the Index) show a Jewish
rage for derivations more fantastic than that of later critics—
though not more so than the finding in Balaam, "destroyer of
the people." A red Indian, running to his lodge whooping
from an ambush with scalps of men, women, and children at
his belt, might take to himself such a title, but Beor never
could have given it to his new-born son.

This error of the Septuagint was set right in our Version, and
long before that, in the Vulgate. It is repeated in "Lange's
Commentary." There it is set right in a note by one of the sense-
keepers set over the American translation, often wiser men and
better scholars than those they translate ; and happily so for true
religion; for this comment often accedes to the wildest unreason
of unbelief—as where it calls Abraham "*a heathen Chaldeo*"
and says, he was about to murder Isaac as Moloch worshipers
murdered their children.

The genealogy of the Shemites opens with styling Shem the

captive. And he took up his parable, and said, Alas, who shall live when God doeth this ! And ships shall come from the coast of Chittim, and shall afflict Asshur, and shall afflict Eber, and he also shall perish forever."—Num. xxii ; xxiii ; xxiv, 15–25.

To comprehend the scene on the hill of Moab when Balaam looked out on the camp of the Lord is to comprehend much of the meaning of all history. Much of the world, as it was then, was there; and our HOPE was in those goodly tents of Jacob. In its "great and terrible wilderness" conspiring against Israel—as now, in its greater and more terrible wilderness, the world is conspiring against Christ—and feeling, with the sensitiveness of the desert, that spiritual power was on the side of Israel, and knowing this moves and determines the course of human events, Arabia * had called to its help other spiritual

---

father of the children of Eber. Of course, the Eber it thus points out must be the Eber it names a little farther on. The Scripture calls that Shemitic people whose history it traces, Hebrews. Between these facts comes in its calling Abraham— children of whom this people loved to call themselves—" the Hebrew : " and yet some deny the force of all this, because they say " nothing is known of Heber—" as if the fact which the Shemitic genealogy at its opening makes known about him, that he was the great forefather of the Hebrews, was nothing ! In the rendering of this oracle the Septuagint corrects its blunder in the other place, by giving as a paraphrase of the same word, 'Εβραίους, Hebrews ; so the Syriac. The Vulgate has, *vastabuntque Hebræos*—shall destroy the Hebrews.

* Of the vast Arabia of modern geography, so much as skirts the west and south of Palestine. This is sometimes called Arabia in Scripture. The people on the western and southern

power. Arms had failed, and another plan had been devised. Four times the princes of Midian and Moab had journeyed across the breadth of the Syrian Desert; his first embassy to Balaam had failed, but "Balak, the son of Zippor, who was king of the

---

fringes of Palestine belonged to this desert, as sailors to the sea. They were all troubled by the landing of pilgrim Israel on their coasts; and, though little or no use has been made of this, it is one of the keys that unlock the history. To prove they were troubled, it is enough to ask, How could it have been otherwise? And the facts are these: Midianites went with Moabites on the embassies to Balaam; the Ammonites had a chief part in this thing, as may be seen from Deut. xxiii, 3, 4; Neh. xiii, 1–3; the Amorites had been scattered by a defeat that probably led to it. Balaam on the mountain addressed Amalek; and the Kenites also, who as a tribe ate salt with the Israelites, but some of whom seem to have made common cause with the other tribes. It goes to show the Jewish opinion that all southern and eastern Palestine took part in the calling in of Balaam, that Philo, when narrating this event, says of the exode of Israel, (though with a touch of his usual exaggeration,) "all the Asiatic nations were disturbed by it." It is curious evidence of this opinion, that in the Septuagint Og is lugged into the history with a violence that dislocates the oracle: "And he looked upon Og and said, Who shall live when God doeth this?" This favorite giant comes in quite unexpectedly in the wild legends of the Jews. Thus, in Gen. xiv, 13, one came to Abraham with news that Lot was a captive. In the Targum of Palestine: "Og came, who had been spared from the giants drowned in the Deluge, and had ridden protected on the top of the ark, sustained with food by Noah." Perhaps this naming of Og in the Septuagint came from the killing of Og of Bashan by the Israelites in an inroad into his country about this time. On these last two facts no stress can be laid; but the twice sending for Balaam could not be a secret, and great publicity was given to it. The desert tribes must have felt an interest in it, and that they all, or nearly all, were active in it, seems proved by the evidence above cited from Scripture.

Moabites at that time," sent "princes, more, and more honorable than they," and said, " I will do whatsoever thou sayest ; " and so at last they had brought with them, " from the mountains of the East," "the greatest of the prophets at that time," "the diviner renowned above all, and his glory spread everywhere," "the rival, the possible conqueror of Moses." *

WHAT WAS THE WORLD, THE TIME, THE CHARACTER
OF THIS MAN, AND THE PURPOSE IN HIS COMING ?

In general history, and even in Church history, there is an under-estimate of Balaam's time, and with some a reticence as to both his character and the meaning of his mission, all of which have tended to make his history needlessly perplexing. Beyond the seas some would not be suffered, either by their ecclesiastical or their secular rulers, fully and truthfully to interpret the history of Balaam to the people ; and there are some, even with us, who would not if they could. It opens deep and difficult questions that here can only be rapidly touched ; yet as it has

---

* See Numbers xxii ; xxiii, 7 ; xxiv. Philo-Judæus, Life of Moses, sec. xlviii ; Josephus, Antiq., Lib. iv, chap. vi ; Stanley's Jewish Church, lec. viii. The two Jews lived in the first Christian century. Some record as to Balaam is quoted by the prophet Micah, chap. vi, 5–9, which is not in the Mosaic Books ; but this was before the exile, some seven hundred years before Josephus or Philo lived ; and it is not probable they had any other means of knowing about Balaam than what are now in the Bible. They only give a sermonizing amplification of what is there. It is of no historical value, save as reflecting the impression the Bible-history made on them. Time itself is the true and only interpreter of this history.

become with so many a scoff and a jeer, which with
those who understand it even a little, it can never
be, it must here be more fully treated than would
otherwise be required to answer those questions
as to the Star of our Lord which arise out of his
Oracle.

WHEN the monuments of history are traced back
for about four thousand years a chasm is reached beyond which nothing can be seen, while on this side
of it there is a quick emergence of civilization. It
is as if some river were traced to where it flowed in
large volume from an underground lake, while beyond the sudden greenness all was the empty silence
of a tenantless desert. The tools, the work, the
sculptured sphinx, the painted mummy-chamber, the
cutting, drawing, and lifting up on high of the hard
and heavy obelisk, the placing and proportions of the
pyramids, show a working in the metals, a skill in the
arts, in engineering and astronomy, that could have
been attained only by a long course of experiments
and discoveries. Evidently, in some long pre-exist-
ing world, the wisdom competent to results of so
sudden and so high an order, was slowly gained ; but
whenever and wherever that world may have been, it
has vanished like " the baseless fabric of a vision."
The Great Flood, whose memory long continued with
many nations,* and of which the record *of an eye-*

---

* Certain as many of the facts of geology are, its theories
come and go like shadows in a wizard's glass ; and *if*, as said
by some, it cannot as yet recognize any traces of *the* Flood, the
honesty of this confession is praiseworthy ; but when it would

witness is preserved in the Bible, explains this fact, that in the earliest historic age there was a some-what high and complex civilization in a thinly peopled world.

FROM the Great Flood the Bible reader passes on to the miracle commonly called the Confusion of Tongues. This might better be known as the call-ing forth of new languages. Of this, the dispersion of those who were to become nations was a conse-quence. Here, as before, there is some evidence outside of the Bible of what it records. Several languages have been classed into one family (to which the Hebrew and the Arabic belong) and into another, called the Aryan, still more, because of resemblances proving that each family has been gen-erated from some one original form. From the original Aryan form have come the Zend of Persia, the Sanscrit of India, the Greek, the Latin, the Celtic, Teutonic, Sclavonic, and other languages ; and since the Dispersion there has been ample time for these changes, as is sufficiently evident from the fact that the Italian, Spanish, French, and English languages are but a few hundred years old.

One nature is common to the Shemitic-speaking Arab, and to the Aryan-speaking American whom he guides through the desert of Sinai. The changes that have come about in the language of either can be

---

wrest this ignorance against the Bible, the older and graver science of history rebukes and silences the younger ; for the Flood itself is proved as conclusively as any historical fact, by records of history, outside of the Bible.

accounted for ; but not the unchanging, original un-
likeness between the two languages.   They are as
unlike in their structure as the palm-tree and the oak.
Their oldest specimens, more than three thousand
years old, differed as sharply as any two of them differ
now.   And the conclusions drawn from these facts
remain substantially unaffected when the one, two,
or more forms into which all other languages may be
classed, are considered.

The Scriptures, which record the calling forth from
the human nature of new forms of speech at Babel,
witness to the unity of that nature ; and, as this
miraculous power acted upon and through the human
nature, its quick results present themselves to the
scientific eye as if produced by the slow action of
natural causes.*   Yet there is confirmatory evidence

---

* Through, and beyond these two propositions, can be seen
the truth, that collision between the Scripture here, and the
Science of Languages is impossible.   For the sake of clearness
in the brief treatment of the subject above, only languages are
spoken of as evoked at Babel ; but, as the special facts in the
miraculous effect are not given in the Scripture, there may
have been a calling forth of dialects as well ; and these might
present some of the stages of the natural growth of less into
more perfect speech.   If, then, the existing forms of speech
should all be resolved into one ground-form, into an elementary
utterance, of which all others might appear to be a growth,
this ought not even to look like a collision with what is here
revealed.

These thoughts touch not the reality of the superhuman
power.   They only bring out the truth that the Divine supernatural usually acts through, and in conformity with the nature
and laws, it ordained for the natural.   This the Scripture points
out, as will be shown hereafter.   The idea itself is so reasonable, that it would seem only to need to be stated to be

of the Scripture in the fact that it is so difficult, if not indeed impossible, to show scientifically how the Shemitic and Aryan tongues could have come from one parent form ; as may readily be shown of the very different looking and widely separated varieties of either.   Thus, to the discoveries of the science of philology, or of the comparison of language, the Scriptures give the explanation.

What was done at Babel was recorded, not to gratify the pride of the intellect, and not as a page of philology, but for spiritual ends ; and yet it is permissible to reason from the record to facts of inference or conjecture.   The economy of power in miracles makes it probable that one language was not changed.   Among the handful in Babel * there were some who could not have been of the Tower-builders, for Noah and Shem were there ; and the speech-effacing, speech-evoking judgment, passing those, may have spared the language of Shem and Noah,

---

assented to, and yet seems not to have been thought of in much that has been said of miracles.

* As every body was there, one is apt to think there were many ; but on the earth then there were only Noah and his children, grandchildren, great-grandchildren, and a few babies of the fourth generation.   Peleg, in the one hundred and first year after the Great Flood, was named from the division of those few kindred families, and so must have been born in the year of the miracle.   This smallness of the number at Babel takes from the grandeur of the mere sense-conception of the scene, yet brings out the far-reaching wisdom and mercy in the Divine intervention.   And it brings out the fresh vigor of life on that " green undeluged earth," shown in that city-building, empire-founding cycle which followed, and felt far down in the later cycles of time, as attested by colossal enduring monuments of early days, scattered far and wide.

which was the language of Enoch and of Adam. On some of the less guilty the judgment, falling less heavily than on the worst, may have called forth the original Aryan tongue, one of whose forms, the Greek, was to voice the glad tidings to all people. In the worst it may have chilled the fount of thought, and hence have come a language fitted, like the Chinese, for stationary or humble forms of society, and comparing with the Hebrew, deep and clear breathing from the inmost recesses of the soul, or with the flexile eloquence of the Greek, as the talk of paralyzed lips with the fullness of human speech.

Those few people in the Plain of Shinar, whose souls were haunted by the roar of the waters that drowned the world, naturally clung together; and there was something of a pitiable weakness in their making their refuge and strength a tower their own hands would build, as well as of a proud consciousness of strength in their will to carry it up into heaven. But the weakness, the sin of the children baffled not the Father's wisdom. *It is the glory of God to conceal a thing;* and the miracle which dispersed those who were to be the nations over the habitable earth, like the appointed doom of labor, was a blessing in disguise. Change, variety, and fullness of thought on some themes are so little consonant with the genius of the Shemitic tongue, unbending and sterile though sublime, that but for this intervention the world would have been more wicked. Thus the Dispersion increased the power of the forces working on toward the time when the knowledge of the Lord shall cover the earth as the waters fill the sea. But for this, that diversified drama, "its four first acts, already past," which now opens through scenes of conflict and terror the sublimity of its last, never could have unfolded so rapidly. That Dispersion was a part of the World-Plan the Spirit reveals; and, recording the Dispersion before the miracle which caused it, it seems to emphasize how it followed the nations as they trend off into darkness and shadow. Then it traces the true line of history, the line of the children of Eber, for of them was Christ to be born, in whom and through whom the separating nations would regain their lost unity. The companion-hour to this hour of the Dispersion seems to be when there came a sound from heaven as of a rushing mighty wind, and cloven tongues like as of fire, and all the apostles began to speak as the Spirit gave them utterance, and devout men from every nation came together, and every man heard them speak in his own language the wonderful works of God. Of what is yet to be, here was symbol, prophecy, and the fact itself. Time will interpret the whole. From Holy Scripture it seems to appear that the Most High doth vouchsafe to those called of him to rule in the earth something of a far opening reach of vision; and on the 4th of March, 1873, our people heard, and all people heard, or yet shall hear, for they have passed into history, these words of one called of the Most High to one of the high places of human power: "*I believe that our great Maker is preparing the world, in his own good time, to become one nation, speaking one language, and when armies and navies will be no longer required.*"

THE Cycle of Time and Thought to which Balaam belonged dates back to the Dispersion of the nations in the fourth generation after the Great Flood, and it ended with him, its last great prophet.* Babel was

---

* The Thought of Time-Cycles is one of those Oriental thoughts not fully comprehended by the Western mind, though known to the Greeks, the germs of whose civilization were quickened from the East. But there are every-where traces of this thought, for nature and life every-where suggest it. Natural time-cycles are made by Life. Those historic time-cycles the Bible speaks or hints of, are made and determined by Truth. Either by the unfolding of the truth within them into a higher cycle, or by its tending to die out, the cycle comes to its end.

When, through the Gospel, the European mind awakened from long enfeebling heathenism it did not firmly grasp this thought. Very great has been the harm to philosophy and science. And history without this thought is a tangled wilderness of facts, trodden with as much difficulty and as little satisfaction as a jungle in India.

In the Bible this thought comes out in facts ; and sometimes in words where this cannot be seen in our translation. "By whom also he made the *worlds*" (τοὺς ἀιῶνας), should read the *time-worlds;* whether it point to the ages of history, or to the Six Great Days in the Creation, or to that Hebrew idea of worlds on worlds of time, to which, of English phrases, "world without end" comes the nearest. Heb. i, 2.

With Noah a world-cycle began, that continues over a great part of the world. Many cycles have unfolded within this. Some of these, like the Greek cycle, have ended ; and some continue, as that of China, of India, of Islam. There is one other world-cycle. It began with Christ Jesus. As this expands, it in part absorbs or effaces other cycles and fills their places ; and it will expand till it covers the world.

The call of Abraham marked the opening of a new cycle of time. That he lived before Balaam, does not disprove what is said in the text, of his cycle. For the arcs of time-cycles intersect. They do not merely touch at a point. Before one is

within the limits of his world, and perchance he may
have seen the unfinished tower yet standing in that
town which long afterward grew to be the great and
mighty Babylon. Balaam spoke the language of
Shem, and his world in the main was a Shemitic-
speaking world. Its boundaries and limits were defined and fixed by nature. On the east was the
mountain-wall of the Zagros, that beyond the plain
of the Tigris and Euphrates runs from the southern
point of the Caspian Sea to the northern point of the
Persian Gulf; on the west was the Great Sea and the
Libyan Desert west of the land of Egypt; on the
north the mountain-ranges that fill up the space between the western shore of the Caspian and the north-
eastern angle of the Mediterranean; and to the south
was the Arabian Desert and the ocean. It was the
flat country of the Tigris and Euphrates, with a part
of the highlands north of it; all of Syria and the
island of Chittim, afterward known as Cyprus; with
the land of Egypt, and some undeterminable part of
Arabia. Beyond the natural limits of his world
there was nothing which now comes clearly within
the range of the eye. On bleak plains, among the
snowy mountains and by the seas of Central Asia,
there was then the germination of races that since
have made the circuit of the world; but they remain
as little known, and as unknowable, as what those
same races long afterward were doing to the north
of the Black Sea, in the heart of the Teutonic and

---

rounded, another begins within it: as the cycle of a boy's life
begins in his father's, and the two run on together for awhile,
the one contracting, the other expanding.

Scandinavian forests, along the coasts of the Baltic and of the German Ocean, before the Celt and the Teuton came into the Roman Empire, there, at last, to be taught again what they had forgotten of truths that were in the religion of that age and world to which Balaam belonged. For in his cycle of time and in his world there were the elements of all the truth there was in all the world till Christ came. That early time, and the time before the Flood, was the birth-time of our religion, which, like our God, is the Ancient of Days.

OF THE RELIGION OF BALAAM'S WORLD AND TIME.

Some Germans, of the class of men so wittily and well hit off by President Grant "as those who do not believe the Bible because they did not write it," have said, the Oracles of Balaam must be the clever forgeries of some unscrupulous Jew who lived much later, for they show a religious knowledge not possible at the time when Balaam lived. There is need to disprove this assertion fully; for the Bible reader is apt to form his idea of that time from the dark and foul idolatry of the Canaanites, and then to transfer this back to the whole of his cycle.* For though it was a long time from the Dispersion to Joshua's conquest of the Canaanites, yet duration is measured

---

* According to the Hebrew text, Abraham's call from Haran was 266 years, and his death 366 years, after the Dispersion. At the time of that call he was 75 years old; he died aged 175. The time from that call to the coming of Israël out of Egypt is given as 430 years; the wandering in the desert was 40 years. The duration, then, of the first cycle of time, as dating from the Dispersion and ending about the time of Balaam's death, in

by events, and as the record of this time is not
filled up it hardly affects us as time at all ; and so
the heathenism that characterized the end of this
cycle, and was intensely evil in Canaan, seems to
characterize the whole of it.   But in Canaan there
was true religion when Abraham was there.   In that
palm-growing tropical plain, where now is the Dead
Sea sunk a thousand feet and more below the ocean-
level, and with a heat reflected back from its cliffs
hotter than that of India, there were corrupt cities
on whom deservedly fell the fire from heaven ; but
on hills that look down on that plain, and beholding
the smoke of burning Sodom, there was the capital
of a king of righteousness ; and a little farther south,
and nearer the great Sea of the West, there was a
righteous people whose capital was Gerar.   It was
during the sojourn of Israel in Egypt that the knowledge of the true God died out in Canaan ; and
Abraham's blunder as to the king and people of
Gerar should have prevented that German blunder-
ing, for Abraham frankly confessed to Abimelech
and said, " I thought the fear of the Lord was not in
this place."

All that the Bible says of the religious character
and history of Balaam accords with all it makes
known of the earliest historical cycle of time.   This
can be shown to be minutely, thoroughly consistent ;
and the source of the wisdom that died with Balaam

---

round numbers would be 750 years, or more exactly, 736.   The
Samaritan Pentateuch and the Septuagint make it longer ; but
the Hebrew text has the higher claims, and the shorter time
makes the sacred history more consistent with itself.

in the land of Midian is no more an enigma than of
that which lived in the line of Moses, of Elijah, and
of John the Baptist.   In the first cycle of time there
was not only truth, but culture as well ; for Noah, who
was heir of the righteousness that is by faith, was
also the heir of the civilization that was antecedent
to the judgment of the Great Flood.   The Bible
points to but a few of the facts that went to make up
the history of that cycle of time, and yet to all
those that are of lasting importance.   Mountain
peaks with sun-light touched bring out the outlines
of a country, when plains, valleys, and cities lie hidden in mist ; and so the scripture-rays touching the
persons of Melchisedek, Abraham, and Balaam, light
up that time.   In Melchisedek its spiritual height
can be measured, and a wonderful height it was.
The Jews thought he was Shem, the son of Noah.
The silence of the Scripture is against this; though
Shem was living somewhere in that world when
Melchisedek and Abraham partook of the bread and
wine—foreshadowing the Christian sacrament.*

Abraham, and Melchisedek, which, by interpretation, is King of Righteousness, also King of Salem,
which is King of Peace, worshiped the same God
of heaven.   This marks the truth in their world ;
and the city of the one west of the Jordan, the
birthplace of the other beyond the Euphrates and
his journeying to the Nile, mark the space-extent of
their world.

---

* Gen. xiv, 17–20.

OF HIS KNOWLEDGE OF THE HISTORY AND RELIGION
OF ISRAEL.

Balaam was of that country by the Euphrates out
of which Abraham came into the West.   He was a
prophet from the sacred East.*   He traced his lineage back to Shem, as did most of those who appear
in his history.   Among all those Shemitic-speaking
nations there seems to have been a peculiar traditionary literature that, with but little help from letters,
was both commonly known and permanently remembered.   With them history took on the form of
genealogy, as it tends to do among primitive peoples.

---

* When Noah died Abraham was fifty-eight years old; and
Abraham died thirty-five years before Shem, who lived through
more than half the first historic cycle. Probably Noah and Shem
both lived in the East, for there is no mention of either in the
West, then the chief scene of the sacred history; and it is not
likely that either of them went beyond their world with any of
those scattered far by the Dispersion.   In the East the sacred
wisdom of the past survived the Flood with Noah for 350 years
and with Shem 502 years. Shem may have known Methuselah,
who was the son of Enoch and may have talked with Adam.
So long as this patriarch lived, to whom were known saints
before the Flood, the East must have kept in the eyes of the
colonists of the West the sacredness that seemed to belong
to it as the site of Eden; and though, even while Shem lived,
religion there, as every-where else, was corrupting, the West
must have long looked back to the East, not only as the Old
Country, but as the chief seat, the primal home of its religion,
the Holy Land. There may have been a tinge of this feeling
in Balaam's saying, " They brought me from the mountains of
the East;" and all these feelings must have heightened that
prophet's fame in the West. With this view of the religious
relations of the East and the West his religious character and
his history agree; and without it, they are hardly explicable.

Among the Shemitic nations this genealogical instinct has the strength of passion and the firmness of principle ; and in the first historic cycle it was stimulated by the activity of that colonizing, city-building, empire-founding time. For what God then said to Abraham, " I will make of thee a nation," he then said to others in his providence ; and thus to the men of that day those genealogies, reaching back to the three sons of Noah, were much more than the dry lists of names that now look so meaningless to some. They were the names of the fathers of the nations then peopling the world ; they were much of all there was of history then ; and even now, the construction and wording of those genealogies teach of the course of empire and the will of God. Those records, which the patriarchs so faithfully remembered, were then of common interest ; and, in some form, must have been as well known to Balaam as to Moses. The bent of his intellect was religious. By nature and by grace he was a prophet in the oriental, which is the true sense of the word ; that is, not one who merely sees into the future, but one, as well, who is wise in the wisdom of the past. Known from the Euphrates to the Jordan, he was a great man in his day ; and he would have been a great man in any day. Such a man must have been acquainted with the brief genealogies of the fathers of his time ; and there could have been little that was doing, or that had been done in his world in the few centuries between him and the Dispersion of the Nations, especially of a religious kind, of which he could have been ignorant.

Balaam must have known of Abraham, though he
lived some hundreds of years after him ; for Abraham
was one of the few historical personages of his own
cycle of time and of his own world ; and throughout
that cycle of time every thing that was going on in
that world, from the Zagros Mountains to the Libyan
Desert, was soon known from one side of it to the
other. People had curiosity then and less to exercise it upon than now ; and in that region they had
about as good means of intercommunication then as
now, and with stronger motive for it ; for now, every
thing there is formed and fixed and somewhat dead,
then, all that world was in motion, colonizing and
settling.* And there never has been a time when

---

* In our own land something like this has been and is passing
before our eyes, in the colonizing from the East of the West, the
Far West, of California and Oregon—a world where some of
the natural features of Asia repeat themselves. Some of the
facts here are on a broader scale ; but in the settling of California
especially, where emigration overpassed unoccupied spaces, and
regions with half a continent between were brought into sudden intercourse, there was the quick calling forth of latent
human energies, the same in kind as in that earlier eastern
world.

The crowding population in the narrow garden-plain of the
Euphrates hearing of the fertile country beyond it, cleared the
desert at a bound. Emigration from Assyria overflowed Syria.
So long as this was going on, intercourse between them must
have been active. There are as many signs of this as should
be looked for in sacred history ; which here is very much that
of the one family, in whom all are to find Him, who is the center
of all history. One of these signs is in the fact (Gen. xiv, 1–16)
that, from beyond the Tigris, chiefs—for, as yet, kings and
nations hardly were, and such grand titles as theirs petty rulers
have often worn—had some hold on colonists clear over beyond

any thing of much interest there, such as the Crusade of Cœur de Lion, or the Landing of Napoleon in Egypt, that was not speedily known from the Nile to the Tigris, through the intervening, quick-eyed, wandering children of the desert, whose tribes have ever telegraphed to each other in ways that were unknown to Morse.

Abraham in his own day was a man of mark. He was treated in Egypt by its Pharaoh with something that looks like equality—certainly with respect; though it should here be added, it clearly appears from this fact, which thus is of much historical value, that the eminent power and glory of the Pharaohs, which some without any evidence would throw back thousands of years, was yet to come. He came up out of Egypt rich in the wealth of that time—in cattle, in silver, and in gold—and this was before his

---

the Jordan. Other signs of this are to be seen in Gen. xi, 31, 32 with xii, 1, 4, 5, 6; and Gen. xxiv, 2, 3, 4, 10, Gen. xxviii, 1, 2, 5, Gen. xxxvi, 37, where "the river" is the Euphrates; and in the sending for and the coming of Balaam from "the East."

At the closing of a later cycle, a conquering activity, like the earlier colonizing activity, spurned the breaks and distances of that world. Eastern Assyrian hordes then overran the Syrian West. The fountains of the great deep of human nature were broken up; an army from Egypt fought at Carchemish on the Euphrates; and, (the eastern bound of the world enlarging,) from the highland that overlooks the flat Mesopotamia, the Persian Eagle swooped over to the valley of the Nile. In a still later cycle, the Greek successor to Alexander's empire in the East had one of his capitals at Seleucia, on the Tigris which finds the Persian Gulf, and another at Antioch, by the Orontes which flows into the Mediterranean. (See "The Wise Men," page 48.) Again, something of the like was repeated in the far-ruling of the Caliphs of Bagdad.

battle with the five Kings of the East. Though not a man of war, Abraham was a warrior in the sense that every noble was in the feudal ages, as now is every emir or sheik marching, spear in hand, before his tribe. The three hundred and eighteen whom he led to that fight were his own people, his own trained men at arms. Not many; only a few more than the Spartans who fell in the Pass at Thermopylæ; but the world itself was but a handful then; and battles are not measured by the number of the slain, as witnesses the fight at Lexington and Concord. The battle that Abraham fought at the Springs of the Jordan was not the least noteworthy of all that in the years since have been fought in the same region, for it must have spread Abraham's name from one side of his world to the other. A quiet, unassuming herdsman, his home a tent, his cattle browsing along the hills and on the plains of a country where the settlements were few, he plowed no field, built no fort, yet every-where was treated as a king. A stranger and a sojourner, he asked only for a burying-place, and the children of Heth answered and said, "Thou art a mighty prince among us; in the choice of our sepulchers bury thy dead."

As Abraham's history must have been known to Balaam, so no doubt the history of his family, as much of this was known throughout a large part of his world. The romantic story of the fortunes of Joseph lost nothing as told by the camp-fires of the children of the desert, some of whose legends of those days, six hundred years after the Christian era, were recorded for the first time by Mohammed in the

Koran.* The marvels of the Flight from Egypt must have been heard of in all of what was then the world. What is it that now on every Sabbath-day so mysteriously hushes the roar of traffic in this busiest spot of all the earth, this mart of nations, and far inland, clear across this continent, from these waters that wash the shores of Spain, to where San Francisco through the Golden Gate looks out on the ocean that encircles the islands of Asia?

> 'Tis heaven's commanding trumpet long and loud,
> 'Tis Sinai's thunder pealing from the cloud.

And can there be a doubt that some echo of those events, now heard of the wide world around, was

---

* " The great interest of this wonderful book, whose poetic form and nature are so little understood, consists in its independent narration of some of the leading events in the early Old Testament history. We cannot here state the argument, but there is abundant internal evidence that the stories of Abraham, of Noah, of Joseph, of Ishmael, together with other ancient events not mentioned in the Jewish Scriptures, such as the accounts of the prophets Hud and Saleh, were not derived from the Bible, but came down from independent collateral tradition among these sons of the desert; and that these traditions date away back to the times of Ishmael, and even to Joktan, who was the son of Eber, the great ancestor both of the Jews and the Arabians."—*The Divine Human in the Scriptures*. By Tayler Lewis. Page 393.

This confirms what is said of Shemitic culture on page 20. The many, to whom Dr. Lewis' unsurpassed mastery of the Shemitic tongues and the close consideration he gives to all he utters is known, will not doubt that the argument alluded to was fully before his mind; and yet, as this mention of the Book of Islam may sound to others as if taken from some of the many passing echoes of the words of other men, the writer may state that he has seen six or seven volumes in manuscript of his notes on peculiar phrases in the Arabic of the Koran.

then thrown back from the mountain barriers of that narrower world, or lost amid its surrounding deserts and seas? In the generation after Pharaoh and his host were destroyed, that woman of Canaan said to the spies, "We have heard how the Lord dried up the Red Sea for you, and your terror has fallen upon us; for Jehovah, your God, he is God in heaven above, and in the earth beneath." *

The religion of the rival prophets, Balaam and Moses, in some sense, was the same; for each worshiped the God of Abraham and of Shem, even as Shem worshiped the God of Enoch and of Abel. More than this, Balaam worshiped the God of Israel. Balaam's own name for God, which in our version throughout his history is uniformly rendered Lord, is no other than Jehovah; as, "I cannot go beyond the word of Jehovah, my God;" and his adoption and use of this name, with other facts, prove some knowledge on his part of the history of Israel in the Desert.

OF HIS KNOWLEDGE OF THE PROMISES TO ISRAEL.

The evidence of his knowledge of the promises made to the children of Israel is equally convincing. The general tenor of the history goes to prove that the King of Moab knew something of these. It could hardly have been otherwise, for Moab and his confederate, Ammon, were descended from Abraham's brother; his confederates, the Midianites, and his neighbors of Edom, traced their lineage to the

---

* Joshua ii, 9, 10, 11.

great patriarch ; so did the Ishmaelites, and one of
the tribes called Amalekites.

No doubt Abraham was silent as to the promise
of the land of Canaan, to those settlers there of whom
he asked for nothing but a grave ; but within his
own family it seems to have been no secret. While
his descendants were in Egypt there is no note of
any intercourse between them and their far away
kindred ; but there is no record of those days ; with
those peoples traditions were history ; all the descendants of Abraham must have continued to know
about each other, for the limits of some of those
tribes ran close over to the land of Goshen ; Egypt
was attractive to the dwellers in the neighboring
desert ; and all the time those wandering Ishmaelites,
who carried Joseph down there, were going backward and forward. With all this agrees the request
which Moses sent to Edom, that he might pass along
"the king's highway:" "Thus saith thy brother
Israel, *thou knowest* how our fathers went down into
Egypt, and the Lord has brought us out ; let us pass
through thy country." *

The emergence of Israel from his house of bondage, and his appearing on their borders, must have
revived the memories of their kinsmen ; and they
could easily have gained a knowledge of all the reasons that led to the new movement. There was a
diplomatic craft among them that would soon have
found out the whole secret. It may seem a mistake
to speak of the diplomacy of those who were tribes

* Numbers xx, 14–21.

rather than nations, whose cities were small and few, whose kings were petty chiefs, whose manners were as simple or coarse or wild as those daguerreotyped in the Iliad ; but though diplomacy is a modern term, the thing is old ; it is in the blood of the Shemitic races ; and the Scriptures show it among the patriarchs themselves.   But no craft was needed to find out the mission of the Israelites.   It was widely known.   That woman said, who had heard of their passing through the Red Sea, "I know the Lord hath given you this land."

To all those oriental tribes who knew of the history of Israel, the Israelites proclaimed in a very impressive and oriental fashion that they were seeking that land of Canaan beyond the Jordan where the bones of their great Ancestor lay; that land to whose border an august funeral long before, but nowhere then forgotten in all that region,* had carried the embalmed body of Jacob, whose son was prime minister of Egypt ; a funeral procession, not the least memorable of all the funeral processions, from that when the Greeks through subject nations bore the body of their youthful general from Babylon to Alexandria, the city he had founded near the Nile,

---

† Gen. l, 1–14.   This "seven days" mourning was beyond the Jordan at the threshing-floor of Atad.   "And the inhabitants of the land said, this is a grievous mourning to the Egyptians, *wherefore the name of it was called Abel-Mizraim*"— the Egyptian meadow.   Abel, *meadow* or *plain*, is a prefix to several names.   Here, the Septuagint by a slight change in the letters needlessly enlarges the meaning of the phrase into *mourning of Egypt ;* an example of what was before said as to Jewish derivations in the note on page 5.

to that funeral where the corpse of the Liberator,
Lincoln, was borne to a still greater distance, through
cities and mourning States, from the Potomac to the
unifying River of the West; that earliest recorded
of all funeral processions, when Joseph went up out
of Egypt to bury his father, and with him went up
all the servants of Pharaoh and all the elders of the
land of Egypt, and there went up with him both
chariots and horsemen, and it was a very great company; for the dying Jacob had said, "Bury me with
my fathers in the cave that is in the field of Ephron
the Hittite, in the cave that is in the field of Mach-
pelah, which Abraham bought for a burying-place;
there they buried Abraham and Sarah his wife,
there they buried Isaac and Rebekah his wife, and
there I buried Leah;" and now there was about to
pass into that same land of Canaan beyond the Jordan the longest of all funeral processions, not measured, as Lincoln's, by weeks, nor as Alexander's, by
months, but moving on for forty years, and its pall-
bearers died on the way and were buried in the desert
sands before it was done; that funeral procession
bearing in his "coffin" the embalmed body of a man
who had much to do with the coming up of Israel
out of Egypt; for when Moses, eloquent not in words
but in deeds, making his last appeal to his people,
lifted up that coffin and "took the bones of Joseph
with him," *then* the children of Israel "journeyed
from Succoth and encamped in Etham in the edge
of the wilderness;" that funeral procession of all
the most sublime, for the children of Israel bore the
coffin of their Prophet through the waters of the Red

Sea, and they set it down before the burning mount
to hearken to the voice of God, when there were
thunders and lightnings and a thick cloud upon the
mount, and the voice of a trumpet exceeding loud,
and Mount Sinai was altogether on a smoke, because
the Lord descended upon it in fire, and the voice of
the trumpet sounded long and waxed louder and
louder ; and through all the desert leading on that
funeral, the Lord himself went before it in a pillar of
cloud by day, and by night in a pillar of fire ; for *by
faith Joseph when he died made mention of the departing of the children of Israel, and gave commandment concerning his bones.*

The Israelites sought the west of the Jordan ; but
their battle with the Amorites, and the seemingly
more pacific but not less hostile policy of Moab,* on
the east of that river, looks as if some whisper had
gone abroad of the promise to Israel of the whole

---

* Just before the calling in of Balaam, the warlike Amorites
had wrested from Moab all their land to the north of the chasm
of the river Arnon, and slain in battle Balak's father.   Their
defeat by the Israelites, in which their King Sihon was slain,
was commemorated in a song that took words of an Amorite
song of triumph for its opening.   It is one of the oldest pieces
of poetry in the world. Num. xxi, 27–30.   The Moabites were
a pastoral community ; they speak of the Israelites as " a people
who would lick up those round about them as an ox licketh up
the grass of the field."   They were not as unsettled as the
Midianites, nor as warlike as the Amorites, nor as fierce as the
Amalekites ; they seem to have been more civilized than their
near neighbors, and more pacific—though we read of " two lion-
like men of Moab," slain by " a valiant man," who also " slew
a lion in a pit on a snowy day," and whom David " set over
his guard." 2 Sam. xxiii, 20 , 1 Chron. xi, 22.

broad country from "the river of Egypt unto the great river, the river Euphrates." And that which, on the whole, must thus be held for certain of Balak's knowledge of the history of the Israelites, and of the promises made to them, is quite as certain of Balaam's. Besides all his other means of knowing of that series of events running back to Abraham's day, which now led to the appearing of Israel on the borders of Canaan, the embassy that was sent to him gave him the means of knowing all that Moab knew of the Israelites. He shows some knowledge of the history of Israel when he says, God brought him out of Egypt; and of their genealogies, or of genealogies like theirs, in the way he speaks of Asshur and of Eber. His own words to Balak seem to show that he knew of the blessing pronounced on Israel, "How shall I curse whom God hath not?" when taken with his words, "Who can count the dust of Jacob?" in which there seems to be an allusion to the promise to Jacob, "Thy seed shall be as the dust of the earth"—a word of meaning to those who had seen the desert of Arabia—and when taken with the words, "Rise up, Balak, and hear"—for not even kings may sit to hear the word from the King of kings—" Rise up and hear; God is not the son of man that he should repent; hath he not spoken and shall he not make it good?" Undoubtedly these last words immediately refer to the blessing which Balaam himself had just pronounced on Israel, and yet both the king and the prophet may then have had in mind this blessing and promise to Abraham and his family : " I will bless thee, and thou shalt be a blessing," though they may not have chosen to remember those other words which only the future-seeing God could then have spoken, " In thy seed shall all the nations of the earth be blessed "—words whose fulfilling to the uttermost is hastening now on all the winds of heaven.

OF THE CONSISTENCY OF HIS HISTORY.

This history, for Scripture, is uncommonly minute ; and every way it is explanatory of itself. The Seer's intelligence of the past may have been one of the conditions of that intelligence of the future which can be referred to no human source, as when he says, " This people shall dwell alone ;" and this conditioning of the supernatural upon the natural also appears in the advance of his prophecy from one stage of it to another. For as the stubbornness of Pharaoh called forth more and more of the Will above the human will, so the unyielding mind of Moab called forth more and more of the Mind that is above the human mind. The first stage of this prophecy is hardly more than the prophet's refusal to curse Israel. In its second stage the prophet hears the shout of a king in that democratic camp, and explains this by saying, " God is in the midst of them." In the third his vision of this king takes on a human form ; and this king in Israel is higher than Agag, the common name of the kings of the Amalekites, as Pharaoh was of the Egyptian kings ; and why they were taken as representative of all kings, comes out when Amalek is called "the first of the nations." His words thus point to him of whom Daniel said, " Behold, one like unto the Son of man came to the Ancient of Days, and there was given him a kingdom, that all peoples, nations, and languages, should serve him."

But all these prophecies together do hardly prepare for the reserve of power that comes out in the last, where the breadth of illumination and prophetic grandeur is in harmony with its belonging to a class of prophecies of world-endings of which there is a series in the Bible; and which, it would seem from other Scriptures, could only have been uttered in the end of a world. But to make this thought more clear, it should be said that time is conceivable only as a cycle or a succession of cycles; and so the notion of any endless rectilinear progress is not only *irrational*, but *unthinkable*. The cyclical idea of time is the only idea of time that we can have, and it is upheld by all the manifestations of created life, each of whose forms is every-where passing through its cycle of growth and decay. In harmony with this law of our thinking and with the whole constituting of nature, there is every-where recognized in the Bible a succession and series of *time-worlds;* or, to take the modern word that comes nearest to its thought, of *ages;* and of successive *world-endings*, more and more resembling that when time shall end —that is, the cycle of duration measured by the circlings of our planet round the sun.

The spirit of prophecy ever seems to awaken the soul of the prophet to discern from afar this world-end in those previous world-endings, each of which, in truth, is a Coming, or judgment of Christ. It was by means of such comings that he described his final coming; and as the Bible-idea of the other world-endings has been much obscured, so has what he says of the end of the world, and what the apostles say of his coming in their own day.

The last of Balaam's oracles is concerning what he himself calls "*the end of days*," that is, of time-worlds. The truth there is in a time-world is its life; it gives to it character, and determines its duration. Balaam belonged to a time-cycle that was then passing away; the truth there was in it died with him;* and his mental relations to the fact that his time-world was ending, may have been one of the conditions of the revelation to him of the endings of time-worlds that were to come farther down in the abyss of Time. For though the Natural seems to

---

* In this revelation of the divine purpose in the Call of Abraham, "In thy seed shall all the nations of the earth be blessed," there is seen the beginning of a new cycle from which others were to unfold till they covered all the earth. Yet a quarter of a century passed before an heir was born to Abraham, and centuries before the new age began to be manifest to human eyes. It was so, when Israel came out of Egypt; it was fully so, when in Canaan Israel took its seat among the nations; and coincident with this, it would seem, must have been the ending of the preceding cycle of time. The prophet Balaam withstood the new age inaugurated by the prophet Moses; and when Balaam died, the past, which in his heart he desired to uphold, seems to have descended with him into the sepulcher. His Oracle is the last religious word of the once sacred, highly favored East. In his history the religion of Shem and of Noah as there corrupted and debased, yet still keeping something of its primal glory and light, found a last solemn expression, that is a monument and a warning. As sometimes there are strange contrasts in the utterances of a dying man—flashes of intelligence mingling with delirium—so there are in this last apparition of the old Religion; and then in the East the silence of death.

have permanence and law, and the Supernatural may seem to be sudden and fitful as the lightning flashing at irregular intervals, it is the supernatural that abides the same, while the natural, even in the heart of the mountain and the depths of the planet, is ever passing through some fraction of its round of change. If, then, in any one case, the conditions can be determined in the multiform and ever-changing natural, in which the supernatural has manifested itself, it is known, because of its unchangingness, that in similar conditions it may again be manifest. Now it was at the ending of a time-world that Daniel beheld the time-worlds that were to be ; and it was at the ending of a time-world that our Lord revealed the end of time. From the mount of Olivet the mountain of Moab can be seen ; and it was the same Lord who, on the one as on the other, caused something of the vision before the Almighty to be made known in the midst of that obstinate unbelief and presumptuous determination in the will of man to withstand the newer will of God, which, ever characterizing the wickedness of a dying world, gives occasion alike for the Prophecy and the Judgment.

It now becomes more clear, from a purely human point of view, why Balaam could not anathematize the children of Israel. He knew too much about them. His bad heart was not bad enough wholly to darken his clear-seeing intellect. And the divine influence which held him back from this sin could act in harmony as well as in conflict within the heart of the man who could pray he might die the death of the righteous, who mingled his wail with his vision

of coming judgment, and felt he should see the Lord
only afar off; and thus, that divine influence could
make him in a certain sense the willing voice of its
purpose; and thus, while the divine control of human
events is here manifest, it is also manifest that even
in that hour of ecstasy, no violence was done to the
human will.

In a way that shows in him some sharpness of insight, Moab discerned this willingness in Balaam,
and it made him very angry. The king "smote his
hands together," yet, respecting the sacred office of
the prophet, and fearing to trust himself, he bade
him fly. Balaam had courage. He firmly stood his
ground till the king controlled his anger; and so
there was occasion given for that last revelation, after
which no more is heard of the king's wrath against
the prophet. They part, for a time, in silence. So
ends a scene which is a true comment on words
which go as deep into the mystery of evil as any in
Holy Writ: "Surely the wrath of man shall praise
thee; the remainder of wrath shalt thou restrain."
It is wonderful how in that old time, and far away
off there on that hill of Moab, these two men not
only do make, but anticipate history. King and
priest have usually found a "holy alliance" convenient and profitable; but when, as often has happened,
there has been strife between them, the pride of a
priest never yet quailed before the anger of a king.

OF HIS DEFINITION OF RELIGION.

The crowning evidence, alike of Balaam's clear,
deep insight into religion, and of truth in his cycle,

which, though dying with him, in other ever-widening cycles lives on forever, comes out in the definition of religion he gave to Moab, the best definition of it ever given—a lightning flash in the darkening horizon of his time, only less vivid than those prophecies of his that light up the horizon of time itself. Hardly less instructive than those words are the circumstances in which they were spoken; and the consideration of the two completes all that here need further be said of the character and the mission of the prophet.

The amity and peace which Israel proffered, Moab would not hear of, for he knew too well what was going on. He beheld what king never beheld before. He saw a new power in the earth, and its leader was like no king. No regal tent was in that camp. No royal banner was displayed before that march. Moab could not fathom the future of that democratic movement, which from that far off *beginning*, " perplexing monarchs with the fear of change," now gloriously moves on in all the earth; yet this apparition of slaves whom Christ had delivered from the kingly and priestly bondage, the splendid miseries, the bitter mockeries, the unrequited toil of what the world called civilization then, as it calls it now, of slaves changed to men and trained to arms, of a people emerging from a desert, was to him a sight of dread ; and this sight of a people awakened in him, as it does in all kings, priests, and aristocrats like him, unfathomable fears.

This ante-type of Philip of Spain and of Charles Stuart of England, determined to crush that people.

The warlike Amorites had been utterly defeated, and when after that the Arabian kings took counsel together, the military was succeeded by the ecclesiastical plan. With wealth and power, power like a king, they at last succeed in bribing the High-Priest of the time:—to carry back a word that in those regions belongs to a later date, but which is the true word here to use, if regard be had to essential likeness of idea in the midst of unlike outward circumstances. In like manner, the peculiar form their policy assumed, the calling in of this prophet to curse Israel, only becomes intelligible when the idea and the fact repeat themselves in ages long afterward. Those princes and kings meant to array against that people the religious feeling of their world, and thus to strike terror into them, to divide them, and to encourage their enemies to assault them as men divinely doomed to certain destruction. The Pontiff of that time was sent for from afar to excommunicate that kingless people.*

---

* The power of a scheme that fails is apt to be misjudged. This attempt of Moab and his confederates to harm Israel seemed to me for a great part of my life (as it may have seemed to others) so childish, meaningless, and feeble, that the intervention of the Almighty would have been beyond belief, had not a reverence for Scripture come in aid of inadequate interpretation of the history. Now, reading with more intelligent eyes, I see clearly that had the prophet in this matter been suffered to forward the evil intent of Moab, as in other instances religious men of evil influence have been suffered to forward the intent of evil kings, it would have united the disunited, irresolute peoples whose hearts were hostile to Israel, in a military frenzy of fanaticism that would have swept before it the army of Moses, as the whirlwind the sands of the desert. The dan-

It was to accomplish this, that Balaam set out from the town of Pethor by the Euphrates, with a retinue of princes ; riding, as in those days and countries kings rode ; as in the end of the next cycle of time another prophet rode into the city of Jerusalem. It was to accomplish this that the king of Moab went out to meet Balaam "in the uttermost coast" of his realm. Here, then, was the same alliance of king and priest which put to death that other Prophet, the true King of men, the only Priest, in the city of Jerusalem ; and has put to death so many of his followers since. Here, then, was the beginning of unnumbered woes All this can be clearly seen in a purely human view of these events ; and when the vail of things else hidden from knowledge is drawn back, and mingling with the light of all other history unearthly light is let in upon the scene, it is not strange that strange things are revealed, that one of those cattle in whose stable our Lord was born, one of those mute creatures whose "earnest expectation waiteth for the manifestation of the sons of God,"* that through the divine will and power "the dumb ass, speaking with a man's voice," rebuked "the madness of the prophet," † the angel drew his sword, and these secret things were brought to light that all might know that in the war against Christ the mute creation, below and around us, and the heavens

---

ger was real and great. To this witnesses the law of the Lord, that because of their calling in of Balaam, an Ammonite or a Moabite shall not enter the congregation of the Lord forever. Deut. xxiii, 3, 4.

* Rom. viii, 19. † 2 Pet. ii, 16.

above us, have an interest in what man is doing;
and that to all might be manifest the unbending will
of man—for the brave bad prophet rode on—and
the will of the Most High ever to uphold and forever to guard against the freedom of the human will.
To guard against the freedom of the human will—
evidently for this these marvels were made to come
to pass ; for, strike them out of the history, and it is
past understanding why on that perilous mountain
this bold man did not give in to those who sent
for him ; why this false prophet did there fulfill the
office of a prophet that was true ; why he did not become as recreant to God then as he did afterward.
He dared not speak otherwise than as God told him
to speak, and so through his own will he became the
instrument of the Almighty's will, for the sword of
the angel brought with it salutary fear. Though,
with the same willfulness that, knowing it was wrong,
had brought him so far, he would not turn back on
his path, yet as he looked forward to meeting with
the king this made him firmly make up his mind to
obey God, not indeed through any high motive, yet
not the less clearly illustrating how the will of God
works its will in the will of man. This was at the
last moment. Moab then was near at hand ; for,
as Balaam's own servants only were with him, the
princes must have gone on to meet the king and
to announce the prophet's coming ; and as at the
close of the words of the angel they were in sight,
they must then have been returning to escort him to
the presence of the king, with whom his meeting
seems almost instantly to follow.

The intelligent belief of Moab in interventions of God is so consistent with the mode of revelation in the first cycle of time, that it is one of the facts which make the supposition, that this history is later than its date, as reasonless to a pure criticism, as it is to that reverence for the word of God, which has too sure foundations to be shaken by any little difficulties in the Scriptures, where, if there were not difficulties both little and great, there could be neither antiquity nor depth. Vision and voice, and the angel of the Lord revealed to eye and ear in human form and act, were in that world; and hence the king's sure feeling there were communications from the Most High that were neither to be concealed nor disobeyed. And yet with this true intelligence there blended a childish notion that the prophet had some power or art to mold to his own purposes the will of the Most High, and that the king might justly be enraged with him if he failed to put this forth. In this thought and hope of Moab there was presumption and folly, and in the prophet's countenancing it—and his coming did so—there was guilt. The next step in sin for a priest is to counterfeit such a power, and for a king, knowing the fraud, to uphold him in it, it being agreed between them that the fraud shall be made to further their common selfish ends. This could be, but not till a later day of riper wickedness. This was to come in ages more atheistic in spirit and deeper in guilt. It was to come, but the time of such iniquity was not yet.

Somewhere in the course of events, which reached its height on the mountain—probably before that, but whether before or after, there seems to be nothing

that tells—the king of Moab, feeling that God was on
the side of Israel, thought to bring him over to his
side by some most costly and precious offering—
a vain, presumptuous thought, yet common and natural in the human breast, though the form of the
sacrifice that Moab thought to make was horrid indeed. Moab was ready to make the same dread
offering that, long afterward, Mesha,* one of his successors, did make of his own son to Chemosh, the
national god of the Moabites ; and let us be just, each,
no doubt, thinking it would be for good. For even

---

* 2 Kings iii, 26, 27. This king having failed to cut his way
with seven hundred men out of the last of his strongholds,
Kir Haraseth, (the modern Kerak,) then sacrificed his son and
heir to the fire-god, on the wall, in sight of his enemies on
the amphitheater of hills so closely encircling the rock of the
town that from them slingers could throw stones into the
citadel. What followed is evidence (though the time was
later) of that quickness of the people of those regions to religious impulses, named when speaking of what might have been,
had the prophet cursed the children of Israel. Though
flushed with the hope of the instant capture of the city and
king, there fell on the beseigers a religious fear, an overmaster-
ing dread, and they all withdrew. Before that town they no
longer dared abide.

This may have much depended on the fact that the victim
was the king's son, for human sacrifices were known in all
that part of the world. There are some traces of this horrid
rite among most of the heathen, as even among the Romans
as late as the Christian era ; yet with Aryan peoples—and probably with the Moabites—it was rare. But this inhumanity
seems to have been a common part of the ritual of some of the
peoples of Western Asia—one of many facts that show the peculiar and remarkable hardness, fierceness, and audacity in the
Shemitic and Hamitic apostasy from the faith, hereafter spoken
of in chapter v, 134–140.

in the cruel thought of Moab there seems to have been something like the feeling ascribed in the religious fables of the Romans to Curtius, when, clad in armor, he leaped his horse into the gulf, which, ever yawning wider in the Forum, the oracle said would close only when the most precious things in Rome were thrown into it. Moab was ready to offer " thousands of rams and ten thousands of rivers of oil ;" and rising to a great height of patriotic self-devotion, and identifying himself with the sin of his nation, he asked the priest, if he " should sacrifice his first-born for his transgression, the fruit of his body for the sin of his soul." So, in the end of another cycle of time, Caiaphas counseled that one man should die for many, knowing in his heart that he was speaking of the best and holiest in the land. Moab spoke of the oldest prince of the blood. As kings usually are when they see an uprising of the people, Moab was terribly in earnest and very sincere. Caiaphas was worse than Moab, Balaam better than either. He rejected the thought of the king, saying to Moab, " The Lord hath showed thee, O man, what is good ; and *what doth the Lord require of thee, but to do justly, and to love mercy, and to walk humbly with thy God?*" Micah vi, 5–8. Sublime words, sublimely applied ! and which seem to be taken— but the Scripture is before you, and let each one judge for himself—from some common authoritative source, known as such both to the king and the prophet.

Certain Germans have said that those words show a religious knowledge that could have been developed

only in later ages.   Those words show a knowledge
of the intent and meaning of sacrifice ; but sacrifice
is a type whose origin reaches back to the beginning
of the human race ; and while others forgot and per-
verted its meaning, there were few more certain than
this great prophet to have done neither ; and that he
saw through the dark heathenism of Moab, and fear-
lessly reproved its injustice, cruelty, and presumption,
accords with his courage, his religion, and with all
the Bible records of the spiritual illumination of the
early ages of the world.

Doubtless Balaam saw, what every clear-sighted
man must see, that all the right doing that man can
do is but his reasonable service, and that he has no
way of making up for his sins.   As the people of
God had ever known this, doubtless he knew it was
an error to think God delighted in burnt-offering; a
debasement, and denial of the typical and prophetic
meaning of sacrifice.   He was too intelligent a
priest to have the slightest confidence in any priestly
thing.   He had too much intellectual honor to cheat
the king.   His words to him set aside the idea that
in the matter of his sins man is to propitiate God in
any way of sacrifice.   In this, true and false religion
differ.   So they differ now, and they have always
so differed.   All this difference is in the wisdom
of Abel and the presumption of Cain.   As in that
beginning, so ever since, the hate of the false to the
true religion, of the pride of the one to the humility
of the other, of its haughty trust in works to the
other's faith in Christ, seldom fails at last to reach
the wrath of murder ; and so those of the true

religion, like the righteous Abel, often seal their witness to it with their own blood—even those slain for
the word of God whose souls from under the altar
cry, How long, O Lord, holy and true, dost thou not
avenge our blood! And many are the signs that do
now foretell that the last conflict between true and
false religion draws nigh.

OF THE CHARACTER OF THIS PROPHET.

Balaam was no more a heathen than he was a
Hebrew. He inherited that temperament sensitive
to spiritual impressions, which belongs alike to wizard
and prophet. He was born when the sky of his
world was darkened, when true religion was inter-
mingled with magic, priestcraft, and idolatry; yet he
knew much truth, he was very religious, and came
very near being good. Were his a human history
only, in his temptations, what now read as words of
God would read as the utterings and pleadings of
his own conscience; but in the Scripture the vail is
withdrawn, and we are permitted to know, what in
like cases with ourselves few of us do know, and yet
what Balaam knew so well, the divine voice that
blends into one tone with the voice of the conscience
till all seems human. He gave in to the twice repeated temptation, when the king said, I will pro-
mote thee to very great honor; thinking to himself,
though I go into this sin I will not sin, which, again,
is translated for us unto a higher than human dialect;
and he goes, intelligent that he can only do the Divine will, yet seeking his own ends, goes with eyes
wide open on his self-determined way to ruin. Yet

it was hard for him, as it is hard for any man, to baffle the wish of the Father in heaven, whose tender mercies are over all the works of his hands, to save him.   He barely escaped eternal life.

Neither Balaam nor Moab was the worst of men. They were like many that have come after them. King-type and priest-type of an evil sort are they; and long the war of king and priest against the people of God, which they began; and much the same as theirs, the means all like them have used. Yet the good in Balaam is brought out in his history as clearly as the evil; making it a true picture of the inconsistencies and contradictions there may be in a religious man; a picture, not the less instructive now because it is a very old picture, of the spiritually minded and worldly minded minister.   The last line is given to the drawing of his character, and he fully justifies the sympathy of the king, when he tells him to use the beauty of the women of Moab and of Midian to seduce the men of Israel to sensual worship.   In this the history marks in him the blending, not unknown in our day, of the clairvoyant and the licentious in the same nature.   It marks, too, that when in this *beginning* priest counseled king, the priest divined how destructive to true religion is religion that gives license and gratification to the senses.   The words, "God is a spirit, and they that worship him must worship him in spirit," every-where do now oppose the *spirit* of Balaam's evil counsel; and yet, while every age has admired his insight into true religion, the experience of every age has justified his insight into false religion; and in this as in many

ways, this history is a magic glass showing before,
the coming time.

Moses was more tempted than Balaam, yet by faith
he refused to be called the son of Pharaoh's daughter,
choosing rather to suffer affliction with the people of
God than to enjoy the pleasures of sin ; esteeming
the reproach of Christ greater riches than the treasures of Egypt, and fearing not the wrath of the king,
he endured as seeing Him who is invisible. Balaam
was a prophet, a poet, and a soldier, as Moses was;
and a man of the world, as Moses was not. He was
a great man ; in death the sacred history gives him
rank with kings, but in trying to combine the character of a man of God and a man of the world he
failed where none will ever succeed.

Some dreamed of old that the Great Cycle of Time
would so repeat itself that all things would at length
come round to the same state again. Nature in its
cycles seemed to hint at something of this sort, as
when the second childhood repeats the first ; and
owing to the cyclical law of all being that is not
eternal, there often are what look like recurrences in
nature and in life. As we look down towards the
close of the next time cycle after him, we see resemblances between him and Caiaphas. Each wield-
ed a commanding religious influence ; each had a
prophetic gift ; each was placed at the intersection
of two cycles of time ; and showing that, as in
these cycles the truth is ever widening and heightening, so the evil is ever growing more intense,
in the earlier cycle kings sought the aid of the
priest, in the later priests sought the aid of kings;

and all had the same intent, to stay the inevitable coming of the future which God ordained.

In that time-world to which Balaam belonged, Melchisedek, the highest form, is of course higher than Abraham, with whom a new time-world began. Abraham paying tithes to Melchisedek is the new time, rendering its fitting tribute of honor to the old ; Melchisedek giving his benediction to Abraham, after his defeat of the five kings, is the old time recognizing and blessing the new.

In that time-world to which Balaam belonged, Abraham represents the spiritual principle in alliance with God. He is firm in faith, cheerful, hopeful, and sure of the coming age. Balaam represents its spiritual principle in alliance with sin ; he is wavering, conscious of guilt, corrupt, and the corrupter of others. He is foiled and slain. The dying voice of the evil of his time is heard from his lips— that wail of sorrow and of fear which is ever wrung from the unbelief of a departing age as it confronts the glory and hope of a new time. Of Balaam's grave no man knoweth, or whether he had a grave ; but the unviolated sepulchre of Father Abraham is with us till this day.

CHAPTER II.

WAS A STAR FORETOLD?

THE prophet's coming sent a thrill of fear through the twelve tribes.* It sent a thrill of hope through the Arabian tribes. They felt as Balak did when his messengers went to Pethor, saying to Balaam, "Behold, there is a people come up out of Egypt, they cover the face of the earth ; come now curse me this people, peradventure I shall be able to overcome them ;" and so the sheikhs of those tribes came to hear this prophet utter his malediction, his *interdict* of the people of Israel, which was to kindle to religious fanaticism the martial hatred of their kinsmen of the desert.† This scheme was so peril-

---

* The Moabites could not have kept their sending for Balaam a secret if they had so wished. Before the failure of their schemes, which they did not look for, they had every motive for making it public, and they did so. Balak went out as far as his last town to welcome Balaam ; and coming with him to Kirjath-huzoth, (the city of streets, Strasburg,) Num. xxii, 36, 39, 40, he there openly did honor to him and the princes with him. About this time there was a good deal of intercourse between the Midianites, Moabites, and the Israelites ; and all that was going with either of these two parties was of interest to the other. The Israelites could not but have found out all about the sending for Balaam ; and, as they were only less superstitious than their hostile kinsmen, they must have feared what might come of it.

† Stanley, lec. viii: " The eye follows the Two as they climb upward from height to height of the extended range ; to the

ous and so wicked as to call in the known intervention of God; and twice, overmastered by superior
influence, the baffled seer told the king the truth—

---

high places (Num. xxii, 41) dedicated to Baal, 'on the top of
the rocks;' the bare hill close above it, (xxiii, 3, 9;) 'the cultivated field' of the watchmen, (xxiii, 14) (Zophim,) on the top
of Pisgah, (xxiii, 28;) to the peak where stood 'the sanctuary
of Peor that looketh toward the waste.' . . . Behind him lay
the vast expanse of desert extending to the shores of his native
Assyrian river. On his left were the red mountains of Edom
and Seir; opposite were the dwelling places of the Kenite in
the rocky fastnesses of En-gedi; farther still was the dim outline of the Arabian wilderness where ruled the then powerful
tribe of Amalek; below him lay the vast encampment among
the acacia groves. Beyond, on the western side of Jordan, rose
the hills of Palestine, with glimpses through their valleys of ancient cities towering on their crested heights." Stanley is the
Claude Lorraine of history. In the Scripture-pieces of each the
figures are lost in the landscape. Without faith in its supernatural, Hebrew history is cloud-land and shadows. In faith
Stanley is deficient and wavering. To the school of Bunsen, of
which he is a disciple greater than his master, there is wanting a clear perception of the truth in this saying of Bolingbroke,
which, skeptic though he was, shows good English common
sense: "The miracles of the Bible are not like those in Livy,
detached pieces that do not disturb the civil history, which goes
on very well without them; the whole history is founded on
them, and if it were not a history of them it would be a history
of nothing." Stanley's calling Balaam "the rival, the possible
conqueror of Moses," is a gleam of historic genius, but nothing
in his lecture explains or confirms these words. He is one of
the great writers on Hebrew history; and his error in speaking
of Balaam and the king as alone on the mountain, is shared by
those I have consulted. It is an error that stands in the way of
insight into the calling in of Balaam. It is an error that is
strange indeed; for, who built the seven altars and slew on
each the ox and the ram? And is it not said in Num. xxiii, 6,
there were with the king "all the princes of Moab?"

true for all time—"there is no enchantment against Jacob, no divination against Israel;" yet Moab would not give up—prefiguring the Heart of Man persistent in its unrelenting determination to wrest the Intellect to the service of its evil desires. For the third time the reluctant prophet is constrained to go and plead with Jehovah, while the smoke of sacrifice ascends, and expectant kings and nobles wait by their red altar-fires burning on the mountain. For the third time the word from before the Lord made known his decrees, but they bowed not their will before the manifest will of Heaven. Therefore, to warn them, to warn many who should come after them, and with appropriateness to this beginning in the long war of the Church and the World, at last there was unvailed before the prophet the Vision of all time. Nothing less can harmonize all there is in the record; and no doom-dealing oracle of Ezekiel, no imperial vision of Daniel, no other prophecy opens with words giving so startling an idea of its grandeur as these, which, twice repeated, go before utterances of Balaam: *He heard the word of God, knew the knowledge of the Most High, saw the vision of the Almighty.*

OF REVELATION, AS OF SCRIPTURE ONLY.

Thus there comes out, even in this early time, that idea and fact of Revelation which distinguishes the true religion from the religions of the world. Well nigh universal has been the thought of some divine influence as possessing seer or sibyl, and opening the future in dream, vision, or ecstasy, as well as kindling, exalting, and purifying utterance, in which form it was prayed for by the poet in his invocation to the Muse; but revelation in Scripture goes so far beyond all this that it becomes something quite un-thought of by the heathen world. It is no disclosure of isolated events, but of the whole plan and purpose of God in time. There was no word that did, or could, have this meaning in classic Greek; nor does any word have quite this full significance in the Greek of the New Testament. The idea had to precede its name, the fact had to become clear to the mind, be-fore any one word could set it forth. It is all Script-ure that enables us to give to the word Revelation the full sense in which we have come to use it; it is all Scripture that has made that meaning so familiar to us that we have become too little sensible to its sublimity, and almost insensible to its novelty outside of the Bible. Yet the thought is quite as conspicuous in the Old Testament as in the New. In neither is Revelation merely the unvailing of moral laws obscured by sin; it is historical rather than didactic; and it every-where points to Christ as the center of itself, as Him in whom the purpose of God in space and time, finds its meaning and its end.

GENERAL INTERPRETATION OF THE LAST OF BA-LAAM'S ORACLES.

As the divine influence smote the Seer, he fell to the ground; and in the sleep of his senses, saw*

---

* In the same paragraph (Num. xxiv, 15, 16) our version twice speaks of the prophet's open eyes; but the Hebrew is not the same in both places, and it is disputed whether in the first it should be translated *open*, or, curiously enough, *shut*. The with "the unsleeping eye of the soul." The awe and terror of what he beheld wrung from the depths of his shuddering conscience words, the same in spirit with those other words of his, " Let me die the death of the righteous ;" these dread words of wailing, " I shall see Him, but not now; I shall behold Him, but not nigh." This real human cry is convincing evidence of the reality of what Balaam beheld ; it puts the human soul *en rapport* with his ; yet were it not for his thrilling outcry that suggests so much to which the human conscience makes response, his oracles at their first hearing would hardly seem to equal the awful promise of the words that go before them. His thoughts come back so quick from beyond the bounds of this world to Amalek and Edom, his far-opening words so suddenly contract, that some hear them as if they foretold a mere smiting of the corners of Moab. They do not see the universal, shining through the particular ; how one word must stand for many as he would utter the unutterable ; how natural the inevitable glimpse revealed of his own new world of feeling and thought ; then that he recalls the star that burned, the scepter that smote ; then that Moab, Edom, Amalek draw the lightning ; while with the personal and the present so blend the far and the universal as to bear out the

---

disputants make the word point to a physiological fact. It is perhaps possible that both words point psychologically, and denote states or stages of spirit-vision. The latter certainly does. On this the best comment is 1 Sam. iii, 1, a verse rich in suggestion. In Israel there came an evil time when " there was no open vision." This verse confirms the meaning above given to the latter phrase, as above quoted from Philo.

declaration, made when little had come to pass to confirm it, but now with the witness of ages, that he saw the Vision before the Almighty: so through the lifting mist is seen the troubled boundless ocean, and felt its power, as landward rolling waves smite with thunder the isles, the rocks, and shores.

Balaam foresaw something of that which the world-conscience ever foresees. He foresaw a series of divine judgments in such long and orderly succession that at last they awakened in his soul a true presentiment of what would be beyond them all—even of the coming of Him by whom those visitations came, his appearing at last to put an end to the guilty world, and to sit in judgment on the quick and the dead.

The want of perspective, this apparent confusion of the far and the nigh, is the seal of truth. The prophet could not set forth under the law of time what was over and beyond all time, nor declare the vision "before" the Almighty in words of men.* Still his broken words are in keeping with the far-determining import of the hour. They open the future, and yet are naturally limited and determined by the circumstances in which he is placed. As he comes out of his trance and struggles clear of his personal feelings, in the group around, gathering close to listen, he recognizes haughty Amalek, chief of the swarthy riders of the desert, and the Kenites, proud of their strongholds in the rocks : "And when

---

* Where our Version has *of*, the Targums of Palestine and Jerusalem have *before*—"The vision before the Almighty." Of this every one must feel the sublimity.

he looked on Amalek, he took up his parable, and said, Amalek was the first of the nations; but his latter end shall be that he perish forever. And he looked on the Kenites, and took up his parable, and said, Strong is thy dwelling-place, and thou puttest thy nest in a rock. Nevertheless the Kenite shall be wasted, until Asshur shall carry thee away captive." Utterance failed; for though his thought

> Flashed o'er the future, bidding men behold
> Their children's children's doom, already brought
> Forth from the abyss of time that is to be,
> The chaos of events, where lie half-wrought
> Shapes that must undergo mortality,

he had no words that could describe the foreshadowed future of nameless nations then unborn. Catching at the hint in the only name that could then point to the track of his thought, history fills out the blank with devastations that, rising out of the East, swept over Syria; judgments that so touch his soul, distracted between good and evil, that he cried out, in words so like all his personal utterances, "Alas! who shall live when God doeth this!"

Still struggling to set forth in the language that was, things that were to be, he makes known, as best he might, what was to come farther down in the abyss of time: "And ships shall come from the coast of Chittim, and shall afflict Asshur, and shall afflict Eber, and he also shall perish forever." Those words were written in a language that was dead before they came to pass. They were spoken

> When Tiber slept beneath the cypress gloom,
> And silence held the lonely woods of Rome,

when the Greek empire existed only in the purpose
of God. A thousand years before the gulf and shore
of Salamis knew the fight that in after ages sent the
world-traversing army of Alexander to the Indus,
longer still before the galleys of Rome bore her
avenging legions to Palestine, those words foretold
that from the shores of the Great Sea of the West,
the Greek would come to humble the pride of the
East, and after him, the Roman to destroy the
Hebrews : * and they also foretold the ruin of those

---

* The wondrous foresight of the oracle here is strangely
limited by some orthodox critics.   They make Asshur stand for
Assyrians on this side of the Euphrates, Heber for those on the
other.   This has no countenance from geography or history.
It may seem to have some from the Targum of Onkelos, but
the language of this is explained by the two other Targums,
which here speak of "the children beyond the river," meaning
Hebrews of the Far East.   Their rendering probably grew out
of the error as to Gen. xiv, 13. (See note pp. 5, 6.)   On the
other hand the "Speaker's Commentary" makes Asshur and
Shem mean "the descendants of Shem generally"—a wide
sweep, and happily with no countenance from Scripture ; for
neither sacred nor common history knows of any fulfillment of
the prediction so wildly interpreted as to include all those
Shemitic Arabs who were never subdued.   Each of these notions runs counter to the interpreting mind and memory of the
Church, as represented by the Septuagint, the Syriac Version,
and the Vulgate, which here understand, *the Hebrews.*

Some refer the words "and he also shall perish forever"
to the Hebrews : but he that is to come in ships, he it is that
shall also perish.   The Greeks so came.   The fight at Salamis
by land and sea is taken to represent that series of victories
which repelled from Europe the Asiatic invasion of the hordes
of Xerxes.   This afterward fired Alexander to conquer Asia ; he
thus unconsciously beginning the fulfillment of the prophecy uttered by Noah, when Noah and his three sons were all the men

who would come from the West in ships, whom the
prophet could not name, for as yet they had no name ;
and thus his words here reach down through the
third and fourth of the cycles of time, through the
Greek kingdom of brass, and the Roman kingdom of
iron, revealed in a vision of the night to the king of
Babylon.

Thus, in the same vision, the prophet beheld the
future glory of Israel, and something of the misery
which has befallen the children of Heber in all the
earth ; his last words, revealing this insight into
future time, being only less wonderful than his first,
which reach beyond all time. Most truthful, too, was

---

of the human race. Gen. ix, 27. These words of 1 Maccabees
i, 1, 2, clearly pointing to the oracle of Balaam, show it was
then understood of the Greeks : " Alexander, son of Philip,
the Macedonian, came out of the land of Chettiim "—the old
form of the word used by Balaam—" smote Darius, King of the
Persians and the Medes, made many wars, and took spoils of
many nations, insomuch that the earth was quiet before him."
That Balaam here prophesied of the Greeks none will doubt
who hold that he prophesied at all. Did he of the Romans
also ? When all the peculiarities of the case are fairly considered, his words seem to encompass all those, nameless to
him, who came sailing from the West, to destroy the Assyrians
and the Hebrews. To this the interpreting mind and memory
of the Church assent in the Targums of Palestine and of
Jerusalem ; and in the Vulgate, which with a bold paraphrase
says, *Venient in trieribus de Italia*, " They shall come in triremes
from Italy." Thus the time-plan of the world as seen by
Balaam is the same as in the vision seen by Nebuchadnezzar,
King of Babylon, which was interpreted by the prophet Daniel,
and as revealed on the Mount of Olives. I ought, perhaps, to
say I did not reach this thought by reasoning back, but, first
having made up my mind as to the reach of the oracle, then
came to see its agreement with later revelations.

Israel, and the conviction sure, that Balaam "knew the knowledge of the Most High," for on the same page, so bright with glories to come, is transcribed from his lips the doom of the Hebrews.

With difficulty the human memory recalls the hour when Amalek was the first of the nations. It was far "in the dark backward and abysm of time" when Balaam looked out on the host of the Lord; yet the presaging pageant, which then, in that far-off *beginning*, foreshadowed the long war of the people of God, still makes known the pre-ordained triumph of the chieftain born in the house of Jacob. Viewed thus in its true historical and representative character, this scene calls to mind the grand Messianic psalm, *Quare fremuerunt gentes*, "Why do the heathen rage, and the people imagine a vain thing? The kings of the earth set themselves, and the rulers take counsel together, against the Lord and against his anointed, saying, Let us break their bands asunder, and cast away their cords from us. He that sitteth in the heavens shall laugh: the Lord shall have them in derision." The scope of the psalm is universal. There are no local or temporary allusions in it. It is a psalm for the Church militant to chant forever. Yet such is the identity and continuity of thought in Scripture, though the thought is ever enlarging and brightening, that it might fittingly have been sung by Israel when Balaam went away to die in the land of Midian, in the last battle fought by the command of Moses.*

---

* Something here should, perhaps, be said on the question, How did the Israelites get hold of the oracles of Balaam? as

SPECIAL INTERPRETATION OF THE ORACLE WITH
REFERENCE TO THE QUESTION DISCUSSED IN THIS
CHAPTER.

The last of Balaam's oracles has nothing of the
familiarity of Dante with sights of his own making ;

---

to which needless uneasiness has been shown. In all history,
whether of yesterday or to-day, there are things that cannot be
explained, because there is always that which cannot be known.
The first thing here to be thought of is this : Num. xxii, xxiii,
and xxiv, recites facts known only to Balaam, and the recital of
the oracles is evidently from him. This record, then, is his. In
this fact, thus far, there is nothing strange. It was the fixed
habit of the Hebrew prophets to write down their prophetic
and sacred thoughts. A late instance of this is the Song of the
Blessed Virgin, as it may be read in St. Luke. Is there any
reason to think that among the Shemitic peoples this was peculiar to the Jews, or of a later date than Balaam ? None at
all. There never was any need to prove to readers of the Bible
that writing then was known ; and the illusion that it was not,
has already passed away. It was one of the phantoms conjured
up against the Bible by an assumed historical knowledge that
was ignorance. That Balaam wrote out his oracles, inter-
weaving with them, as Daniel did with his, something of his
own history, is almost as certain as that he uttered them. I
have seen the conjecture that, after he parted in silence from
Moab, he may have gone over to the Israelites for a time : this
is barely within the wide limits of possibility ; but if he had he
would never have gone back alive. There is no need to resort
to any thing improbable. The calling in of Balaam has been
proved to have been a public thing, well known to the Israelites ; and this being so, the Israelites must have been bent upon
getting hold of his version of his oracles, and there may have
been so little of difficulty about it that they never thought of
stating how they did it. They must have had their spies among
the Moabites, and easily enough their gold could have bought
of Balaam his oracles. My last thought here, which naturally
might have been my first, but which came after this note was

and yet, its reach and unity are beyond Dante's genius. As natural with his awe-struck conscience, his overburdened brain, his words are few and broken; yet they so cohere as to shadow forth the unutterable whole; and what they speak of being known in the past through history, or foreknown through revelation, it is clear that his vision was suited to the evil heart of the man. In words that make him personify the human Intellect as it wages its unavailing war against Christ, wailing he cries: I shall see him, but not now: I shall behold him, but not nigh. Of this outcry the next words give the cause, in disclosing the symbolism through which the idea was given him of the One whom he could not see: "There shall come a Star out of Jacob, and a Scepter shall rise out of Israel, and shall destroy all the children of Sheth." Balaam had seen the insignia of the Son of man, each of the epochs of whose kingdom is a day of judgment, his spiritual coming to judge the nations, and each and all of which prophesy and prefigure his last and visible coming. The ensigns of a divine being had been shown to Balaam, and *these were all that he could have beheld.* These, and no more, can be shown to the intellect.

---

written, shows how readily some historical difficulties as to Scripture might vanish if every thing were known, or, rather, if all the Scripture tells were thought of—*when Balaam was killed in battle his effects may have fallen into the hands of Moses.* Josh. xiii, 21, 22 : Sihon, king of the Amorites, which reigned in Hesbon, Moses smote, with the princes of Midian : Balaam also, the soothsayer, did the children of Israel slay with the sword among them that were slain.

What is behind them it cannot see. Only the pure heart can see God.

> Dies iræ, dies illa
> Solvet seclum in favilla :
> Teste David cum Sibylla.
>
> The day of wrath, that dreadful day,
> Will melt the world in flame away :
> So David, so the Sibyls say.

Per sepulchra regionum, "through the regions of the sepulcher," the trumpet will send its call ; the immortal Seer will stand up superior to and amid his brethren of all time, and then the prophecy in his dread consciousness will be fulfilled. The wizard intellect of man, in him prefigured on the hill of Moab, will then confess its king, when every eye shall see the Son of man come in his glory.

To his friends his kingdom is "fair as the sun and clear as the moon," to his enemies "terrible as an army with banners." This contrast of feeling thus comes out in the Apocalypse : while kings lament when they see the smoke of a great burning, and the merchants of the earth, weeping and wailing, say, Alas ! that great city that was clothed in scarlet and decked with gold, then was heard a voice, saying, Rejoice, thou heaven and ye holy apostles and prophets, for in her was found the blood of saints ; and there was heard the voice of a great multitude, as the voice of many waters and as the voice of mighty thunderings, saying, Alleluia ! for the Lord God omnipotent reigneth.

The prophet beheld the march of Christ's kingdom as in the thought of its king when he said, *I am come to send fire on the earth.* In the symbolism through

which these things to Balaam were revealed, there
was a Star and a Scepter. Soon as the prophet frees
his soul of its personal forebodings he names this
star and this scepter; and, so doing, he makes known
the way in which the idea was given him of that Invisible King from whom his soul recoiled in sorrow
and in fear. Evidently in that star and that scepter
centered that which overmastered his courage; the
Star, perchance, setting the world in a blaze, and
lighting up the wide desolations, while the Scepter
smote kingdoms to dust.

Did this foreshadowing imagery, besides its office
of revealing a kingdom, did this star and this scepter
point also to realities directly answering to themselves? As this vision through its revelation of the
things done in time attested to the power of Christ,
I look into the Gospel to find what there may answer to the Scepter, and there, so answering, is the
Cross. If this be so, the air-drawn scepter pointed
to a literal scepter, and something as visible and real
must have been prefigured by the Star; whether it
were some light that, looking like a star, might be
described as such, an optical star; or whether it
were—and this is a great question hereafter to be
earnestly thought of—whether it were one of the
stars of heaven.

I am persuaded that the scepter prefigured the
Cross; and yet there seems to be need further to
prove that the star and the scepter foreshadowed
things literally answering to themselves. This symbolism did foreshadow a real kingdom; but did it
also point to other real things to be seen in their

foreseen order, first a Star and then a Scepter? This office of the imagery in addition to what assuredly it did prefigure, and to the use it would seem must have been made of it in the vision, this wheel within these wheels, may seem to complicate matters ; and yet there are three arguments in proof of this, each of which seems to be decisive.

If those who heard the oracle, interpreted what it says of the star and the scepter as foretelling what would literally come to pass, then it must be so interpreted by us. In the interpretation of inspired words no idea is permissible which they did not *in some degree* awaken in the minds of those to whom they were given—a rule that again and again will have to be applied in the course of this volume. As often and as far as this plain rule of common sense is disobeyed, the Scripture is made over after man's device. This has often been done ; Scripture has often become a *palimpsest,* where, the sacred text rubbed out, something else is written over it. This is often so unconsciously done, that it were harsh to call it forgery of Scripture, though nearer to it than it is to interpretation.

This may seem to make the Bible a book not to be read by the people with edification ; but there is much in the Bible to which this rule has no application ; that is to say, there is much in it which does not call for what is styled interpretation ; much as to whose meaning a scholar has no advantage over other men, and where he is sometimes comparatively at a disadvantage. In other cases, where in the reading of the Scriptures some critical knowledge of old

forms of thought and of ancient ways is needed, the
Scriptures themselves are the great storehouse of
material for their own illustration. They contain
within themselves so full, so clear, so living a portraiture of that old world under whose forms of
thought they were given, that the Bible through all
the changes of the world is a self-interpreting book.
The more it is read, the clearer it grows; and this
not by reason of its morally illuminating power only,
but of its mentally illuminating power also. Working to the same end, the providence of God may be
seen in the fact, that the Scriptures must be read by
the people in a translation. Much of all that scholarship can do to make their old forms of thought intelligible is done in a translation by rendering them
into corresponding forms of later thought; as where,
to give an almost trivial illustration, it is said, He
gave to every man a *penny*. With the Scriptures
translated, the common reader has in this matter
much the greater part of all the help that language-
learning can give. Dead languages can suffer no
more change, and so are the only languages that live
unchanged forever. When the languages in which
it was written became dead, the Scripture could not
change; and the language in which Scripture was
written became dead, not that the people might not
understand the Scripture, but that they might understand it better. The translation of the Old Testament into Greek, made at Alexandria some two
hundred years before the birth of our Lord, conveyed
to those Jews who spoke only the Greek language
much of all the light that scholars could then throw

on the meaning of the old Hebrew words. For the English speaking world the like is done by the English version ; and the great argument for its revision is, that the later results of a somewhat finer and truer insight into the meaning of some few words may thus be incorporated into it. A translation tries to embody the interpreting mind and memory of the Church by reproducing in another language the word of God precisely as it was in the language in which it was written ; and this by giving each word as uttered in the old time its exact equivalent in the new. To this end all the old versions are consulted, all recorded thought bearing on the subject is interrogated, and the agreeing voice, so far as it can be ascertained, is the translation. Should, then, a Bible-reader know something of the old thought-world in which the Bible was given ? a Bible-reader cannot but know something of this. Nowhere else is that world so portrayed as in the Bible. Open its pages and you are in it, you breathe its air, you become familiar with it. As you read the book, the world of the book opens around you. In the translation you have much of the best means of understanding the Bible, the very essence of comment, once scattered in thousands of volumes or piled away in hundreds of libraries ; you hear the voice of the universal, ever-living Church, repeating to you in your own tongue, word by word, the holy Scripture.

Some of my readers may say, the interpretation that has been given of the oracle of Balaam does the very thing the rule laid down condemns ; if this were so, it would be fatal to that interpretation, but in it there has been no putting into the oracle of more than could have been in the thoughts of those who heard that oracle ; and the modern comment, that denies its prediction of a real star, leaves out what must have been in their thoughts. In the light of these latter days its burning words have ceased to be luminous ; and to decipher them we must sit with those of old in the evening before the dayspring visited the world, till from the darkness the letters once more come out in fire. For though more may now be seen in the prophecies than was seen by them of old time, not only must that more be essentially the same, but the very condition of rightly seeing this, is first to see what they did. Otherwise, all that seems to be seen may be illusion ; but if we go back to their stand-point, and look along the same line they did, we then may behold the same truths, with further, larger, brighter vision, for along this true line the increasing light brightens forever.

But can the meaning this oracle had, to those who heard it so far back in time and within the circle of a darkening and heathenizing world, now be reached ? Direct means of ascertaining how Moabite, Ammonite, or Amalekite, how Edomite or Kenite understood this oracle there are none; and there never will be any, not though a dozen Moabite stones were found or forged ; yet this can be reached, though no other line of their literature now exists, and no monument of theirs as ancient as this oracle. For what their interpretation of this oracle must have been is very clear when their thinking is known on certain other matters, as to which the thought of the ancient world at all times and every-where was similar, so far as it can be traced, and which can be traced so far and wide as to leave no reasonable doubt it was universal. They were heathenized men who heard this oracle, but this similarity of thinking made its meaning much the same to Israel and to Moab.

Of old the sky seemed not beyond the reach of men. A tower might be built up into it. To the heathen it was the dwelling place of superior beings who sometimes walked the earth, and of heroes who from the earth had gone up among the stars. As the over-world seemed near to them, so did the under-world. Of this the ancient universal notion is pict-ured in these words of a Hebrew to the ghost of a king of Babylon: "Hades from beneath is moved for thee, to meet thee at thy coming: it stirreth up the dead for thee, even all the chief ones of the earth. It hath raised up from their thrones all the kings of the nations." Into that under-ground cavern of the dead, men had gone down and come back. Coming up from thence Samuel's ghost was seen by her of Endor,* and heard to warn the king of Israel that on the morrow he should be there with him.

To the men of those days their oracles were the highest and the surest kind of truth. Into them they looked with the fixed, undoubting eyes to which

---

* 1 Sam. xxviii, 3–25: The heading of this chapter in the Vulgate says, *Saul consulit Pythonissam*, "Saul consults a Pythoness." The choice, whether wise or not, of this word, Pythoness, shows that between Greece and Syria the translator recognized the similarity just spoken of.

alone the secret things of prophecy appear; and men
of spiritual insight, in that darker time, readily divined
their deeper, hidden meanings, where now, through
excess of light, the lines are faint almost to invisi-
bility. In this ancient oracle of Balaam the lines
were then sharp and clear; and with their notions of
the over and the under-world, those who heard the
fearful outcry, "I shall see him but not now," must
have caught the idea, deepening with every other
word, of some demi-god whose rule would be from
the bright realm of ether to the dark under-ground.
In a way easy and natural to them, they would have
combined in their thoughts of him the divine and
the human; nor would it have seemed to them incredible or passing strange, that in some way he
would be of mortal birth, and this world the scene
of his reign. Were this oracle a newly discovered
fragment of old mystic lore, it could only read as a
prophecy of some personage at once human and superhuman, standing in some close relation to Israel, and
whose dominion, to all save Israel, would be a vision
of dread. This meaning in the fragment would at
once be present to our minds, far removed as we are
from that cycle of time in which such thoughts were
familiar things; and thus far, the modern and the ancient sage would interpret such an oracle much alike,
however much more it might have, for the former, of
intensity of interest and vivid reality of truth. Yet
the modern and European reader, would see in the
star and in the scepter only a prophecy of dominion,
and not look for any thing literally to correspond
with them. Not such would be the thought of an

Oriental reader, then or now. The symbolism through which the power and glory of this divine-man was portrayed, would seem to him at once symbolism and literalism. The staff, or wand, or scepter of a magician king, such as Solomon is always said to have been in the legends of the East, has every-where been held in the East, to be both the symbol and the instrument of his wonder-working. In the legends of the Jews, which, in the Targum of Palestine, are enshrined in their Scriptures, that is, are interwoven into a free translation or paraphrase of the sacred text, it is said that after the world was made, "between the suns at the coming in of the Sabbath," ten wonders were created, and among these "the rainbow, the cloud of glory, the ten tables of the law, *and the rod of Moses.*" We may be sure, then, that the thoughts of those who, on the hill of Moab, listened to the wizard, were fastened intently on that rod of empire, foreseen though undescribed. They would have said to themselves, of the shape or the powers of the wand of so mysterious a being we cannot know ; but they could have no doubt it would be as real as the king himself. With those words ringing in their ears they could no more have disjoined the thought of such a wand from such a king, than we can disjoin from such a king the thought of power.

The like is true as to the star. They thought the starry world was co-ordinate and sentient with the human world ; they thought the stars foreshaped and fixed the human destinies ; and even without any word suggesting it, they would have thought the birth of one whose power was to be so new and great in the earth would be marked by an outshining star. What was said of the star must have given this idea to them ; and as this was its meaning to them, it must be its meaning as designed by the Spirit who revealed the vision and inspired the words.

That they did thus interpret those words literally is proved by their literal interpretation by the Jews ; for, as to the single question now before us, Was a star foretold? if we can be sure of the interpretation of this oracle by any one ancient Oriental people, we may be quite sure of that of all others. In the Gospel of St. Matthew alone, there is sufficient evidence that the Jewish interpretation of the oracle was at this point a literal one.* Mark the words of the Magi, " Where is He that is born King of the Jews, for we have seen his star ? " These words do not sound as if the idea of a star at the birth of this king was strange and new ; and the evangelist records them without explanation, evidently because he thought they needed none. These words, then, and still more *the record* of them, prove the expectation of a star at the Messiah's birth was common among the Jews. But, save the oracle of Balaam, nothing in their sacred books warranted this ; for though the figures under which the Lord is spoken of in their Scriptures are many, as when he is called a Sun, a Tower, a Shield,

---

* There is farther evidence of this in the fact that the leader of the Jews in the rebellion in the reign of the Emperor Hadrian, which led to the extirpation of that people from Judea, (A. D. 120,) took to himself the name Barchochab, that is, the Son of the Star.

the Rose of Sharon, the Rock of Ages, yet there He is never called a Star. This was a natural figure in a country where the night is more grateful than the day, but the oracle of Balaam stood right in the way of its use ; and the fact that nowhere else in the Hebrew Bible is the Messiah named with a star, proves that the Hebrew belief in a star at his birth, a belief spread so widely as to be known to Persian Magi, had its root in this prediction.

Thus, while this oracle, "A star shall arise out of Jacob and a scepter from Israel," to us would only be a purely figurative prediction of some glorious and kingly personage, with the modes of thought that must be attributed to those to whom it was given, it was also to them naturally and inevitably a prediction of a star at his birth. Their kindred, a people of similar language, and, as touching this matter, of similar modes of thought, understood this oracle as a prediction of a star. As clearly as in this language and imagery there is to us the prediction of a king, so, *with this, there was to the Jews of old the prediction also of a star;* and they looked as certainly for the fulfillment of the oracle in the one respect as in the other. A star, which according to this antecedent Hebrew interpretation this oracle did predict, according to the Gospel, did appear at the birth of Jesus the Christ. And it greatly strengthens this threefold argument, that the Fathers, who read this oracle with notions as to the stars somewhat like those of the time when it was given, gave to it, at this point, the same interpretation as did the Jews; and held it to be fulfilled in what the Magi saw.

There is one argument more: The life of his people of old more or less foreshadowed the life of
Christ, because the spirit of Christ was in them.
Their lives, and even that of the Hebrew nation,
were in some measure controlled for the purpose of
making this prophecy of him more expressive and
complete ; his life was the theme of revelations sup-
plementing these ; and thus very many of its events
were naturally, or supernaturally, foreshadowed or
foretold: of his infancy, that he would be born of a
virgin, in the family and town of David, that his life
would be in danger, that he would go down into
Egypt and be called from thence ; of the close of his
life, that no bone of his should be broken, the casting
of lots for his vesture, the laying of his body in a rich
man's tomb.   It would seem, then, that the celestial
sign at his birth, whose appearing was interpreted
afar off, the Star heard of by the nations with joy,
must have been predicted of old.*

REPLY TO INQUIRIES THAT MAY ARISE.

1. Some may ask, How could Moab, or Amalek,
or Edom, have aught to do with Christ : they were

---

* There is some disposition in the Church to limit Messianic
prophecy to a few verses, and some in the world, *caused in part
by this*, to deny all prophecy.   Together they indicate an omi-
nous darkening of spiritual insight.   More "open vision" will
come mainly through the heart.   Messianic prophecy is not
of intellectual perception merely.   As the spirituality of the
Hebrew Scriptures is more deeply felt, their Messianic prophecy
is more clearly seen.   Messianic prophecy is their life-giving
and life-preserving element.   The revelation of the Lord pervades the Old Testament as it does the New.   As it is all *from*
him so it is all *of* him.   It was *the Old Testament* which Christ

long before his time? Into the making of a World, the element of Time enters as really as the element of Space. He by whom the world was made "dwelt among us" near the close of the four thousandth year of history, but the day or the year of his birth no man knoweth; so little have clock-measured days or sun-measured years to do with Him, who is "the same yesterday, to-day, and forever." The all-time is the time of Christ.

2. Others may say, to believe in the far-reaching prevision ascribed to Balaam is unphilosophical. If philosophy had humbly refrained from daring and fruitless inquiries into things beyond the human mind, and explored more of the fathomless depths and untold wonders of the soul of man, it would have much less of a controversial spirit in things religious. As a matter of words, foresight in the soul may be a dispute without end; as a matter of fact, all men act upon it. To Balaam there was a miraculous revelation, yet in his trance there may have been a supernatural exaltation of natural power; for, at this very hour, the spirit there is in man hath a prevision of the onburning of the fire the Lord kindleth in the earth, as real, and as really terrible to the world, though foreseen but in part, as the whole, when foreseen by the world's greatest prophet. And something of what he beheld in vision, every generation has beheld in fact. Balaam beheld in vision the onburning fire that ever runs before the Lord. What,

interpreted, when beginning at Moses and the prophets he expounded in all the Scriptures the things pertaining to himself. Luke xxiv, 13–32.

as a whole, he saw in vision, this generation beheld in part, as a dread reality, when it consumed slavery at Gettysburg, and the empire at Sedan. Call it un-philosophical to believe in his vision, the fact remains. It can no more be dissolved in any scientific melting-pot, than the mountain on which the prophet stood—that same Pisgah whence Moses saw the Promised Land. Long before some of the events by Balaam foretold came within the horizon of time, the language in which his vision stands recorded ceased to be spoken among men ; and every age bears clearer wit-ness to its reality as the dream of the world draws nearer to its waking.

3. Others may say, If the star seen by the Magi had been foretold, St. Matthew would have said, as elsewhere he does so often say, Then was the Script-ure fulfilled. This idea has bewildered some Chris-tian critics, and *needs a decisive refutation.** The evangelist does not always use this formula when he might. He does not use it, in this very chapter, when he says, "They are dead that sought the young child's life ;" words recalling like words as to Moses, and bringing out a correspondence between him and Christ. In his time the few and costly manuscripts were committed to memory, and oral teaching stood for the printed page. On the Sabbath the Scriptures

---

* On the other hand, Hengstenberg maintains, as the learned and judicious Archbishop Trench well says, "with great in-genuity and, in the main, success," that the other facts in this part of St. Matthew's Gospel are selected to show how the history of Christ has its roots in the Old Testament ; and, if so, then, this coming of the Wise Men, moved to undertake a pil-grimage by a star.

were read aloud, and the Hebrews, the only people of old who had common schools, were so familiar with their scriptures (as any one may see from the New Testament) that some references to them would then have been more clear than now.

Most of St. Matthew's references to the Hebrew Scripture are to verses not likely to have been familiar, or not understood as he understood them, or not so applied as he applied them; neither was the case here. The Hebrews knew the story of Balaam well. In all their history little could have been better known. More space was given to it than to almost any other event in their Wandering; and it was referred to in several other places in Scripture. All there was of interest about the man was told. The name of his father is given,* and his country and town are twice named. An ordinance, unparalleled in the legislation of Israel, an ordinance without repeal, and reaffirmed after the return of the Jews from Babylon, shut out the Moabites and the Ammonites from the congregation of the Lord forever, because they called in Balaam against Israel. All that pertained to that event was minutely told, and the interest of the story deepened with every scene. It touched the national heart when the malignant enemies of Israel

---

* Given in the New Testament also—2 Peter ii, 15—slight evidence, and yet some, of how the particulars of Balaam's history were written on the Hebrew mind; so too, that in the Books of Philo in six places there is some note of Balaam. He is also named by St. Jude, verse 11; and by our Lord. Rev. ii, 14. Besides, there are a number of places in the Old Testament where, on closely comparing the words in the Hebrew, there are seen to be allusions to the oracles of Balaam.

were confounded ; it touched the heart of faith when the bright spirit of true prophecy overmastered the self-willed, reluctant seer. It kindled national and religious enthusiasm when it foretold the Messiah's dominion. It had the fascination of the weird and wonderful. It was a life-long memory. Beneath the star-lit night, on the house-tops of Judah, Benjamin and all Israel, outside of the black hair tents of Reuben, Gad, and the half tribe of Manasseh, in the open fishing-boats of Zebulon and Naphtali as they sailed over the Sea of Galilee, it was a tale to children told; and once heard could never be forgotten.

There were such resemblances between Balaam and the Magi as diviners and foreigners, and their histories were so related to the Messiah that the one could not but recall the other. The fact, then, that the evangelist does not say the oracle of Balaam was fulfilled in the star the wise men saw, is one of the minor evidences of the truth of his Gospel. For the words of the Magi so point to the popular belief in the oracle of Balaam, that this would have been worse than useless. Even those boys of Jerusalem, who watched round the gates of King Herod's palace to catch a passing glimpse of his princely guests, well knew those Magi had seen what Balaam had foreseen. From thence onward to the burning of the city and Temple, the popular interest in the Messiah ever deepened, and had St. Matthew directly connected the words of the Magi with the words of Balaam, he would have affronted the intelligence of those for whom he wrote.

Thus it has been shown that those who heard the

oracle of Balaam must have interpreted it as foretelling a real star ; and that it was so interpreted by the Jews. This interpretation was verified in what the Magi told. The Fathers all agree that, at this point, such is the meaning of Balaam's prophecy, such its fulfillment ; and in the criticism of these days there is nothing that can be set against this view of the oracle as its words stand undisputed on the record, and as they have been understood by the consentient wisdom of all the past.

CHAPTER III.

THE STAR OF OUR LORD ONE OF THE STARS OF HEAVEN.

THE foretelling of the Star of our Lord a thousand years before, suits not the common notion that the star was some sort of a miraculous jack-o'-lantern, flickering for a while and then going out. Yet, such is the almost universal, almost unquestioned error; and it were hard to tell the difficulty or the need of effacing this prevailing folly from the mind of Christendom.

Out of this delusion some few have escaped into the delusion that the Star was a conjunction of planets. In times past, some have fancied the star was a comet; others that it was the brightness of an angel. These conjectures, with the common one of an exalted, marvelous jack-o'-lantern, all go forth in as happy-go-lucky freedom from the control of the sacred text, as if the evangelist's name for what was seen in the sky when our Lord was born had very little to do with determining what it was.

Even if it might, perhaps, be doubtfully granted, that in the high-wrought poetic language of prophets, a will-o'-wisp might, possibly, have been called a star, here the question is, What does that word mean in the plain prose of St. Matthew? And against the notion that the Star was some optical apparition which was not a star, there is a strong presumption arising out of the fact, that the meaning of the word is as sharply defined, and as well fixed to one meaning, as that of any word well can be. It is not a name for every thing in the sky, not for the lightning, cloud, or storm; not for the zodiacal light, nor the northern lights; nor for a meteor, nor a comet. If used for a meteor or a comet, it is with the aid of an adjective, as, a "shooting" star, or of some other word or phrase. So nice is the instinctive discrimination of speech, that if, using the word out of its common meaning, one cries out, I see a star! the tone, the emphasis tell of an uncommon light. Ideas have differed as to what are those points of light which look out nightly all over the sky; but the word for them is one of those terms whose meaning is so fixed by nature herself, that the name for them in any language has always had its exact equivalent in every other.

The Magi tell of a Star, and, save their words imply it was a new star, these astronomers speak of nothing else which distinguishes it from the stars of heaven. But the legend-making love of the marvelous has ever been at work inventing such things. Thus, some have wildly dreamed the star led the pilgrims all the long way, not much less than a thousand miles, from the East, around the Syrian desert, to Jerusalem. If so, the star's leading them from Jerusalem to Bethlehem, towns six miles apart, is a little thing in comparison. Consistently with this notion, the apocryphal Gospel of the Infancy makes no mention of any special guiding on the way to Bethlehem, that being only a short section of the miracle thus long drawn out. This it draws out still longer by making the star continue to lead the pilgrims, *donec in patriam suam, revertentur,* "till they got back to their own country." These long journeys were made by daylight, but what of that, if "round the Star," as St. Ignatius wrote to the Ephesians, "the sun, moon, and stars formed in a ring, and its light outshone the whole." These inventions, and the notion that the star was a conjunction of planets, are good illustrations, whether in the second century or the nineteenth, of how the simple and precise words of Scripture may be· transformed into legends, of how the word of God may be made of none effect by poetic or scientific traditions.

The error that the Star guided the Magi on all their long way to Jerusalem has been common enough ; and still more common has been the error, that the star faded out when the Magi were in the East and they saw not its like again till the night of the journey to Bethlehem. So far as this error arises out of what is told of that journey, it will be considered hereafter ; *here* the inquiry is limited to what is said before the Magi left Jerusalem. This is very little ; but in the art of saying much in a few words the ancients are the despair of the moderns. Modern history tells us what to think, how to feel, and shapes the facts to the sermon. In ancient history, and in sacred history more than any other, the facts tell their own story. "Where is He that is born King of the Jews, for we have seen his star in the East, and are come to worship him?" are words that hold much of meaning in their small compass. They give the impression it was a new thing ; a feeling which the evangelist strengthens by the cry of wonder, "Behold! there came," so quickly followed by the mention of the star; and this was enough, as the thought of new stars was familiar to the popular mind,* though the fact was something so out of the common course as to be a wonder and sign. But thus telling the star was a new one, the Magi by their silence tell something more than this; for had it disappeared, assuredly they would not have given the contrary impression. Their words gave that impression then; for though a light suddenly shining and suddenly withdrawn, its mission being only to mark the birth of the Lord, would now, wherever astrological thoughts have vanished away, answer to their words, *it would not have so answered there and then.* Any such notion comes far short of the astrological thoughts of those times—universal then throughout all Asia, and there universal even now†—and so it

---

* No doubt familiar to the scientific mind also. The Roman naturalist, Pliny, refers to the fact as assuredly known.—*Hist. Nat.*, lib. xi, 22. *In ipso cœlo stellæ repente nascuntur*—In the firmament stars suddenly are generated. New stars may have been noted in the astronomical tables of the Chaldeans, as to which, see "The Wise Men," p. 110.

† Sir John Malcolm, one of those who built up the British empire in India, being charged with a difficult mission to the Shah of Persia, waited on horseback, with all his retinue, outside of the capital, Teheran, till the minute when the Persian astrologers, whom he consulted, said the stars would be propitious; and then he crossed the city line. To this all Iran attributed the success of his mission; a success natural enough when an Englishman had the tact thus to compliment a powerful class and to humor a popular illusion. In his History of Persia (1815) he says, "Astrology is cherished throughout the

comes far short of the meaning of the Magi to those who heard them. There could then have been no thought of so evil an omen as His star's fading out.* The shepherds saw a light in the sky, but when they saw it fade they could not have mistaken it for the star of the Messiah. According to the popular thought of the time, the new star must shine while the king should live. *That beautiful thought was true, and the King lives forever!*

If the Magi discovered a star, they had so to name it, and the name was its perfect description. If it was not a star, they were not shut up to this one word. They had any number of phrases with which to describe it ; or they could have said they had seen a wonder in heaven. To say they called it a star to connect it with the oracle of Balaam, the Seer of the Gentiles, as they called it that of the King of the Jews to connect it with the great prophecy of Daniel, chief of the wise men of the East, does not do away with the force of this ; for though this was the fact, still there was no sufficient reason why they should have made this one word their sole description of it, unless it were a perfect description.

---

whole of Asia." He says that, even from Europe, belief in divination by the stars has but recently passed away ; and in proof of this in France, with other facts, he cites the statement of Voltaire, that an astrologer was secreted near the bed-chamber of Anne of Austria when Louis XIV. was born ; and that Louis XIII. was surnamed the Just, because he was born under Libra, the sign of the Balance.

* The fading out of a birth-star would have been a dreadful omen. It would have portended the greatest calamities, such as captivity or death.

OF ST. MATTHEW'S KNOWLEDGE OF THIS PILGRIMAGE.

As such a description their historian sets it forth.
As will soon be made to appear, this is very decisive of what it really was, if St. Matthew well knew
all about this pilgrimage. There should not be a
doubt that he did ; and yet this needs to be clearly
and fully established ; for most of those who have
touched upon it (and none have done more than
this) betray the feeling that on several points St.
Matthew was much in the dark as to this pilgrimage ;
though his tone and language do not at all warrant
this ; and the fact that they are in the dark does not
prove that he was.

Lest, however, I seem to undervalue the fair success of much that has been written as to the Gospel
of St. Matthew, let me say, that while the beauty of
the story of this pilgrimage touches the eye of a child
like that of a rose or a star, and some of its truths
write themselves on every heart, the lost meaning
of some of its words and phrases has been a problem
so baffling that its solution was possible only to the
thought of years, and needs for its full appreciation
so much of the same qualities by which it was
wrought out, applied to the same end, that the exact
determination of its true value, as did that of Kepler's
discovery, abides its appointed time.

My re-discovery of the answer to the questions,
Who were the Wise Men ? and How came they to
Jerusalem ? was made through the conviction that
each of St. Matthew's terms had a definite meaning
in his own mind ; while back of this was the cer·

tainty that the Gospel is not, as some hold it to be, a conglomerate of sayings and doings rounded into something like unity and completeness by the pious labors of many, and stamped at last with an apostolic name, not in attestation of its authorship but of its truth ; the certainty that it is not, as others say, the work of St. Matthew, yet as a history not much better in point of style than the crude, unsatisfactory chronicles of the Dark Ages ; and the certainty it is the Gospel of one who proceeds throughout according to the highest method, whose grasp of his theme, whose wisdom in selecting and stating his facts, every-where approve him worthy of his election as one of the apostolic biographers of Christ.   Had not a study of his Gospel, as a whole, given to this knowledge a certainty that could know of no increase, the continuous thought I gave to his history of this pilgrimage would have strengthened it.   For this made it certain to me, that St. Matthew knew every thing about the pilgrimage which the historian of so remarkable an event ought to have known.   St. Mark, St. Luke, and St. John say nothing of it, as though St. Matthew had left nothing to be said.   His narrative answers every question concerning it that need arise, and almost every question that reasonably can arise. This it does when the difference between a great and a little historian is understood.   Each supposes himself, and is supposed by his readers, to be able to set forth a sufficiently full account of the subject of which he treats.   Each tries to do this; but the little historian fritters away in petty nothings those grand impressions in which the highest truth of history consists.   What the one labors in vain to give through many words, the other conveys through a few ; and, this done, he will neither stoop nor stop to answer idle questions. The great historian instructs by his silence as really as by his speech ; and to impute that silence to ignorance is to mistake the man and his method.

To illustrate this : Let us suppose that, looking only to vain thoughts that cling to St. Matthew's narrative like barnacles to the keel of a ship, and in this case are sometimes mistaken for a part of its cargo— looking only to idle notions that are common enough, let us suppose it possible that we could now approach St. Matthew and reverently address to him these inquiries : "Did some commissioned angel, or some dream divinely sent, or word from heaven, reveal to the Magi that what they saw was the Star of the King of the Jews ? Did the sign fade out as soon as seen, or did it guide them all their long way from the East to Jerusalem ? Was it in fact no star at all, but only a conjunction of the planets Jupiter, Saturn, and Mars ? Or was it a meteor, or some sort of a comet ?" No doubt these inquiries would astonish him as much as the answer it is to be supposed he would give—"Had any of these things been, I had said so"—would astonish those who have entertained these vagaries, instead of learning from his silence as well as from his words.*

---

* It will be easy to belittle the force of this by saying, After all, St. Matthew may not have known *every thing* about this pilgrimage ; for example, the conjunction of planets, through which the Magi identified the new star. Yet his silence proves there was no supernatural cause for their knowledge, and,

Standing much alone in my opinion of the fullness of St. Matthew's knowledge of this pilgrimage, I dare not weaken the strength of the evidence of this, for fear the manner of presenting it should be misunderstood. The strength of that evidence discovers itself only in this proposition : If St. Matthew's knowledge of this pilgrimage was not very complete, then there never was any such pilgrimage ; that pilgrimage was a very public thing in Judea, if there ever was any; the people of Jerusalem were greatly moved by the coming of those men from the East, if those men ever came at all ; what kings openly do is no secret in their realm, and Herod's parliament never could have assembled at his summons to answer a question that stirred every Judean heart like the noise of a battle, and the facts which caused its convocation have been forgotten within fifty years, while yet the city, the palace that gave audience to the Magi, the hall where the Sanhedrim met, were untouched by fire, and some still living who had seen the priests, scholars, and nobles assembling in that council ; these facts, not in themselves to be soon forgotten, were written on the hearts of the Judean mothers and children of that generation ; St. Matthew, whether as a man, a historian, a Hebrew, a Christian, an Apostle, or as an Evangelist, must have felt great interest in this matter ; not far from the time when he wrote,

---

therefore, he must have felt a strong interest in its natural causes. He may have known them, and have thought that in his Gospel they were out of place. Yet, of course, what conclusions from a writer's silence are certain, and what are more or less probable, it is for common sense to decide.

probably at the time, there was in Jerusalem, at the house of St. John, the blessed Mother who had talked with the Magi, and whose recollections of that interview are in his narrative ; and since these things are so, to think that St. Matthew was ignorant of any fact as to this pilgrimage, such as any intelligent man, who professed to treat of it, would properly be supposed to know, is treating it as an idle legend.

The bearing of all this on the question, What did the Magi see ? is decisive, when the historian's method, at this point in his history, is understood. For much the Magi must have said in reply to the many eager inquiries in Jerusalem as to what they had seen. The masterly hand of St. Matthew, than whom no writer was better able to give a comprehensive statement in fewest words, compressed all of this he thought there was need to record, into a very few words of theirs. Had they said, the sign faded out from the sky, or said any thing else inconsistent with its being a star, it is very certain he would have recorded the fact. *It was a star*, is, then, the answer the Magi gave to the persistent questionings in Jerusalem as to what they had discovered in the sky ; according to the Evangelist, it is, substantially, their complete and only answer. It tells how it looked, what they thought it was, all they knew about it. And their word for it St. Matthew makes his own ; the Evangelist sanctions it ; throughout the history the inspired Evangelist names it a star.

THE STAR ONE OF THE LIGHTS OF THE HEAVENS.

So far as we have gone in the study of this history, the conclusion seems to be certain that the Star of our Lord was one of the great lights of the immeasurable heavens; first seen by the eye of man when, in mercy to the need of the human heart, God revealed himself in human form; a star whose rays, journeying thitherward through long preceding time, touched the firmament of the human world with glorious light when the Word, by whom all things were made, came to dwell among us; a star now shining in that firmament, and there to shine till, at the word of Christ who called it into being, that firmament shall pass to whence it came. In the material world which exists for, and in conformity with, the higher world of spirit, that spiritual world hath its marks and shadows; and the shining of this star into the human world was to Man the sign, in the material creation, of that union of the spirit of man, whose frame is of the dust, with the eternal Word, which visibly brought together in its Creator and Lord the whole material and spiritual universe.

The appearing of this star prophesied of a sphere higher than that of miracles. Miracle is of the present cycle of time, but the work of Christ goes beyond this. The Word, in the form of the man Christ Jesus, opened a new era in the eternal kingdom of God. He came to create a new race of men, a new heavens and a new earth. This being so, the harmonies of truth require some open visible manifestation of his creating glory when his purpose began to pass into open visible accomplishment. As certain astronomers, studying the harmonies of the planetary movements, rightly said, there must be a planet in a certain quarter of the heavens, so, the

Reason would affirm, that decisive moment was marked in the material universe by some sign of the new glory of the all-creating Word, even had the fact been outside of the province of revelation, and so wanted its absolute confirmation. To this sign the Magi witness. This sign the Evangelist records. It points far onward. It intimates that the influences of the Incarnation reach beyond the paths of the planets. It prepares for the prelude to the Gospel of St. John, revealing that by the Word who became flesh all things were made ; and for the words of St. Paul, *By him were all things created, that are in heaven, and that are in earth, visible and invisible; all things were created by him, and for him.*

THE BURDEN OF PROOF ON THOSE WHO DENY THIS.

If any will say, This is not so, it is for them to prove, that in defining that which shone into the firmament of the human world when Christ was born, the sole witnesses thereof to all the world forever, the Magi and the Evangelist, improperly named it a star. Against this the protest of common sense and of reverence is so strong that it can be established only by strong evidence. Nothing else will suffice for this save to prove it is impossible they properly so named it.

As new stars have appeared, this cannot be proved solely, or directly, by the fact that it was not seen before; still this might be confirmatory evidence of it, if in some other way it appeared it was not like a star. It is said, This does so appear ; for the narrative is to be taken as a whole, and then these verses make it certain the evangelist does not use the word properly: "They departed; and, lo, the star, which they saw in the East, went before them, till it came and stood over where the young child was. When they saw the star, they rejoiced with exceeding great joy. And when they were come into the house, they saw the young child and Mary his mother, and fell down and worshiped him." It is said: First, these verses show that the Light seen by the Magi beyond the Euphrates was not seen by them again till they went from Jerusalem, and, therefore, could not have been a star: Second, that what these verses say of its Guiding proves it could not have been a star.

Against the first of these propositions there is the fact that the history does not say the light disappeared. There is also against it the presumption, before noted, from the name of the light, and here this is somewhat strengthened. If the facts were as this argument supposes, then, with the accuracy only of any well-written history, the statement would have been, Lo! a light like the one they had seen in the East went before them; for, on this supposition, the light seen on the night-journey to Bethlehem, though it might have been similar, could not have been the one seen in Babylonia months before; and this supposition almost compels us to take up with the childish notion of the Apocryphal Gospel of the Infancy, that the Magi saw an angel, no other light than one emanating from such an apparition well answering to the narrative as thus understood. But the evangelist here knows nothing of any angel, or of any magical

light ; and only, in both times and places, of one and
the same Star.

*The Scripture thus said to teach that the light unex-
pectedly reappeared not only does not say so, but was
written in the manner and form it is written for the
very purpose of forbidding this idea.   But so lax are
the usual ideas as to the binding force of a writer's
words, and of his method, in a description where form
is of the substance,* that I have to prepare the way for
the argument in proof of this by some

𝔗𝔥𝔬𝔲𝔤𝔥𝔱𝔰 𝔬𝔫 𝔏𝔞𝔫𝔤𝔲𝔞𝔤𝔢 𝔞𝔫𝔡 𝔍𝔫𝔰𝔭𝔦𝔯𝔞𝔱𝔦𝔬𝔫.

Writing may have the certainty of figures.   Oftentimes nothing is less sure than what is written, giving
rise to endless lawsuits ; but this touches not the
rare precision to which language can attain.   In
masterpieces of utterance, such as the best verse of
Milton, *the place of each sentence, clause, and word*, as
well as the choice of each word, is determined by
laws which, consciously or unconsciously, genius
obeys ; and any change at all in any of these can
hardly be made without some loss of meaning or
variance of effect.

Some may grant this of poetry in its perfection, but
not of prose; but while there is a plain difference
in form between poetry and prose, it is not easy to
fix upon any essential distinction between the two ; *
and though poetry may be the higher achievement,

---

* *Wordsworth*—Preface to Lyrical Ballads—says : " It would
be a most easy task to prove that some of the most interesting
parts of the best poems will be found to be strictly the language
of prose, *when prose is well written*."

there is some reason for thinking it is not the most difficult. It goes to show this, that song is known among barbarians. It goes to show this, that poetry is earlier than prose ; Homer coming before Herodotus, the rhyme of Spenser before the prose of Dryden. So, too, that it seems easier to conceive of the ideal of a song, an ode, or an epic poem, than of an essay, a biography, or a history. Is it said, this is because there are good models of these, and not of those—if it be so, the inference is the same :

> Empires have moldered from the face of earth,
> And tongues expired with those who gave them birth,
> Without the glory such a strain can give
> As e'en in ruin bids the language live :

but of prose this is still more true. In Greek there may be some as little perishable as any Greek poetry ; but of the English-speaking races where is the master whose prose, because of its *perfection of style*, will live as long as the best English verse ?

In music there is harmony, another name for order, and this, again, for obedience to law. Music is the most free because the least lawless of all the soul's voices, and so is the symbol of the social joy of heaven. So far as it is free obedience, the music in the soul, when breathing out in verse, has a symbol in rhyme or rhythm. This rhythm tends to forbid whatever is out of proportion, or out of place. It were hard to tell the secret of its magic, to bound the compass of its power ; but one plain consequence of this accompaniment of the thought is that exactness of expression in poetry to which we now look, the better to know the possibility and the fact of its like in prose.

Poetry, though one of the voices of emotion, is self-regulating, and the best is the most so of all. Unconsciously, or without seeming effort, its movement is like that of a child at play. One of the conditions, unmarked it may be, of what is so admirable in each, is *precision*, without which there is neither safety nor grace. Prose is less exact than poetry, but there is no need of this, for poetry is the chosen utterance of emotion, prose, of judgment. Feeling pervades the one, deliberation is more characteristic of the other ; and it has more of self-conscious will and a freedom in the choice of words that makes up for the self-regulating magic of rhyme.

There is nothing mechanical in any utterance of the soul, whether distinctly rhythmical or not. Life is the secret of this fountain. The *word* of the soul, outspoken, or heard only by itself and God, is ever going forth, ceaseless as the beating pulse. The relation between *thought* and *word* resembles that between the soul and the body. Thought and word, soul and body, are alike inseparable unities. The body is the limit of the soul, and so is the *condition* of its personality. The *word* is the limit, and so is the *form* of the thought. If we would think of a soul without its body, or of a thought without its *word*, it eludes us. Whether it can be said to be or not we cannot tell, for in either case there is only that which is formless and void. To think of a thing is to form some image thereof; and there can be no image of a spirit without body, for that is a spirit without form ; and so there can be no image of a thought without its *word* either audible or inaudible. The possibilities of thought, like those of feeling and will, which belong *to the complete idea of the word of the soul,* are limited. Those possibilities, whether thought of as present or future, actual or ideal, are the same as those of utterance, without which they have no form, that is, no being of which we can form to ourselves any idea.

Trying to fill out the farthest bound of its thought, the life of the soul in the thought determines its form as more or less full, and as more or less real. If this life be weak and ghostly, the utterance will be imperfect or shadowy. Intense life, of which high emotion is the sign, tends to clear form. Hate lacks not precision of words, nor does love, nor prayer.

Overwrought feeling breaks out in incoherence ; but this is the breaking down of the soul from a higher to a less dangerous mood. When death is in the house, how clear of sight the still feeling before the spirit, sinking down into wailing, blurs its vision with tears. If that deep clear seeing speaks, its words are more than eloquence ; as when St. Matthew tells of the passion of his Lord.

One body embodies the all of one soul ; so may one form of words the all of one thought. Of this some of the sayings which have passed into proverbs are good illustrations.

Man is body and soul. In his audible and inaudible utterance, in every *word* of his never voiceless being, there is the material and the spiritual. The life of the soul makes the material breath of its

words imperishable things ; and by our words shall
we be justified, and by our words condemned. *The
word of the soul, here including in it looks and deeds,
that is, the whole of its manifestation,* is an intelligible
image of the man, who can be known only through
this *word.* Further than this no man can pierce
into the spirit there is in man. It is unseen and un-
seeable. No light can make it visible. It is unknown and unknowable. Its being is manifest only
through its *word;* and this mystery of human utterance is a sign, very nigh at hand, even within us and
inseparable from our being, *of one of the high mysteries of our holy religion.*

The written or printed page is an intelligible image
of the soul's utterance in words which lie back of it ;
and still back of this is something of its thought,
feeling, and will, or of all the soul's only revelation
of itself. Each so represents the other that communing with the written or printed page is as near
as possible to communing with the soul itself. If
God, who made man in his own image, so touches
the spirit there is in man as through its thoughts, feeling, and will, of which its words are the sign, to speak
intelligibly to other souls, then communing with the
page, which is the sign of that divinely human utterance, may thus be communing with God.

The sacred writers stand apart from other men in
a class by themselves. To them Inspiration was
given, and to them alone. Of this word the meaning has been dangerously lowered. It has been reck-
lessly applied to other writings than to those to which
alone it belongs ; and with many Revelation, a word

of less effect, has come to be greater than Inspiration. It may exist apart from it; for to St. Paul things were revealed which he was not inspired to utter. Dream, vision, and ecstasy are states which are below that of inspiration, and revelation issuing from them does not take rank with words of inspiration. There is revelation now, there always has been, and in the future there will be more than in the past; for of these last days God hath said, "I will pour out of my Spirit upon all flesh: your sons and your daughters shall prophesy, your young men shall see visions, and your old men shall dream dreams; and I will show wonders in heaven above, and signs in the earth beneath." (See Acts ii, 17–21.) But the sacred writers have no successors. Their office was to portray the word of God, even Christ Jesus, who is "the same yesterday, to-day, and forever," and with the Holy Scripture their work was done. By inspiration they wrote what God willed should be written in the Bible, and this whether of things within their own knowledge, or of things which only the Spirit could have revealed. The book is what God willed it should be; and when taken as a whole, so that what is incomplete in one part is made complete in another, it has a divine completeness, as well as a divine authority, that can belong to no other writing. To set up any device of men—whether creed, confession, law, or usage of the Church—as of equal authority savors of blasphemy, for Holy Scripture is clothed by our Lord with the same divine authority as his own divine words. Our Lord never set up the authority of the Hebrew Church in attestation of any

truth ; he repeatedly and openly denounced its teachings, and unloosed the conscience from their binding ; while often and usually he spake of the Scripture
as having power to bind the conscience, declaring it
to be the word of God, as he did his own words, and
making them of the same effect.

Authority is often claimed for the apostles which
they disclaimed for themselves ; for the Apostle Paul
wrote to the Corinthians saying (2 Cor. i, 24) he
had "no dominion over their faith ;" but over faith
the Scripture hath dominion, for it is not the word
of men but the word of God. The apostles completed this Holy Word. For this they were chosen
as disciples, and then as apostles. They were to
"bear witness" of Christ, and the reason is thus
given by the Lord himself, "Because ye have been
with me from the beginning." For this he promised
them the Spirit, saying, "He shall bring all things
to your remembrance whatsoever I have said unto
you." (John xv, 27 ; xiv, 26.) Thus they were em-
powered to complete the "volume of the Book." By
them and through them this was done, though in
this work others had a part—the blessed Mother
of our Lord, the evangelists Mark and Luke—and
the New Testament, attested to the Holy and Universal Church by the apostles, was received by the
Church as of like divine authority with the Old
Testament, which our Lord declared to be the word
of God ; and when St. John, the last evangelist and
the last apostle, died, the Church knew the Scripture
was finished, for there was no one then, commissioned of the Lord, to add to it by his own writings,

or by his sanction to the inspiration of the writings of others.

Inspiration is spoken of in Scripture as a divine inbreathing. It is not possible to interrogate the sacred writers, nor, if it were, is it to be supposed they could disclose more than this. In that which was written by inspired men there is, then, a divine element which makes it the word of God; and yet it is a human utterance intelligible to human beings. Of that divine element in itself we can know nothing, and any attempt to pierce into it is presumptuous and utterly vain.

It seems to be otherwise as to the limits and the laws of human utterance; but all that my purpose requires or admits of, is to waken up the soul to see that *certainty of meaning* is possible in human utterance; and that in proportion as thought is clear, feeling strong, and the will firm, so sure will be the words, their intelligible image. This must be so, as far as the spirit there is in man can find utterance in language; and the possibilities of any language, despite all poets, orators, or philosophers ever born, are unknown; for they are as exhaustless as the soul, which is the fount of thought, and of the words through which thoughts have form and being. Since, then, there *may* be in language certainty of meaning, there *must* be in the language of the Scriptures; for the soul is an instrument so fashioned as to be capable of self-regulating and perfect utterance, and there its chords are struck by the creative hand.

What is called the artlessness of the evangelists may seem to make against their precision; but if by this artlessness be meant that they use common words, and write out facts in their utmost simplicity, with no embellishment and no comment, this is the way that witnesses, thoroughly in earnest and entirely sincere, tell of things so great that in trying to state them, just as they were, they lose all thought of every thing else. In this natural kind of writing, each word, the turn of each phrase, and *the place of each clause and sentence*, is significant; for in it the facts are written out just as they wrote themselves on the soul. If by their artlessness be meant that they have no order, or only of the slightest kind, this is at once refuted by the fact that, beyond all other writings, theirs give a oneness of impression.

It is true there is the greatest ease in the narrative of the Gospels ; but, as has been seen, *precision*, far from being opposed to this, is one of its conditions. The union of symmetrical effect with such freedom that the story seems to tell itself, may find one of its conditions in the fact that these writers are freely and entirely obedient to the laws of utterance within their own souls ; and it may be, that so far from *thinking of inspiration as freeing from those laws, it should rather be thought of as keeping the soul up to them.*

This might be with unlearned men as easily as if they had been trained in the rhetoric of the schools, for the words of the uneducated go more straight to the mark than those of book-learned men ; and though the words in a language may be multiplied by its culture, those later words have not the pictorial charm, the naturalness, freshness, and force of those that make up the less copious but more living language of the people.

In virtue of its endowment of speech, and of its perceptions and feelings, there are in the soul, even of a savage, the principles of the grammarian, and something of the system of the rhetorician. Grammar merely writes down some of the forms of utterance as it has heard them; rhetoric notes this for others; but neither makes them; and if either tries to do so, it is worse than useless. The order, then, in the Gospels, so far as it has for its sole cause the full and free exercise of human faculties, is in the line of the art of the grammarian and the rhetorician, though far beyond all reach of art; and this order, so far as it comes from a power above the human faculties, comes from no violence done to the laws of the soul, but is like the order in nature, which is wrought out, not over, but through, the qualities of natural objects.

The ideal of human utterance is actualized in the Gospels; yet it has been often said they have no style; and, though far from wise, this is natural enough; for thoughts are shown in a good style as things are in the pure light of day, while that which shows them is unthought of. In the style of the Gospels there is very much more than this inimitable transparency. In them there is an order whose secret is past finding out, even as there is in nature. The hills group themselves freely, at their own will the streams wind along, carelessly grow the woods along the uplands; yet the outline of every mountain, the path of each river, the place of each wood, why it is that moss grows on this side of the rock and not on the other, why these shrubs fringe this thicket and those reeds and grasses grow in that meadow, are all determined by laws, through which comes that order in nature felt as beauty, that peace which comforts the heart of care and gives the wounded spirit healing. The ever-varying heavens are ruled by laws quick as their own changes, keeping the unbroken harmony of the earth and the sky. Nature is not lifeless. Therein is the presence of the Word of God, through whom in the beginning it arose out of the formless and void, a presence whose indwelling within the forms of material things is felt by the living soul. Felt or unfelt, it is, alike in Scripture and in nature, the assurance of that known under other names, in its comprehensible manifestation, as order, harmony, or obedience to law. As there is a reason why a fern grows here and a flower there, why pine and not oak crowns yonder headland, a reason for every wind that blows, a reason for the shape and color of every cloud, a reason for every thing and *for the place of every thing in the world of Nature, even so it is in the world of Scripture.*

OF THE ERROR THAT THE STAR UNEXPECTEDLY REAPPEARED.

Almost irresistible evidence has been given to prove that the New Star of whose appearing the astronomers of Persia told, was one of the great lights of heaven; evidence is to come that will confirm this; but I would not hide from my readers that if the exceeding great joy of the Magi on the night of their journey to Bethlehem was caused by an unexpected reappearing of the Star, *all this evidence goes for nothing.* If here the argument fail, the reader must make a better one; or else may as well close this book, so far as one of its main lines of thought is concerned.

There is a divine element of certainty in the language of Scripture; yet my argument will assume *no greater accuracy in the Evangelist's description of the journey to Bethlehem than properly belongs to any good writing;* that is, the argument is the same as if the description were found in Herodotus, in Tacitus, or any well-written ancient history.

The words, "when they saw the star they rejoiced with exceeding great joy," are generally thought to prove the Star unexpectedly reappeared. But this is explained by the common want of appreciation of the *fullness and precision* which the description of this night-journey combines with *brevity;* together with the fact that these words so often float in and out of memory apart from the context. For, if the narrative be not rightly understood, and these words be remembered by themselves, as usually they are, they do suggest this. But when the whole description is before the mind, they forbid the idea, if the rejoicing be placed where the Evangelist places it, not when the Star began to move, but *some hours afterward when the Star stood still.*

The evangelist's mention of the exceeding joy of the pilgrims is not at all in the nature of a pictorial embellishment. It teaches truths well worth the knowing. The height of their joy when the house was pointed out by the Star to those pilgrims who went from the holy city by night and alone, marks the depths of their disappointment in Jerusalem. It also reveals the witness to their history of one who had talked with the pilgrims after they came to Bethlehem ; doubtless, of some one who within that house heard their joyful outcry in the stillness of the night. It is but a little less than certain that this was the blessed Mother of our Lord, who from these words in the Gospel of St. Matthew, and from those chapters in the Gospel of St. Luke which no other could have written, is gladly and reverently to be hailed *Regina Evangelorum*—Queen of the Evangelists.

The whole picture of this night-journey covers less than a hand's-breadth ; but in a little picture, even more than on the broad canvas, there is meaning in every touch and shadow of a touch. The more this picture is studied the clearer it becomes. As out from under the gloomy archway in the wall of strictly-guarded Jerusalem the pilgrims ride into the gathering night, suddenly the star goes before them. Whether they had seen the star every night, or but once before, their feeling must naturally have been that of astonishment. It is the Evangelist himself who marks this ; for the cry of wonder is his, and so is the identification of the Star, which, in his description of the scene, is a thing of course. It is most natural to suppose their state of mind must then have been that of *silent* astonishment. A great outburst of exceeding joy would hardly have been natural then. The portent was too surprising, too

10

unaccountable. The awe which the manifestation
of the supernatural ever awakens must have been
upon them. With throbbing hearts, wide-open, eager
eyes, even those kings in the world of thought must
have followed the portent going before. A blending of many feelings hushed them to the silence
of breathless expectation, as, with wonder, hope, and
religious fear, they questioned within themselves what
this strange thing might mean, where this would
end. The Star leading the way, they come to the
village of Bethlehem. The Star leading on, they pass
along the silent street. It stands still over a house.
Expectation changes to certainty, all doubt is gone.
As well as if a voice from heaven had told them,
they knew, before they went into the house, the Star
"stood still over where the young child was," and
that is the moment when "they rejoiced with exceeding great joy." By placing these words where he
does, the evangelist marks the instant *when*, and he
gives the reason *why*, their souls kindled to ecstasy ;
and at that instant their joy is so natural that we
might have been sure of it had we not been told.

The word-picture of this night-scene reproduces
the feelings of the pilgrims, because the facts are
written out just as they wrote themselves on their
souls. Scott could almost have expanded the one
into a romance, Shakspeare the other into a drama,
and have said nothing unsuggested by its swift and
simple words. Even in the line, "over where the
young child was," there is much wisdom in word-
painting. Change it to "over the house" and light
suddenly fades from the picture. A good deal of

meaning is gone from it at once. The less definite phrase leaves the mind more open to think, as the pilgrims then thought, wholly of Him, whom both the guiding and its description honor. It marks that before they went into the house the pilgrims felt sure he was found, as well they might and must have felt. Some have called this a very in-definite line;* but in it great definiteness of feel-ing is expressed. The soul of the pilgrims shines through it. No speech, no language, no voice, yet the star told them, He is there! and no wonder they broke out into loud rejoicing, knowing their long pilgrimage was happily ended.

Then to this picture the full touch of precision is instantly given, "when they went into the house they saw the young child." Minds corrupted by books cannot appreciate a style like this. Its brevity mis-leads them as to both its fullness and its precision. The book that Hamlet was reading† is the book now read; the grain of gold is beaten out into pages of glittering tinsel; and this story-devouring genera-tion is so used to having the work of the imagination all done and ill done for it, that it has scarcely the critical sense left to reason from the structure of a description so perfect as this.

There are mosses and little flowers, fair, fragrant, and full of grace, that disclose all the wonders of their fabric only when enlarged under the microscope,

---

* Alford and some others say, it may mean over the town of Bethlehem.

† Hamlet, act ii, scene ii. *Polonius.* What do you read, my lord? *Hamlet.* Words, words, words.

which changes nothing of proportion and yet brings out a world of wisdom. Let something like to this be done with the description of this night-journey—it requires no scientific apparatus—only let each word be followed to where it leads, only let the mind pause and dwell upon each line till it fills out to its fullness the meaning, and the fact that the joy of the pilgrims was caused by the star's pointing to where they knew the child was, and not by an unlooked-for appearing of the Star, comes out with the certainty of a proposition in Euclid.

The identification of the star being a thing of course, the description of the scene fixes the reader's mind upon the Guiding, even as upon it the narrator's mind was fixed. The cry of wonder marks not the star, which they had seen every night, but this unexpected miracle; lo! the star which they had seen in the East, *went before them*. To this miracle the description continues to hold our attention. It went before them *till it came and stood over where the young child was*. Not till after all this guiding has been thought of and thought out to the end; not till after we have gone, mile by mile, with these pilgrims star-led on their unknown way through the strange scenery and the night; not till after we have kept company with them for wondering hours while the narrow camel-track wound steep down the hill-side, over the dusky plain, and along the vale of Bethlehem; not till the star's out-shining in that evening sky is miles behind in space, and hours away in time; not till the house is in sight and the guiding star stands still above it—*not till then* is the joy of the pilgrims named. The Evangelist does not say they departed, and lo! the star they had seen in the East appeared again, and they rejoiced with exceeding great joy, and it went before them; he separates his mention of the joy from the coming out of the star; he places it after the star's guiding; he connects it immediately with its standing still over where the child was; and thus the evangelist marks that the star's pointing out the house caused the rejoicing.

Nowhere does the Evangelist give any countenance to the notion that the wise men had not seen the Star since they were in Babylonia. Nowhere does he say the star of the Lord was the passing phantom of an hour. His silence as to any such fact proves that he knew of no such fact; and if he knew of none such, there was none. Only let some little justice be done to St. Matthew as a man, only let there be some little appreciation of his merit as a historian, and it is clear and certain that by the form and manner of his narrative the Evangelist forbids the heresy that the star of the Everlasting Lord, shining once into the world of man, shines not there forever.

ITS GUIDING CONSISTENT WITH ITS BEING A STAR.

That astronomy forbids the belief that the light which led to the house in Bethlehem was a star seems to be a common opinion, and from this error comes the Second of the two propositions before named: Its guiding proves it could not have been a star. More fully stated, the argument here is this: If the Magi saw a star, its guiding was the result of motion imparted for this especial purpose to a world further away from the earth than the sun, and at least equal to it in size. This is not to be thought of, because the power thus put forth would have been so utterly out of all proportion to the thing to be done. It would baffle the calculus to compute, the imagination to conceive, the contortions and complications of the star's motion before it could have piloted through the crooks and turns of the six miles from Jerusalem to the house in Bethlehem. It is irrational to think that a world so independent of the earth, so great, so far away, was thus wildly perturbed. It is irreverent to believe that even the Almighty would have put forth such power to do a thing so easily done in other ways as clearly supernatural.

The very sound of this argument is imposing, but there is nothing in it. It is merely a wrong inference from the language of Scripture. It is almost a sufficient reply to it to say that, like some other arguments against Scripture, it takes for granted what cannot be known. It takes for granted that this miracle was wrought in the way it points out, and could have been wrought in no other way. If no other way could be pointed out by man, it might be modest to remember that God might know of some other. But here faith need not fly for refuge to the grand old truth, that his thoughts are not as our thoughts, his ways as ours. A way, other than that supposed, can be pointed out in which this star may have led the pilgrims, and yet the great orb in its far distant height have been no more disturbed than the great God himself by the putting forth of the power which accomplished the miracle, however that power

may have been put forth.   For it is more than possible, it is probable, that the power which wrought
the miracle of the Guiding was not put forth upon the
body of the star, but only upon some few of its rays
after they had come within the atmosphere of the
earth.   This supposition is so in harmony with the
common and proper use of language that it perfectly
answers to the words of the Evangelist. For when a
man speaks of seeing a star, he always means seeing
it in and through a few of its rays that touch his eye.
And yet he rightly says, I see the star, because his
Creator so made him as thus to think, and so to
speak.   According, then, to natural usage, uniform in
every language under heaven, when the Evangelist
speaks of the star's guiding, he speaks of a guiding by
some of its rays.   Just so much the words of the Evangelist affirm, and this is all that his words do affirm.
The Scripture in no way, further than this, commits
itself to how the guiding was brought about.

   To get rid of the incredible power it is supposed
must have been put forth to bring about guiding by
a star, the theory of a supernatural light, looking so
like a star that it might be described as such, is
now upheld ; but the difference between the power
on that theory, and the power if the miracle was
wrought in the way pointed out, is not worth esti-
mating.*

---

* If it be assumed that the early Christians thought the star
was within our atmosphere, (which it is probable they did,) and
so their belief came nearer to that of a transient meteor, a
luminous globe, an optical, a seeming but not a real star, than
to that which holds it to have been one of the stars of heaven

If the guiding were wrought in the way pointed out, this touches not the reality of the miracle, and it touches the greatness of the miracle but very little if at all. For a miracle affects the soul not chiefly by the quantity of power supposed to be put forth, of which it has poor means of judging, but rather by the feeling that is above the height of human power ; and this is, perhaps, as vivid if the miracle were wrought in its rays as if they were wrought in the body of the star.

If wrought in the way pointed out, the miracle was accordant with the analogy of Scripture. In the miracles of Scripture there is that which looks like economy of power. When the Lord clove a path through the sea, and its waters were a wall unto the Israelites on their right hand and on their left, supernatural power allied to itself natural power, for all that night the waters were divided and the sea made dry land by a strong east wind. This economy of God, like every thing else revealed of Him, teaches a lesson to man. It is one of the marked differences between the miracles of the Bible and those in legends and myths. The analogy of Scripture, then, all things else being equal, leads to a preference of that idea as to the power in a miracle which reduces

___

it may be said, they could not make the wide distinction made by us between those stars and any such passing light. To them the stars of heaven seemed not far off, and not large. They knew comparatively little about them ; and yet, doubtless, would have said, It matters not what they are, the Scripture teaches this Star was one of them—which is the fact, now, from astronomical considerations, denied.

it to the smallest limit, rather than of the one that carries it to a greater height.

If the miracle of the guiding was wrought in the way pointed out, it was wrought only in those rays of the star which touched the eyes of the pilgrims. Thus the sense-conception of the grandeur of the miracle may seem to be lessened, but its moral worth is greatly increased. For here, the true idea of this miracle, as wrought in the rays of one of the stars of heaven, opens an idea applicable to three other miracles where, to many, there seem astronomical difficulties in the way of believing them that are insurmountable; yet those difficulties vanish before this idea in connection with what else has been said of this Guiding. Those miracles are, the standing still of the sun on Gibeon; the going back of the shadow on the sun-dial of Ahaz; and the sickening of the light over the land of Judea while the Son of God was dying on the cross.

Through the fact that it was seen only by those it led, and was known to others only as witnessed to by them, this great wonder and sign at the opening of the new age was a type and prophecy of that guiding by the Holy Spirit which was to mark the coming time; and which, even in one of its most peculiar characteristics, was thus foreshadowed in the guiding of the Star of our Lord.*

---

* Some further evidence that this star was one of the stars of heaven will be given in the chapters on The Relation of the Universe to Christ, and on The Astronomical Doubt as to Christianity, which follow the two on The Miracle of the Guiding.

CHAPTER IV.

THE MIRACLE OF THE GUIDING.

WHEN the firmament of the Christian soul is all darkness the Star of our Lord shines out as real to the spirit as when it led to where the young child was. So bright is the assurance of divine sympathy and aid for all who seek the Lord, which ever abides in the gospel of the guiding of his Star! This is the most touching, the most needed, and the most universal of all its many lessons. It teaches this of itself. None need to point it out; and every Christian is a witness to its truth. The experience of the many is in the words of one,[*] who, changing the imagery, but not the truth, in the Evangel of the Star, thus wrote from his heart:

Once on the raging seas I rode;
   The storm was loud, the night was dark;
The ocean yawned, and rudely blowed
   The wind that tossed my foundering bark.
Deep horror then my vitals froze;
   Death-struck, I ceased the tide to stem;
When suddenly a star arose—
   It was the Star of Bethlehem.

It was my guide, my light, my all;
   It bade my dark forebodings cease;
And through the storm and danger's thrall
   It led me to the port of peace.

---

[*] Henry Kirke White.

> Now, safely moored, my perils o'er,
>   I'll sing, first in night's diadem,
> For ever and for evermore,
>   The Star, the Star of Bethlehem!

Oftentimes there is evidence of the inspiration of the Scriptures not only in their truths, but even in the way they embody those truths in words.   To me this seems to be so here.   For, studying the word-picture of the guiding of those pilgrims traveling in the night the unknown road, in the unknown country, seeking the unknown Christ, I see this night-journey is naturally told just as it struck the narrator's mind : first, the thrill of wonder at the star's motion, then its moving on till by its standing still it pointed out the house, and *then* that great rejoicing ; I see that a few more words easily thrown in would at once have made clear to the first glance of every eye the time, the place, and the reason of that exceeding joy ; and I also seem to see that here the very form of words was pre-ordained as the one best fitted to awaken just such emotions in just such hours as gave birth to that hymn.   It may also have been a thing ordained, that until this, the most common, the most personal, and the most helpful of its teachings should be universally and lastingly inwrought into the heart of the Church, the eye should be held from beholding, in this variously teaching sign, other truth which shines from it in consequence of the astronomical disclosure of the greatness of the stars.

A FURTHER ASTRONOMICAL DOUBT AS TO THIS MIRACLE.

Astronomy has made a star of heaven a most fitting material emblem of the spiritual glory of Christ ;

and yet, as it now becomes certain and clear that the guiding light which pointed to the house in Bethlehem was one of those stars, there will be some, who, instead of rejoicing in the beautiful lessons of this beautiful miracle, where nature in its grandest form led to Christ, and not seeing that nature apart from its spiritual uses is of no account, will feel as if, by a star's leading to Bethlehem, violence were done to the scientific idea of the universe. It is the harder to do away with this and with all the other astronomical doubts as to the Bible, because of the fact, almost without a parallel, that while usually the shock of new ideas is dissipated and new truths are adjusted to the old in some short space of time, the astronomical heavens so come anew into the youthful wonder of each generation, that the human mind seems ever to be surging with the emotions of the sixteenth and seventeenth centuries. And yet the distance and grandeur of the heavenly bodies can have no rational power to dissuade from belief in the miraculous guiding of the star, if with the scientific we hold on, as we should do, to the natural thought of the world. The astronomical thought is, that our earth belongs to the solar system; the natural thought is, that the sun, moon, planets, and stars belong to our world. It comes, in a measure, from that apparent circling of the heavenly bodies around the human world, which no doubt prefigures some high truth as to man; and it seemed to be upheld by it, until, in the sixteenth century, the Copernican theory of the solar system referred the seeming motion of the sun to motion in the earth itself. But the apparent circling of all the starry host around the earth, as if to do it honor, is not essential to the evidence for the natural idea of the earth, and, though set aside, the proof of it still remains. This natural idea of the round world is just as true as the scientific; for the sun, planets, and stars are parts of our world, as really so as the earth is part of the solar system and particle of the universe. They are parts of the world by their uniform presence and uses in it. They are indispensable to its idea. Our world would not be a world without them. They give light and heat, and without them there would be no life. They mark times and seasons ; and, regulating time, they regulate thought. They adorn the sky of our world. They lead man over the desert and over the waters. The science that whispers to his awe-struck mind something of their far-off glory but heightens for man those ministrations, in virtue of which they are his.

The star-struck mind may wonder that the Lord should have made a world millions of times larger than the earth, and millions of miles away from it, the guide of men ; but did not the Dipper point the unlettered bondman to the North, and may not we, like him, recognize a guiding office in those far-off worlds ? Things like this guiding on the way to Bethlehem, the creating Lord meant the stars should do ; and things like this they have ever done, from the time when Abraham journeyed from Chaldea to Egypt, star-led, across the naked plains of the deserts, until now, when, freighted with the wealth of nations and trusted with priceless lives, navies are crossing

the seas, star-led, from continent to continent.   Ever
since upward-gazing man was on the earth it has
been the office of the stars to guide ; and this guiding by a star to Bethlehem, *so far from being unnat-
ural*, only carried what nature has always done to a
supernatural height in honor of the Lord of nature.
As the Lord so made the stars as ever to light and
cheer the way of man, it is as credible now as before
the blue arch melted into an infinite expanse, that
He, who from evening to evening guides by his stars
the wanderers on the sea, the redeeming Lord, lifting
his mercy in the realm of nature to higher glory in
the realm of grace, for the encouragement of all who
should come after them, should have made his own
Star miraculously guide the pioneers of the long
procession of numberless, benighted, heart-tired, sin-
weary pilgrims who have sought, are now seeking, or
shall hereafter seek, not the lowly house in Bethlehem, but that where He now is, that house not made
with hands, eternal in the heavens.

CHAPTER V.

THE MIRACLE OF THE GUIDING STAR: CONTINUED.

THE gold, here and there on the earth's surface, was thrown up from unknown depths holding wealth that man will never explore. This gold, once thought to belong only to the place where it is found, runs traceable in continent-traversing veins, and systems of veins, related to ranges of hills and to the plan of the globe. As the globe is traversed by gold veins and systems of veins, so the Bible is traversed by veins and systems of veins of miracle. These veins of miracle-gold have been wrought on the surface. But their lines of direction, unity, and purpose have not been traced as far and well as they might be. Nor have shafts been sunk very deep into their unfathomable caves.

In the world of Nature, each event is a part of the whole; each event has fitness of time, of place, manner, and occasion; and each has some lesson or lessons to teach. The like is true in the world of Grace, and very true of those eminent events, the miracles.

OF THE FITNESS OF THIS MIRACLE.

The Miracle of the Guiding Star was every way suited to the character and the circumstances of those before whom it was wrought. Star-gazers were led by a star. "The shepherds, as of Jewish extraction, were guided by an angel, but the wise men by a star; those by a revelation which was familiar to them, these by nature, with whose aspects they were familiar." The pilgrims who had come to Jerusalem to worship its King, were now to find him for the Holy City. For the Jews, strangers were to find the son of David, the son of Abraham! a prophetic fact, pointing far onward to what even now is to come; every way a strange fact, and a trying one to the faith of those foreigners. They were severely tried, but they stood the trial. Learning less than they thought to have learned, this they did not despise. A path was shown them, and though they had little encouragement to follow it from those who should have gone with them in multitudes, on they went alone. The high-wrought persuasion of the truth of their art, common to astrologers, may have had something to do with this, and yet all heaven been glad to see it. In high resolve there is often safety from unknown dangers, and their quick decision saved them from the perilous honor of an escort of spies of Herod; but their sudden departure must alarm the tyrant, and his emissaries will soon follow them. They need straightway to find the Child and to go from the country. They need a sign from heaven, not for guidance merely, for other they might find, but to guide them quickly. They need a sign from heaven to cheer their hearts. If ever men did, they deserved one. It was to such men, in these circumstances, that the guiding of the star was given. And it was given in the hour of miracle—for that the supernatural was very manifest at the birth of our Lord is the most natural of all things.

Because it was the most spiritual of the nations, great wonders were shown to Israel; pre-eminent signs were displayed before the most spiritual three of the disciples; and so, to the most spiritual men of the world the guiding of the star was given. This miracle was as well suited to the calling, to the virtue, and to the instant need of these men as if only they were thought of; and yet, has world-wide lessons, fitting to the world-wide time, and to their character and office as representatives of the mercy of God in all the earth, and as witnesses of it to all the nations.   It has lessons of truth that reach out far toward other truths, and lead far into the mysteries of the kingdom of heaven.

THE LESSON OF THE MIRACLE AS TO NATURE-WORSHIP.

The witnesses of this miracle were of the nations; and its immediate great lesson was appropriate to the nations, rather than to the people of Israel.   This great lesson was uttered against Nature-worship; and to comprehend it the mind with patience of thought must strive to comprehend Nature-worship—then, and now, the worship of the majority of the human race.

Nature is a word not easy to define.   It is used with different meanings, and with different shades of the same meaning, in consequence of man's vacillation as to what he would express by it.   Sometimes it means the whole scheme of things; sometimes its laws ; sometimes it means that which makes a thing what it is in distinction from every thing else ; some-times a semi-deity.   Its meanings, all taken together, point to all that is not God.   This includes them all, and fills out the widest compass of the word.   The root-meaning of the word is, that which is *born ;* and this idea in the word brings out a contrast between the idea of Nature and the idea of Him who *is*.   For, as Nature exists but in birth and change, it is in this an antithesis of Him with whom there is no shadow of changing.

Worship includes in it Reverence and Service ; and, as hereafter used, Nature-service is to be under-stood as having in it some touch of Reverence ; for, even in Christendom, men serve passion and pleasure with a love, zeal, a self-abandonment, a prostration of soul, a sacrifice of themselves and of others, that, essentially, is *worship*.   Christendom is a great and a real fact, but those who come into it from Persia, India, China, or Japan find in it much of heathenism. The religious symbols of the old gods have passed from Christendom, but not the old gods themselves. In Christendom no temples are consecrated to Bacchus, Venus, or Mars, but the sacrifices to Wine, and Lust, and War are costly, and the worshipers of Mammon are many.   It is written, Covetousness is Idolatry : there is, then, a Service of things in Nature, that is, a Worship of them ; and, in its widest meaning, Nature-worship has two forms, one expressed in religious rites, and the other not.   It means all Service, as the word is here used, paid to aught save God, and thus denotes the Life of fallen man.

OF THE PREVALENCE AND POWER OF NATURE-WORSHIP.

It is not the least curious of all the many facts found out in this century, that long before the Christian era some of the Hindoos held that in all the varieties of Nature-worship, as expressed in religious symbols, there was unity of idea.   In this they were right.   Deep down beneath all facts or forms of idolatry, at last is found the underlying *hope* that the World is God, or that God is the World ; *feelings* distinguished as Atheism or Pantheism, yet coming to the same thing, *as each is unwilling to say Creator, or Father.*   The hope that nature is all and there is no God beside, and the hope that God is the only substance and all else that seems to be is illusion, are the two sides of the same lasting heresy.   The latter was the more prevailing feeling in the Hindoo heart. This dream of ancient India was never fully dreamed out in less speculative Europe while Nature-worship as a system of religion there survived ; but, every way strangely enough, a little after the middle of the seventeenth Christian century, at Amsterdam, the pantheistic spirit of Indian heathenism took possession of Baruch Spinoza, a Jew by birth, but disowned by his own people, and some time after it entered into a succession of thinkers, his kindred in soul though not in blood, the most famous of them three Germans of the present century, Fichtè, Schelling, and Hegel, men of subtilty, of patience in crooked thinking, and " mad at the root."   Each of these patented the old heathenism as a new invention of his own.

Each petted it in his own fashion, and uttered it in words of his own coining.   In various disguises, and with oracular speech, they sent the old heresy forth on travels far and wide ; and no small part of the culture of Europe has listened to it as the opening of every secret, the sum of all knowledge, the latest and the last word of truth.   Yet, in the long time this ghost was working his way underground from the Ganges to the Rhine, he gained little in ideas and lost in clearness of speech.   On through interminable volumes his unholy, barbarous jargon runs, while devotees mistake obscurity for wisdom, and the less they understand the more they admire.   This philosophy is so extravagant in its claims, so clumsy and so dark in its utterance, that it only becomes intelligible when it is clearly seen that its aim is to explain the inexplicable mystery of Creation.   This being its aim, it must and does, in all its rival sects, start from, and it must and does come round again at last to the old Hindoo assertion, that the Creator and the created are the same.   This assertion is the beginning and end of all this Teutonic Brahminism, whose philosophical explanation of Creation is *merely a denial of the fact*.   Between the point from which it starts and to which it comes back it does nothing but reiterate this assertion through all the realm of Nature and all the realm of History.   Its positive, its obscure, and its continuing reiteration of it, it takes to be the proving of an assertion which contradicts the reason born with us.   Even the words that set it forth contradict it.   They cannot do otherwise, for there are no words that do not contradict the foolishness of the Atheist or the Pantheist. Language cannot do their godless bidding. They torture, they mar, and they barbarize it, but all in vain; Language is not the slave of the human will; the soul is so made that its utterance *cannot* but witness to its Maker.

In this barbarous philosophy a very wide circle of error in space and time is at last rounded by Hegel into completeness. But here neither its history nor aught else about it has any place, save the one fact that it is a justification of all idolatry, a resurrection of heathenism, which in Europe, though not every-where buried out of sight, was long ago charitably thought to be dead. In its weird uprising it repeats, as before, that God is the phantom of the mind, the soul's own being, every-where projected before and around it, and mocking it from the stars, the waves and all that seems to be, and is naught but the soul itself—one's own shadow on the wall; self, wall, and shadow equally Him who being every thing is noth-ing. The conclusion, then, of this philosophy is this: When man, by as unintelligent an impulse as stirs the winds or the tides, is moved to worship, he may worship one thing as reasonably as another. Thus rises the Pantheon again, on a foundation broad as the world. What heathen Rome, or Greece, or As-syria, or Egypt did, is more thoroughly done. Every hill is consecrate, and grove and stream, each bird or beast, each reptile bred in slime, and creeping, biting, stinging thing.

Of this philosophy, which comes here from over the sea, as the cholera bred in Hindoo filth came

from Europe, ship-borne to these shores, breathing
death, the crowning dogma is, that God rises to consciousness in man. It has an incoherent, contradictory, jumbled notion (if it can be called even a
notion) of a universal something which, within the
ground, is the constituting principle of the ground, and
also the very ground itself; which blindly outstruggles
in mastodon, or crocodile, and all the reptile crew;
and, as out of the ocean the flying-fish darts up into
the world of light and air, rises into a higher world
of being in man. This philosophy may here seem
to appropriate to itself somewhat of the old heathen
notion of the Soul of the World; but in the center
and height of this nonsensical blasphemy, namely,
that *God comes to self-consciousness in man* there
is an egotistic vanity, a crazy arrogance, an utter
foolishness that classic heathenism would have been
ashamed of. By one who knows any thing of himself, or of the Allwise Creator of men, this heresy is
apprehended with difficulty; and any one who appre-
hends it at all, and is not morally insane, must recoil
from those who utter it, abhorring their low thoughts
of the Most High, and loathing their silly conceit of
their miserable selves.

But, again, nothing of this madness concerns us
here, save the fact that this philosophy makes each
low passion, each vile man, *divine.* Thus the altars
to Tiberius, at whose sins Rome shuddered, thus the
altars to crazy Nero, rise again. The madness of
Caligula, who would have compelled the Jews to
worship him in the Temple at Jerusalem, becomes
respectable, he having the wish to enforce the wor-

ship of himself, while they, who scorned this degradation, were stiff-necked because of their ignorance. Thus, with an arrogance in sin which the bounds set to human guilt do not permit to be greater, the Culture of that strange old transatlantic World, where men seem ever learning and never able to come to a knowledge of the truth, gives an exhaustive justification of their groveling and polluting idolatries to the half-civilized and barbarian worlds. *Most manifestly, then, the wickedness that, denying the living God, builds temples to Nature, and though in body exorcised from Christendom thus comes back in spirit, can be rooted out of the Earth only with difficulty.*

OF THE PURPOSE TO DO AWAY WITH NATURE-WORSHIP.

The soul hides from its Maker behind every other object of worship. Creation worshiped is creation interposed between the soul and its Maker ; and if he would reclaim his erring creature to himself he must do away with all such worship. His purpose to do away with the worship of Nature, and his purpose to do away with the *service* of Nature, that is essentially a *worship* of it, so blend, that when the one is attained the other may still be furthered by the revelation of the means used for the former. This is possible, because whatever enforces the truth that the Creator is the only object of Worship sets him forth as the true object of Service. These two purposes went on together ; but the former was the more prominent for a time ; and the first chapter of the Bible, the first command of the Ten, and the bent of the Miracles of old, were directed against Nature-worship.

It seems probable that Nature-worship would yield long before Nature-service showed signs of any very great impression being made upon it. And when the set time was fully come for doing away with Nature-service, God sent his own Son into the world, the Holy Ghost came from heaven, and the whole Bible was given. Since then nineteen hundred years are well-nigh gone, yet the waters of sin prevail, the earth is without form and void, darkness on the face of the deep. Very long and very difficult the doing away with the Service of Nature! So long, to human thought so slow, that to some the work seems to have begun only to fail. And shaken is the faith of those Christians who try to measure, with the radii of the circle of a year or a life, the Time-cycles of Him who inhabiteth eternity. Let such remember the difficulty of doing away with the worship of Nature among one people only. Of that difficulty the sacred history of that people is one continuing illustration, for a time not much less than that from the coming of the Holy Ghost until now. When the glory of the Lord was like devouring fire on the top of Mount Sinai the children of Israel cried unto Aaron, "Up, make us gods!" Seven hundred years later, He who "worketh hitherto," ever in earnest, and hastening on his purposes with all the resources of omnipotence, had only in all Israel reserved unto himself seven thousand men who had not bowed the knee in worship of the sun. Yet He speaks of this in words of cheer to Elijah, the most fiery soul that ever Israel knew, yet so disheartened, even after the great public miracle on Mount Carmel, that he wandered down into the desert where the fathers of those priests of the Sun whom he slew by the river Kishon heard the thunderings and the trumpet exceeding loud, and there, poorly screened by a bush from the burning eye of God's great rival, he laid down to die. Whoever is so in sympathy with this overtried man as to feel what he had to contend with, whoever will enter into the spirit of the long war with the Worship of Nature from when Abraham abandoned heretical Assyria to when his children for their idolatries were dragged back there, captives of the Assyrian gods, will not faint at the slow doing away from the human heart of the Service of Nature, though ten times ten thousand years should pass before the earth is filled with the beauty of holiness.

The idolatry of Western Asia with which Israel had to contend, through its faith in itself, had strength known to no other. No sufficient idea can be formed of it from the idolatry of the classic world; none of its wickedness from the sober morality of the earlier Romans, none of its strong fascination from the fairy-like mythology of the Greeks. Israel struggled with it, like a bird struggling with the charming of a serpent. It could be met only by miracles, swept from the earth only by the whirlwind of war. Even miracles did not suffice to hold back the heart of Israel from the sins of Moab, of Philistia, Phœnicia, Egypt, Assyria, and Babylon; nor did they withstand their enchantments till they witnessed the punishment of that guilty world by the Persian, whom, *in words luminous for history*, God said he would raise up, "that they may know from the rising of the sun and from the west that *there is none beside Me.*" Thence onward there was no prophet in Israel till one cried in the wilderness of Judea, "Prepare ye the way of the Lord." From this point of view, the signs and wonders of old Hebrew history, from those wrought in Egypt by Moses to those wrought in Babylon by Daniel, are so appropriate to what had to be done and was done, that, to the Christian reason, the natural in that history is good evidence that the miracles recorded in the Hebrew Bible could not have been otherwise than so.

OF THE THREE CLASSES OF MIRACLES.

Of miracles there are three great classes or processions. Those wrought by his Spirit before Christ came ; those wrought by Him in person ; and those wrought by the Holy Ghost. There are significant differences between them. The sphere of the first is Nature, of the last, Spirit. The class that intervened partook of the characteristics of each. Its miracles are transition miracles. They bridge over the chasm between the first class of miracles and the last. In some things they are like the first ; in all things they are types and prophecies of the last.*

---

* The Edinburgh Review, October, 1864, says: "The Romanist believes in the miracles of Scripture ; he believes, also, that a continuing Church continues to possess the power of working miracles. The Protestant believes in Scripture miracles, but he believes that the power to work such miracles ceased

When the first class of miracles is compared with that which followed, it seems adapted to an earlier stage in the reclaiming of man. The former impress the senses, the latter the reason. The former seem more stupendous, the latter are more convincing. To minds trained up to appreciate the higher procession of miracles which Christ led forth in his own person, *and that invisible procession of miracles, higher than either, now led forth by the Holy Ghost,* the earlier miracles seem unspiritual though stupendous. Thus they *should* seem, for the object was suited to the subject ; the miracles were fitted to unspiritual ages that were Titanic in conception, colossal in achievement, the ages that wrought the wonders of Thebes and Babylon. The colossal miracles of old were for the purpose of abasing Nature-worship. The colossal miracles of old were to teach man that he was not made to be the idolater of Nature. With many aims, this was one great aim, one great Lesson of the Miracle of the Guiding Star. And in this point of view it belongs in the same class with the miracles of old ; though in them, in the first instance, regard was had for one people, and in this for all.

OF THE GREATNESS OF THIS MIRACLE.

As the divine method in the reclaiming of man discloses itself in the world-history, one of its rules seems to be, to train up a few to be teachers of the many. Of this the history of the Hebrews is the

---

after the time of the apostles, *for which he can give no very cogent reason."* Evidently, the writer would insinuate, that no reason ever has been, or can be, given.

grand illustration and evidence ; and as soon as there were men fit to give full scope to the truths learned by the Hebrews, and for truths for which those had prepared the way, this work was given those men, small as their number was.   There was a varied and wonderful preparation for their doing this work ; but all thought of this must here be restricted to the fitness of the miracle of the star to aid in the Christianizing of the Roman world.

As this Nature-humbling miracle was the closing miracle of a long series directed to one end, and summed up all the Lesson as to Nature-worship which Israel had learned in all the past, would it not transcend all the miracles before it, and be the greatest because the last ? a question which merely indicates the line of the thought that is to be followed and not a predetermined conclusion.   I am not of those who know what the Infinite One should do, and say, and do, and then judge the Gospel by it.   I force no ideas upon the miracle.   I learn from the miracle what the miracle should be.   The Greeks said, a circle is the most perfect form, and therefore the heavenly bodies must move in circles ; but the planets, paying no heed to either assertion, moved on as before, while their circles covered the skies with a maze of confusion.   Astronomy was content to trace the elliptical paths of the planets.   The lesson is a good one, and whether in the world of Nature or in the world of Grace, let us get at the facts if we can. This I try to do.   I disclaim all speculation.   I report what I see.

THIS MIRACLE COMPARED WITH THAT OF THE SUN.

The comparative greatness of the Miracle of the Star is brought to its proper test when it is compared with the standing still of the sun on Gibeon, the moon on the valley of Aijalon.   This was the last of the procession of miracles that marched with Israel from Egypt into Palestine, and it was pre-eminent over them all, as if thus only could it bring that epic cycle of signs and wonders to its fitting close.   Its occasion was greater than that of any of the train of miracles that preceded it, for that battle-day grew out of all the past of Israel and secured all the future. The battle-day of Marathon is no more to be compared with it than Miltiades with Joshua.   What was gained at Marathon and at Yorktown is to be universal and immortal only through what was gained at Bethhoron.   What should we have been had Israel been hurled down into the chasm of the Jordan, and driven back into the desert, where it had been training for forty years to fight this very battle ?   When on the verge of that desert the sand-cloud told of Pharaoh's coming, and from it rode out the horsemen, till on either hand, and behind, was the circling enemy, and the sea was before those frightened slaves, then deliverance rightly came by miracle, for so only could it come.   Then by the waters of the Red Sea it was the hour of the right hand of God.   In the pass at Bethhoron it was the hour of man.   To the good conduct of the children of those herdsmen of Goshen, bondsmen of Egypt, was then trusted the world's deliverance from Idolatry, which, tracing the vivifying of Heat in every thing under heaven, then as now, universally culminated in the worship of the burning sun. The battle it was given them to fight at Bethhoron, they were left to fight without the aid of miracle.

There is a life in nature of which little is, or perhaps can be, known; but as it seems to have sympathized with its Lord when he was dying on the cross, so here it may have been in sympathy with his purpose in this deciding hour; for when the faithful people were driving the apostates from the living God down the long pass that leads to the Philistine border of the Western Sea, the Lord suffered the wild fury of the elements to go forth against the flying infidel. It is the pleasure of Christ that nations, like men, shall work out their own salvation; and that prayer of Joshua's, which perhaps might not have been heard had it been for help in a battle that was to be fought, was a prayer that he might secure unto God the fruits of a victory won. On that day God found, what in the long war with infidelity he has hardly found again, a man in sympathy with his own intensity of purpose to destroy it. When Joshua heard the roar of the elements begin to mingle with the roar of the receding battle, the spirit of the captain of the host of the Lord so rose to the thought of the Almighty that the Man was as great as the moment. Then, for once, there was in a man fullness of sympathy with God; and so there was the intense feeling, the courage like a grain of mustard seed that can move the mountains. Then, there was, for once, in a man the faith before which it is the

Almighty's pleasure that the Laws of Matter shall dissolve like blazing flax. Then there was that without which *the Scripture would be incomplete.* For when the Jesus of old commanded the Sun to stand still on Gibeon, the moon on the valley of Aijalon, then, there was, for once, in that old prophetic world, that mystic garden where were sown the seeds of every future, the full quickening into life of the spirit there is in man, which in some far Hereafter will approve itself superior to all the orbs of heaven. On that great day the greatness of the great Wonder and Sign is not in the Sun, it is in the Man. By the prayer of such a man well might the Sun be made to complete the discomfiture of its worshipers. No better thing has it done since it began to mark times and seasons. Find another such hour and another such man and you shall behold an equal miracle. Vain the search! the Spirit of all wisdom said "there was no day like that before it or after it." * So great the occasion, and to it the greatness of the miracle corresponds.

The occasion of the Miracle of the Guiding Star

---

* Volumes might be written on this text. All history approves its truth. Or rather, it will, when it is written as it ought to be. As yet there is very little, outside of the sacred volume, that deserves the name. It is enough to show how far that which passes as such comes short of the true idea of history to point, among the English, to Gibbon, Hume, and to Macaulay ; and as further showing the prevailing want in this order of literature of any true idea of that in which the true life of history consists, Professor Creasy's Fifteen Decisive Battles of the World—a book which as well as most historical essays deserves a place in a library—may here be referred to. From this book the Battle of Bethhoron is left out.

was greater. One cycle of time was ending, another cycle of time was opening. A conquest, wider than that of the land between the Lebanon and the Desert, the Jordan and the sea, was about to begin, even of the Canaan of the Globe, under the Captain mightier than Joshua, who said, " All power is given unto me in heaven and in earth. Go ye therefore and teach all nations, baptizing them in the name of the Father, and of the Son, and of the Holy Ghost; teaching them to observe all things whatsoever I have commanded you; and, lo, I am with you alway, even unto the end of the world."

THE EFFECTIVENESS OF THIS MIRACLE THE TRUE TEST OF ITS GREATNESS.

It would seem, then, that the Miracle of the Star must have been the greater. But surely not in publicity, not in quick effect upon the imagination; for in these respects the wonder wrought by day above one army flying and another pursuing, in the great Light of our heavens, seems to take precedence of the miracle wrought by night, before a few pilgrims, in a star. Yet, as the effectiveness of a miracle may be a better test of its comparative greatness, then, while the miracle at Bethhoron may have been the more astounding, the miracle on the way to the house in Bethlehem may have been the greater.

The older struggle with the idolatry of the Shemitic races in Western Asia, though mainly within one people, was more severe than that which broke in pieces the idolatry of the Aryan races in the Roman Empire; and in that older struggle there were mani·

festations of supernatural power, that, seen from this altered world, look so strange, that with many belief in them has changed into wonder and doubt. As the correspondence between those miracles and that world is better seen, this wonder and doubt lessens. And, as tending to relieve those miracles of an air of exaggeration and unreality, somewhat of that correspondence will here be shown : but while, for this reason, more will be said on this subject than otherwise would have been, it will also serve to show somewhat of the difference in spirit between the idolatry of the older Bible times and that of the Roman Empire at the time of the Miracle of the Star.

THE FITNESS OF THE OLD MIRACLES TO THE TIMES OF OLD.

In one night one hundred and eighty-five thousand of the soldiers of Sennacherib were slain by the angel of Jehovah. In suddenness this humbling of the military pride of Assyria was like that of Egypt. But at the Red Sea Israel could have been saved only by the quick intervention of superhuman power, while Sennacherib had withdrawn his soldiers to some distance from the Holy City to abide the onset of an army marching against him from Upper Egypt. The need, then, of the later marvel is not so clear ; and the reason why

> The might of the Gentile, unsmote by the sword,
> Melted like snow in the glance of the Lord,

is, in part at least, in the audacity that characterized the Shemitic apostasy from the faith. A clear proof of that audacity is the message delivered by Sennacherib's herald in the name of his king to the citizens of Jerusalem: "Who are they among all the gods of the countries that have delivered their country out of mine hand, that the Lord should deliver Jerusalem out of mine hand?" Sennacherib's belief in the God in Israel was as real as his belief in the gods of his own country, and his theological controversy with the citizens in Jerusalem was only concerning their comparative power. But whom of the gods of Assyria does he set forth as superior to the God in Zion? Mark, in the words of his herald, Sennacherib's claim that he himself was a god superior to the God in Israel. Mark, also, *the close* of these words from Isaiah's magnificent Psalm of Triumph on his death. Poetry more grand has seldom been written, but in it there is history as well: "The whole earth is at rest and is quiet. They break forth into singing, yea, the fir trees rejoice at thee and the cedars of Lebanon, saying, Since thou art laid down, no feller is come up against us. Hell from beneath is moved for thee to meet thee at thy coming. It stirreth up the dead for thee, even all the chief ones of the earth; it hath raised up from their thrones all the kings of the nations. All they shall speak and say unto thee, Art thou also become weak as we? art thou become like unto us? Thy pomp is brought down to the ground and the noise of thy viols; the worm is spread under thee and the worms cover thee. How art thou fallen from heaven, O Lucifer, Son of the Morning! how art thou cut down to the ground that didst weaken the nations! For thou hast said in thy heart, I will ascend into heaven, I will exalt my throne above the stars of God ; I will ascend above the heights of the clouds, I will be like the Most High."

Even though it be clear to the intellect, a thought or feeling is apt to have an air of unreality when there is no sympathy with it ; and it is hard to understand an exaltation that borders on and passes over into madness, for to understand any phase of the soul, one should have a little fellow-feeling with it.   Sennacherib thought he was a god ; he felt he was as truly so as Jehovah ; and though his thought and feeling have now become strange, unreal, incomprehensible almost, that thought and feeling were real to him. His people thought and felt as he did ; and so, no doubt, did some in Israel.

In the annals of Greece or Rome there is nothing quite equal to this. Against nations protected by their own deities the Romans went forth to wage victorious war, but always in the name of the gods of Rome.   It was the Genius of the Eternal City, the Jupiter of the Capitol, that humbled the local deities. With the Greeks it was the Olympian Zeus.   In his own name went forth Sennacherib to wage war with the gods of the nations.   Thought he they were not gods ?   In his time there was no such thought outside of the peculiar people, and it was not believed by all even of them.   The message of the King of Assyria claimed that he had proved himself stronger than the gods of the cities he had conquered, and in it he more than evens himself with the God of Zion. It was in form and in fact a personal challenge to that Deity.   Sennacherib so meant it, and it was so understood by the citizens of Jerusalem, who heard

his herald, as they crowded to listen on the battle-
ments of Zion.

That the king is a representative and vicegerent
of God has ever been a feeling common to all Asia,
and there it has ever tended to pass into worship of
the monarch. All of any similar feeling in Europe
as to the divine right of kings has been but a faint
semblance of the intensity of this feeling in the Oriental heart; while in Europe the worship of the
monarch has been almost unknown. Alexander's
affectation of divinity, and the senatorial decrees
awarding divine honors to Roman emperors, were
spiritless mimicries of Asiatic frenzy, hollow tricks
of state-policy, laughed at in private by those who
took part in them in public. Not such the feeling
of Sennacherib, Lord of Assyria and Babylon, proud
inheritor of the daring spirit that built the tower of
Babel.

Within the memory of living men antiquity was
the classical world. Rome and Greece filled up the
field of clear vision, and what lay back of them was
so indistinct that they only seemed to be seen. Then
the dark confused background of the time-picture
cleared up. A world opened behind the world. The
Greeks and the Romans seemed nearer to us, and
more like ourselves. As when the traveler from
Geneva to the Valley of Chamouni, journeying through
hills like those of New Hampshire, suddenly beholds
far up in the sky the sharp and bristling points of the
higher Alps, so sudden the apparition of a world older
than Rome or Greece.

Before this, in the world of Hebrew Scripture

great and awful forms, with nothing like them within
a range of sight, that seemed to reach to the beginning of history, awoke uncomprehending wonder.
This was not very trying to faith until in this century
a desire to make the past real, stirred like a new
sense, not in travelers only like Burckhardt, or enthusiasts like Du Perron, but in the common heart.
Then it became far otherwise. For a generation
trained up to feel that the world began with the
siege of Troy, and familiar only with classic history,
could hardly make real to itself the older world of
Abraham ; or think of Moses, of Balaam, of Elijah, or
of the star-led Eastern Magi, as men of flesh and blood.
Christ ever grants new confirmations of his Truth to
meet the ever-varying phases of the human mind ;
and while the new frenzy of inquiry, misled by false
analogies, was explaining away the marvels of Hebrew
history as it had the *pre-historic* myths and fables
of Greek and Roman story, He changed the whole
aspect of the case by enlarging the bounds of recorded Time.

For a long while I could never make out why such
abiding memorials were wrought, at so many places
on the face of the earth, in the Ages after the Flood ;
why to Egypt the power was given to build temple
and pyramid that so dominate over the imagination
and haunt the memory, human memorials that will
abide the coming of the Son of Man. I now see
that through these we commune with their builders ;
and know the Time and the spirit that wrought the
more perishable but equal wonders of Nineveh and
Babylon, and the later marvels of Persepolis. In a

divine frenzy, those early Times wrought for the Times that are, those monuments of themselves, once so silent, now so eloquent.   With history reaching only to the classical world, the Tower of Babel and the Pilgrimage of the Magi were possible only to faith. The Tower of Babel, impossible in Greece, on the plain of Shinar was possible.   Pharaoh, that hard man, so lifelike yet so unlike life, impossible in the modern world, equally so as a Roman Consul or a Greek General, was possible as the Lord of Egypt. Sennacherib, impossible as a Roman Emperor, was possible as a Babylonian King.

Divine manifestations, suited to the men and the times that have risen from the dead, must have been unlike those in subsequent ages.   Through the resurrection of a world so unlike the classical, or the world that now is, the miracles in Hebrew Scripture admit of becoming as reasonable to the Reason as they are certain to Faith ; and this will at length be clear to all, save those who think that nowhere, in no circumstances, can God have ever done any thing they have not seen Him do.

GENERAL EVIDENCE OF THE EFFECT OF THIS MIRACLE ON THE ROMAN WORLD.

Inasmuch as the fervor of idolatry in Europe never was equal to that of the Shemitic races in Western Asia in the earlier cycles of civilization, the Miracle of the Star, though less astounding than that of the Sun, as wrought against European heathenism, may have had the superior grandeur of greater effectiveness.   The strong impression that it had is all I can

attain to.   It is not a matter of rigorous demonstration.   Yet thus much is certain: while there is no
evidence that the Jewish heart was so touched by
the Miracle of the Sun as especially to distinguish it
from the other Signs and Wonders of their history,
the Miracle of the Star had an especial effect in the
struggle of Christianity with the heathenism of the
Roman world ; and though its power cannot be separated from the many other influences combined with
it and measured as a thing apart, yet there is good
reason to think this miracle *had more to do with the
Conversion of Europe than any other.*

To limit the evidence of this to the Guiding of the
Star is too narrow.   All the facts that gave occasion
for the miracle, or that were connected with it, should
be taken into the account ; in a word, all the second
chapter of St. Matthew.   This chapter was peculiarly
fitted to conciliate the Roman world to Christianity.
Before the age of the Apostles, the people of whom
Balaam truly prophesied, " they shall dwell alone,"
had been dispersed "among every nation under
heaven ;" and the Gospel, going forth from Judea and
preached by Jews, had to contend with a common
and bitter prejudice against the Jews and their
religion.   The second chapter of St. Matthew is so
well fitted to take advantage of one of these feelings,
while trying to overcome the other, that the wonder
is some of the celebrity-loving men who have tried
to do away with the Gospel have not set up the
charge that it was most adroitly forged for this very
purpose.   In it the Persians are wiser than the Jews ;
Ctesiphon than Jerusalem ; the Magi know of the

birth of the Messiah while it is unknown to the
Capitol and the Sanhedrim of the Jews.

The Roman and the Greek had come to doubt their
own mythologies ; but their moral sense survived the
decay of their religions, and they were proud of their
intellectual powers. There was a void in their hearts ;
but they did not feel they were wholly without Truth,
and there was no reason why they should. St. Paul
availed himself of those feelings when he preached at
Athens. What there he did, and much more, was
done by this chapter. In the story of the Magi,
looked at with reference to the human element in it,
there was an opening of the way for the reception of
the Gospel, by a recognition of the Truth among the
heathen, that was conciliating to a reasonable self-
respect. Heathen philosophers could see that in it
heathen philosophy was honored. Those who were
not philosophers could see those Magi, so much
wiser than the Jews, like themselves were not Jews.
The human element in the history was purely such
up to the time the Wise Men left Jerusalem. No
miracle pointed out the New Star. It was a human
and a heathen discovery. And so, too, was the immediate finding of the Child, so far as the Jews were
concerned.

The divine element in the chapter was equally well
fitted to conciliate the heathen mind to Christianity.
The exclusiveness of Jehovah was his reproach
among the nations. The feeling that He was so,
though most unjust, was very natural to the Jews.
From them it passed into the Gentile mind ; and it
was intolerable to the polished Greek and the strong

Roman that he should prefer the Jews to them.   In his wonderful guiding of the Magi to the cradle of his Son this feeling met with a corrective.   The beautiful fact was better than long arguments.   It touched the heart of a heathen as it could not touch the heart of a Jew; and it gave to the heart so touched a sense of the thoughtful kindness of God, such as a heathen could not gain of any one of his own deities from all the fables of his mythology. The Gospel of the Star conveyed to him in a most beautiful way a thought as beautiful as it was new. And this chapter was for him.   Jacob's part in it was very little.   This chapter was for him, the Gentile. It was his Gospel, and it was all his.

That the conversion of whole nations ceased after the tenth and eleventh centuries is worthy of more thought than seems to have been given to it.   One of its causes was political.   Europe, then more or less Christianized, was barred out from Asia and Africa by the Mohammedan powers.   From the Black Sea and the Caspian, on the East, round to Egypt and along the southern shore of the Mediterranean Sea into Spain, they drew a military cordon which the Crusades failed to break through.   After those aggressive movements, Europe, in its turn, had as much as it could do to protect itself from the Turks down even into the seventeenth century.   The ocean road, from the western coast of Europe around Africa to the remote and ancient East, hardly began to be used before the seventeenth century, and the old route thither by the Red Sea and the Indian Ocean was not reopened till this century.   Thus, through

causes felt as early as the seventh century and lasting almost to our own day, Asia and Africa became
almost impenetrable. This problem is here referred
to, merely to show, by pointing to one of its various
causes, that its explanation cannot be altogether the
same as the explanation, whatever it be, of another
that looks somewhat like it : namely, that missions
in this century have resulted in no such sweeping
changes as did those down to the tenth century. It
is with no wish to disparage what these later missions—whose end is not yet—have thus far accomplished, but because the full presentation of my
argument seems to require it, that it is here said,
the heathen (or, to give the meaning of a word that
should oftener have been translated, where it has
been transferred into the English Scriptures from
the Greek,) the Nations may have been addressed
by the missionaries too much as if they had never
had the Truth, or were now wholly without it. If so
this be, it gives countenance to the heresy that
denies the unity of the human race; and to the heresy that denies the scriptural account of the Dispersion of the Nations. A truer view of the nations
sees in them the younger brother to whom the Father
divided the inheritance. With the utter spending of
this comes a keen sense of want ; and where this is
not felt the inheritance cannot be all gone. The
thoughts of some of the more Eastern peoples are
slow ; providentially so ; for this is a consequence of
the languages they spoke after the miracle at Babel ;
and as their thoughts are very slow, so their thoughts
are very old. Some of these peoples are not without

some reminiscences of the truth ; not without the presence in times past, or it may be now, of providential teachers ; and none of them have ever been without moral sense ; and none without the mercy of God. The Chinese, one third of the people of the world, the roots of whose ancient civilization can be traced into the patriarchal age, the Mohammedans, one tenth of the people of the world, whose religion is an offshoot from Judaism, seem not further gone from the Truth, perhaps not so far, as the Roman Empire was in the days of the Apostles.

The Apostles were never denunciatory. At the Pentecost St. Peter went to the edge of the truth when, in words showing how grandly his soul was exalted above all natural bitterness of feeling toward those who murdered his Lord, he told the Jews they did it ignorantly. At Athens the tone of St. Paul, the Apostle to the Gentiles, was conciliatory and appreciative. Still more instructive and decisive is the fact that divine Wisdom so ordered the course of events in the Kingdom of Grace that the Gospel should, in its opening chapter, bear witness to a like spirit in the religion of Christ.

There is no reason to doubt the substance of this second chapter of St. Matthew was well known and much thought of by the earliest converts to Christianity. Though printing then was not, thinking was ; and the facts of the new religion were much thought and talked of. The Gospel to the nations was the Life of the Lord ; and the apostolic recital of this must often have been carefully committed to memory in the sacred congregations. This must have begun before any of the four Gospels were written, and have continued afterward ; and so the Gospel then, like the Lord's Prayer and the Ten Commandments now, was written on the heart.*

There is not one direct reference to any one of our Lord's parables, not to one of his miracles, nor, save his birth, transfiguration, passion, resurrection, and ascension, to one of the many events of his life in all the Epistles. The entire absence of any such references to any of the many events recorded by the Evangelists is startling, yet *how accordant with the supposition of the oral, memoriter teaching of the Gospel in the apostolic age!* So accordant, that it is good evidence of such teaching, when it is well understood what the Gospel then was. As the word is now used, what is the Gospel? or rather, what is it not? The Gospel then was the Life of Christ. In the middle of the first century the Scriptures were the Old Testament, and the Gospel-truth in them, forewritten in types and ceremonies, inwrought into history, or uttered in prophecy, was shown to the people in preaching—of this the Epistle to the Hebrews may be taken as an example. Preaching then reproved sin, corrected error, encouraged righteousness—of this the spirit may be seen in all the Epistles ; but the Gospel itself was the Gospel

---

* The written Gospel of St. Matthew went forth before the others ; and so the fact that the Pilgrimage of the Magi is not mentioned in those later written Gospels does not even raise a presumption that it was not a part of all the apostolic preaching of the Gospel, and has no bearing on the question of its effect on the nations.

of the Son of God, or, in the words of St. Paul, Jesus Christ and Him crucified. The story of his life in such form and order as the Apostles gave it, and as committed to memory by others from their lips, this was, at first, the Gospel. Then, after a time, and often using *words and phrases current in that un-written Gospel, and so familiar to the Evangelist in his preaching of it*, came the Gospel according to St. Matthew; its peculiar title, followed in all the others, being in harmony with the facts as here stated. Then came the Gospel according to St. Mark; and this essentially, is the Gospel according to St. Peter, as thus it might very naturally have been. Then the Gospel according to St. Luke, which, in like manner, may be held to be essentially the Gospel according to St. Paul; and when the last Apostle was nigh a hundred years old there came, as from the bosom of the Lord, the Gospel according to St. John. What the unwritten Gospel was may be known from the written Gospel. In this written Gospel, no utterance of human feeling was permitted, not one word of gladness when the angels sang Glory in the highest, not one word of wonder when the widow's son rose up on the bier, not one word of ad-miration when the Sermon on the Mount was done, not one word of pity when Jesus was scourged and crowned with thorns and nailed to the Cross, not one word of wonder by his empty grave. What Christ Jesus said and did, not what even inspired Evangel-ists felt and thought about it, this was the Gospel that evangelized the world. Even before Christianity be-came the established religion of the Empire, it tended

to make heathen philosophy thoughtful and moral.
This apostolic mode of teaching and hearing the Gospel may be the secret, untold by Gibbon or Guizot,
of that rapid spread of pure Christianity among
the common people to which the Catacombs attest.
When it is again taught and learned in the same way
the Gospel will again have the same power. Restore
this method again, by making Church-members learn
by heart the Gospel according to St. John as their
profession of faith, by making the children learn by
heart the Gospel according to St. Matthew, and the
Gospel, not according to man's device but as given
by the Spirit, will convert the world.

SPECIFIC EVIDENCE OF THE EFFECT OF THIS MIR-
ACLE ON THE ROMAN WORLD.

Thus far, only general evidence has been given of
the effect of the second chapter of St. Matthew on
the Roman world ; and from the scantiness of the
memorials of the early Christian ages, specific evidence of it is hardly to be looked for ;* yet I find

---

* Of the early and great effect of St. Matthew's narrative on
the imagination, the exaggerations of it in the Gospel of the
Infancy, and in the Epistle of St. Ignatius, (see pages 79, 80,)
may be evidence. Since this chapter was written, I have marked
in the Anti-Nicene Library, vol. ix, p. 195, a Narrative of events
in Persia. As to its date, I have no sufficient means of judging.
It there appears among " Fragments of the Third Century."
Like much of the Apocryphal Gospels it is sheer romance,
though claiming to recite what is "inscribed upon golden plates
and laid up in the royal temples of Persia :"—a country as to
which the writer shows the ignorance spoken of in the Wise
Men, page 4. The Persian King goes to a temple, which is

such in the history of the feast of the Epiphany. Among the sacred events in the life of our Lord, commemorated in the early Churches by set observances, such as His Passion and Ascension, was the Manifestation of His Divine Nature; and it would seem that the occasion chosen for this might well have been His Baptism, when the heavens opened and the Spirit descended and rested upon Him.   The East-

---

quite after the Greek or Roman style, and is told by the priest that all the gods are in commotion because Juno hath conceived. The statues begin to sing, "whatever creatures were within, whether quadruped, or fowl, in silver or gold, uttered their voices," and a star descends and stands above the image of Juno.   Of course, the King calls for all his interpreters ; and he sends to Judea "some of the Magi, the star showing the way." They find the mother, whose "color was like that of ripe wheat, and she was of a round face, and had her hair bound up;" and the child, "who was in his second year," and was "in part the likeness of his mother."   To him they offer gifts.   The Magi say : "As we had along with us a servant skilled in painting from the life, we brought with us to our country a likeness of them both, and it was placed in the temple with this inscription upon it : 'To Jove, the Sun, the mighty God, the King of the Jews, the Power of Persia dedicated this.'"

Evidently the inventor of this extravagance meant to set forth a conciliatory recognition of other religions, though firmly holding out the supremacy of the true, for when the Star descends "all the statues fall on their faces."   As evidently, he seeks to take advantage of the popular dislike of the Jews ; for he makes the interpreters say, "Of Judah a Kingdom has arisen that shall subvert all the memorials of the Jews;" and he makes the Magi report, that in Jerusalem the priests would have bribed them to hush up the whole matter.   The fragment ends with these words, supposed to have been spoken by the Magi: "We saw Christ our Saviour, who was made known both as God and man : to Him be the glory and power unto the ages of ages. Amen."

ern Christians did elect this occasion for the feast of the Epiphany. The Western Christians accepted this feast, but changed the occasion of it from the Lord's Baptism to the Worship of the Magi, and this change was acceded to in the East. Every way this is remarkable; for in three of the Gospels not one event is named in the life of our Lord while he dwelt at Nazareth, in the other but one event is named; and thus the Gospel emphasizes the contrast between the secluded life of the obedient child or humble workman before His Baptism, and the public and wonderful life afterward. This, together with what took place at His Baptism, explains its commemoration by the feast of the Epiphany; and, at first thought, there seems nothing that can be put in its stead, save the Birth of the Lord, the Miracle at Cana of Galilee, or the Transfiguration. Neither of the latter two were chosen; and, the Birth of the unconscious Infant not fully answering to what was to be commemorated, the feast of Christmas left a feeling which still required that of the Baptism, whose intent was to mark the showing of Christ to the World as God manifest in the flesh. The Gospel almost seemed to conjoin those two great moments, the Birth and the Baptism, by leaving all between them so much of a blank. The reasons, then, determining the Eastern Churches to commemorate the Baptism by the feast of the Epiphany were weighty; and the Worship of the Magi, at first thought, suggests little reason for the change in the occasion of the feast, or for its selection at all. Though it is not to be supposed that the change is thus wholly explained, yet

one who traces the course of natural causes as conjoined with spiritual, must in part account for it by
the personal interest the heathen converts, who in
the West especially were the great body of the
Church, felt in the Worship of the Wise Men. They
must have had a peculiar and strong desire that this
might have a place among the sacred festivals ; for
the manifestation of the Lord to the Magi seemed
His manifestation to themselves, and their wonderful
recognition of Him His recognition by themselves.
This fastened their thoughts upon it, till it seemed
to them the great event it really was.   It quickened
a divine instinct till they felt, a spiritual perception
till they saw the manifestation of the glory of Christ
to the Magi, as proved by their Worship, should be
commemorated as the Epiphany rather than any thing
else ; and the place be given to it which was before
given to the Baptism.   Hereafter, in the chapter on
the Manifestation of Christ to the Nations, a fuller
explanation will be presented of the worship of the
Magi than I have elsewhere given ; and, with reference
to this, I would that my readers should here mark in
this change in the occasion of this Feast the feeling
of the Church that in this Worship, or rather in that
of which it was the effect and sign, there was that
which gave it a high place among the mysteries of
Redemption.

Another of the holy festivals found its occasion in
the second chapter of St. Matthew.   This is, also,
peculiarly convincing evidence of the deep impression it made on the early Christian converts ; for the
philosophic mind must be struck with the commem-

oration of the Massacre of the Innocents; an event on its human side so dark and pitiable that it might seem wiser to have kept it out of sight than to have so held it up as to fasten upon it the public gaze. Here, again, it is so far from my heart to deny that a true spiritual perception led to the election of this mysterious event for special commemoration, that in a chapter hereafter I hope to disclose confirmation of this never before brought to light. But what concerns my immediate purpose is, that the natural cause of this festival may have been that the mind of Christianizing Heathendom in the freshness of its new emotions loved to dwell in an especial and peculiar manner on this chapter; and that each of these feasts is evidence, and the more convincing the more it is thought upon, of the strong and deep impression early made by the train of events which began with the outshining of the Star of our Lord.

In the view that has thus been taken of the second chapter of St. Matthew's Gospel, its teachings may seem to have been directed less to the abasing of Nature-worship than to other ends; but in the Pilgrimage of the Wise Men there was the "manifold" wisdom of God working at the same time, and through the same means, manifold results. Even while it disarmed the bitter hatred of the Nations toward the Jews and their religion, its Lesson against Nature-worship was far from being needless to any of them, and in the ruder districts of the Empire was as much needed as ever.*

---

* See Acts xiv, 11–18: "And when the people saw what Paul had done, they lifted up their voices, saying in the speech of Lyca-

THE EFFECT OF THIS CHAPTER ON THE TEUTONIC RACES.

Besides this, the great work of the Conversion of Europe was not finished when Constantine proclaimed Christianity the religion of the Empire. I am not speaking of how thorough the Conversion of the Empire may have been, but of the struggle which followed with the heathenism of the Teutonic races, of the Goths, Vandals, Lombards, Burgundians, Franks, Saxons, Danes, Normans, and other peoples, such as the Huns, from whom the Goths fled as from barbarians more barbarous than themselves. Some labor has been wasted of late in trying to show that the earlier Conversion of the Roman world was no great thing; but it may have a good effect if it turn attention to the longer, and, perhaps, even more arduous struggle of Christianity with the Northern hordes that overran the Empire, and made it necessary to convert Europe all over again. It was a little less than three hundred years from the Pentecost to the decree of Constantine, but the time of the conversion of those heathen was more than twice that number of years. Among those forest-born dwellers in the bosom of Nature, the worship of Nature was not nerveless and decaying, as within

---

onia, The gods are come down to us in the likeness of men. And they called Barnabas, Jupiter; and Paul, Mercurius, because he was the chief speaker. Then the priest of Jupiter brought oxen and garlands, and would have done sacrifice; which when the apostles heard of, they rent their clothes, and ran in among the people, and scarce restrained they the people, that they had not done sacrifice unto them."

much of the pale of Greek and Roman civilization. Every feeling of theirs was full of vitality. Here, again, it is not possible to trace out by itself the effect of the second chapter of St. Matthew on their quick imaginations and sensitive hearts; but it can be seen, that while there was no prejudice with them against Christianity as proclaimed by Jews, for they knew it only as the religion of a vast Empire whose grandeur, even in ruins, inspired veneration, yet to them, as heathen and worshipers of Nature, all the story of the Magi must have had special instruction and peculiar charms. And that it did appeal persuasively to their hearts and dwelt much in their thoughts will not be doubted by one familiar with the legendary lore which early in the Middle Ages accumulated around this Pilgrimage, with all the volume of feeling that at last found so grand an expression in the Cathedral of the Three Kings at Cologne.

The Sun stood still, the Star moved on, and as it moved drew nations to Christ. Such was its glory then. Such again shall its glory be. In the cold eclipse that is beginning to shroud the intellectual heavens this Star will so shine out again, and with a light unknown before:

> The Brightest and Best of the Sons of the Morning
> Will dawn on our darkness and lend us its aid.

The Sun stood still, the Star moved on; nor is it trifling to note this difference, for in the world of Scripture, as in the world of Nature, nothing is trifling. This difference between the two miracles is the breadth of the difference between the vegetative and the next higher cycle of life; between the rooted trees, whose waving boughs prophesy of the gift of motion, and the animals who, shorter-lived and less grand to look upon, yet born into a higher life, are free to roam among the majestic oaks that stand in the same spot for centuries. This difference between the miracles accords with the fact that the latter was wrought as one cycle of miracle was passing into another and higher. By the one miracle Nature was arrested in her course, by the other she was made to go before man. In that early age, as in the ages since, Nature led man away from God. In the grandest visible manifestation of the divine energy in one great cycle of typical events, Nature all represented in the center of that light and heat without whose effluence there would be no life, was stopped in her course. In the corresponding putting forth of divine energy in the beginning of a new Time, Nature was made to wait upon man as a servant. The latter miracle was *prophetic of that service of Nature to man*, so wonderfully coming about through Science, as born anew through Christianity. And it accords with this, that the witnesses to this prophesying Star were men of Science in that old world then beginning to give place to the new.

THE FINAL EVIDENCE OF THE GREATNESS OF THE MIRACLE.

These thoughts uphold the Miracle of the Star in its test comparison; and yet, after all, it might have been forever a perplexing fact, that, by all the superior splendor of the sun, the miracle of the Jesus of old should have seemed greater than that of the Jesus of whom he was but the type, had not astronomy confirmed the records of faith by disclosing that some of the stars surpass the great orb that lights the solar system. Astronomy here brings aid to faith. It shows this miracle may have been wrought in a star with which the sun compares as the glory of the Jesus of old with the glory of his Lord. And, it will hereafter be proved, the Scriptures make this certain by revealing that the miracle on the way to the house in Bethlehem was wrought in the symbol in the material universe of the all-creating Lord, in the Bright Star of all the worlds.

Thus, of the long procession of Nature-humbling Miracles this wonder and sign was the mightiest, as it was the last. It summed up the Lesson of them all. And it is grandly accordant with the long procession of the miracles against idolatry, that the Lord, who sent them forth by his Spirit of old, Himself in person closed the series, before he opened that higher procession of miracles that bridge over the chasm between the miracles of the old Dispensation and those miracles that distinguish the new Dispensation, wrought not in the unintelligent creation, but in the heart of man.

From the first the Lord by his free handling of nature broke up the bondage of man in nature, and freed him from that idea of its immutability before which he sinks into worship. The heavens were the noblest shrine, the orbs on high the universal objects of idolatry. Well directed then the sweep of the Infant arm that swept every heathenish constellation from the painted sky.   At the opening of the Universal Kingdom of the Lord no more appropriate sign could have been shown to the nations not yet free from Nature-worship.   No more fitting lesson could have been taught to man, than that Nature, which before he had blindly worshiped, was thereafter to serve him.   It is more than this.   It is a prophecy of man's dominion over Nature, this day fulfilling.   It is a prophecy that in higher spheres of being is to have a still higher fulfillment.

The sign thereof was not conformed to the limited ideas of the time, but while answering to those, was conformed to the highest conception man would ever form of the starry heavens.   It was shown to the Representatives of the Human Race, themselves the sign that all nations in their appointed time and order would move on to Bethlehem.   It was shown to them as they were about to come into the presence of the Lord.   It completed the cycle of the miracles of ancient days.   It closed the first volume of the Book of the Redemption of Man.

CHAPTER VI.

THE CREATION OF THE STAR, AND THE RELATION OF THE UNIVERSE TO THE LORD.

AS Archbishop Trench has well said, on the story of the Pilgrims star-led to Bethlehem, the Church "meditates with an interest ever new, a wonder ever growing, as it more and more perceives how deep are the mysteries of faith it presents in simplest historic guise."

WAS THE STAR CREATED AT THE BIRTH OF CHRIST?

Two facts seem to make against this. The seventh of those Days, not measured by the sun, which are classed together in Genesis, is not yet ended; and thus it is known from the Bible that the generation of the earth was going on for a vast indefinite time. Astronomy tells us that the light of some stars is thousands of years in coming to the earth. If, then, the New Star was like one of these, or the time of its generation like that of the earth, is not the idea of its creation at the Advent of our Lord an illusion of the fancy and not a fact for the reason? This may depend on which meaning of the word "create" is taken; for by a world-creation the whole world-making may be meant, or the completion of the process; and so the Star may be said to have been created at the Incarnation if its making was then finished; if that which was not so before then became a world.

Nor would the emission of light by the Star prove that it was, in this sense, created before, for it is revealed that the element Light, of which heat, electricity, and other forces are manifestations, is the form-giving force in the generation of a world. The revelation, that in the sixth great Day "the heavens and the earth were finished and all the host of them," is perhaps more decisive ; yet, as the Earth, with all that to the senses seems to belong to it, and so far as belonging to it, was finished then, and as this chapter is, in the main, a picture of the generation of this round world, it may be these words are to be understood of this finishing.

But, from pressing such hard inquiries the mind is relieved by the truth, that the unknown and the uncreated are so much the same to man, that a star may be said to be created for him when, coming within the grasp of his senses, it visibly becomes a part of his world ; and, so, whatever truth the absolute creation of the Star at the Incarnation might reveal, is revealed through its being then made known to man. The coincidence of the two events has the same significance for him as if the star were then absolutely created ; for a sign to human beings must be conformed to the human faculties. The existence, then, of the Star before the Nativity does not do away with the significance of its shining into the world at the Birth of Christ. Its pre-existence to that event makes it a more speaking symbol of Him who was " before the world was."

THE TRUTH SIGNIFIED BY THIS COINCIDENCE.

To some the coincidence between His manifestation in the world of man and that of His Star may
seem a thing minute beneath the dignity of God—as
if, indeed, such a thing could be—but the fact, that
when the movements of all the worlds were ordered
to an instant, this Star's shining into our sky was
adjusted to a foreseen event—the ground of its
prophecy—accords with what science makes known
of the nicety of the Creator's work, alike in small
things and in great. Things called great on things
called small do so depend, that for the distinction
between them there is hardly a sufficient reason;
and none will think the coincidence of these two
events a small thing who see the truth it signifies.
To think it accidental, is almost equivalent to thinking that all things are given over to blind chance;
to think it unmeaning, is almost thinking the Father
deludes his children with signs to which no realities
correspond. That some truth, or truths, are shadowed forth through the simultaneousness of these
two events is one of those ideas which bring with
them their own evidence. *What truth, or truths, then,
does this coincidence signify?*

THE THREE SCRIPTURES AS TO THE STAR.

Thrice, and thrice only, in the Bible is the Lord
named with a star. Once when Balaam prophesied
of a King, whom he should see after his own death,
who would be Lord of the realm of the dead, Lord
of the celestial sphere, and yet be a man. He foretold that one of his ensigns would be a star; and

when the Man was born, who could not be holden of death, and when a New Star shone out in the heavens at his Birth, the Gospel recording this answers to the words of old ; and the truth of the oracle is vindicated by its fulfillment. Of these three Scriptures, the next is the second chapter of St. Matthew. The phantom-star in the vision of the seer, which foretokened the real star at the Birth of the Lord, and the real star alike signified that *the dominion of Christ would reach beyond this planet.* Thus, separate in time from later and clearer revelations of it, at each of the two epochs, the entry of Israel into Canaan and the Birth of Christ, there was a foregleaming of this fact. There was at a third epoch also ; at the beginning of His ministry, in the Title of his Kingdom ; and before passing on to the last of the three Scriptures, let us here consider the space-extent of the meaning of this Title.

OF THE TITLE, "THE KINGDOM OF HEAVEN."

In the Greek it is, " The Kingdom of the Heavens." It is found nowhere but in St. Matthew's peculiarly Hebraic Gospel. In the rest of the New Testament it is, so to speak, *translated* by " The Kingdom of God." The reason of this may be, that " The Kingdom of the Heavens" would not have given to the heathen the ideas it gave to the children of Israel ; for when the Psalmist cried, " O Thou that dwellest in the heavens !" he thought of " God alone," " glorious in holiness ;" but to the heathen the heavens were the abode of a crowd of deities, the like of some of whose deeds if done by men were punished by the laws.

This translation of the title, "The Kingdom of the Heavens" by "The Kingdom of God," brings out with authority the chief of the ideas in it; yet our Lord used both titles. The one is not the exact equivalent of the other, and it still leaves us to inquire into its meaning.

It is no casual title. John the Herald cried, "The kingdom of the Heavens is at hand;" the King made the same proclamation; and when He sent out his Disciples, he told them to cry, "The kingdom of the Heavens is at hand." The title by which this kingdom was thrice solemnly proclaimed must be its official Title.

The official title of a kingdom is apt to be manifold in meaning. It usually sums up several facts. It speaks to all, but says more to the historian, or statesman, than to the peasant; and as the same title has more of significance in the same generation for some than for others, so the significance of the Title of an everlasting kingdom might differ, in like manner, for different generations. Conveying from the first some common ideas, its meaning might open more and more as its eternal year rolled on; and if those who heard this kingdom proclaimed did not receive from its title an idea it could convey, this might be a natural, perhaps even a necessary, consequence of its everlasting significance.

In the minds of those who heard it proclaimed, the title of this kingdom awakened thoughts as to its meaning that were somewhat determined by their thoughts as to the heavens, and still more so by their thoughts as to the Messiah. Those thoughts were imperfect, and are imperfectly known. The bearing of each of these on the interpretation of this Title will hereafter be inquired into; but they are not the full measure of its meaning.

THE HEAVENS A COMMENT ON THIS TITLE.

The thoughts which the boundless firmament was meant to call out from the human soul are of real moment in determining its full significance ; and if you would decipher all you may of its hidden wisdom, look up to the skies and listen to what they are saying.   That "the heavens declare the glory of God," is no late discovery of the telescope.   The heavens have ever been the theme of the musing, religious mind.   Believers in the Living God have ever felt they were his dwelling-place ; a feeling that is the medium of some unutterable truth, for the Scripture saith, " Heaven is God's throne."   The heavens were divinely appointed to awaken feelings that else might not awake.   They shadow forth what the soul cannot grasp, and of which there is no other picture than the encircling heavens, above, over, beneath, and around all, the picture-symbol of the all-encompassing, all-embracing infinitude of God.   By day the blue depths of ether whisper of this mystery.   In the night its shadow passes across the mirror of the soul.   Beyond the widest reach of thought, every way expands this image of the infinitude of Him whom the heaven of heavens cannot contain.   Heaven is God's throne, and each planet and each star, as truly as the earth, is his footstool.

Some undevout astronomers seem to themselves

to have dispelled this most religious idea. It looks to them like a childish notion. They scale the heavens! Up into the clouds they carry the Tower of Babel! Through the space-penetrating telescope they look along the fraction of an inch on the dial-plate of the universe, and report, not the light in which dwelleth the King Invisible, but the blazing of unnumbered worlds. Yet their discoveries touch not the heavens of the musing, religious mind. Those all-encircling heavens, where all those worlds float like clouds in air, remain. The telescope, widening their circle, makes them but the more expressive symbol of the

> Being above all beings! Mighty One!
>   Whom none can comprehend, and none explore
> Who fill'st existence with Thyself alone,
>   Embracing all, supporting, ruling o'er:
>   Being whom we call God, and know no more.

The Heavens shadow forth the mystery of Creation. The ancient thought of Night as the mother of all things—a dim reminiscence of the story of creation as divinely told—was upheld by the daily birth of the visible world from the Darkness. The solemn, religious Night ever awakens the feeling of the Infinite; and when from the Night goes forth the Day, then passes before the soul a semblance of the miracle, when, through the creation of the world, "the invisible things of God were clearly seen." When from the unknown the known appears, when from out of the formless Darkness shines the form-giving Light, then shines out in the soul the thought of the Creating Word coming forth from His unsearchable hiding.

Thus, in the light of thoughts and feelings which the skies awaken, this title, "The Kingdom of the Heavens," is deciphered as meaning the Kingdom of the Infinite One, who hath revealed Himself through the goings forth of the Word, who was in the beginning with God, who was God, by whom all things were made, and in whom the Life in Nature was visible when He became flesh and dwelt among us.

THE OLDEST OF THE DIVINE NAMES.

In connection with this title it is well to trace in the Bible one of the Divine Names, a name in use long before the Hebrews were a people, and once common to all the earth. This name, *the Highest*, or *the Most High*, expresses "that earliest thought of God which rises in the mind of man as he looks upward to the firmament of heaven and is led to believe in One on high, *above* him in the infinite distance, above him and all created things in the infinite perfection of his nature."* Its first recorded use is in the Scripture, telling that Melchisedek and Abraham together worshiped the Most High ; from which it is certain that west of the Jordan Abraham found the same religion he brought with him from east of the Euphrates. Balaam, like Abraham, came to Pales-

---

* See " Biblical Studies," by E. H. Plumptre, Professor of Divinity, King's College, (London, 1870, pp. 17–37,) which has here for the most part been followed in tracing this name in the Scriptures. He does not speak of any relation between the Title of Christ's Kingdom and this name, nor of its use in the more remote East. He thinks there may be a trace of it among the Phœnicians and their descendants, the Carthagenians.

tine from beyond the Euphrates, and he "knew the knowledge of the Most High."

In the Books of Moses the name is again heard in this verse, which contains the whole philosophy of ancient history, and whose unbroken thought, passing, in the Gospel, over from the typical nation to the Christian Church, contains the philosophy of all modern history as well, in its suggestion of the fact that the bounds of the nations, and if so, their language, laws, and development, are ordained of God with reference to his people, as the parts of the human body are framed, co-ordinated, and distributed with reference to the heart: "When *the Most High* divided to the nations their inheritance, when he separated the sons of Adam, he set the bounds of the people according to the number of the children of Israel. For the Lord's portion is his people; Jacob is the lot of his inheritance." Deut. xxxii, 8, 9. The world-wide significance of the name, the Most High, here comes out with great clearness, for the Founder of the Hebrew Commonwealth uses it when speaking of the Creator as God of all the children of Adam, while in the same breath he uses the name Jehovah when speaking of him as God of the children of Israel.

In the historical and prophetic books this name is not found again,* until the Israelites knew the empires rising beyond the Euphrates. From the Book of Daniel it seems to have been in common use in those Eastern regions: "There fell a voice from

---

* But this name occurs in seventeen of the Psalms, where, generally, it is used of "the wider sovereignty, the universal providence of God." See Psa. xlvii, 2; lxxxiii, 18.

heaven, saying, O King Nebuchadnezzar, thy dwelling shall be with the beasts of the field until thou know that *the Most High* ruleth in the kingdom of men. At the end of days, I lifted up mine eyes unto heaven, and mine understanding returned unto me, and I blessed *the Most High*, whose dominion is an everlasting dominion, and he doeth according to his will in the army of heaven, and among the inhabitants of the earth." Daniel was taught in the king's palace the learning and tongue of the Chaldeans, and with him this was the most common of the divine names : "The kingdom and dominion and the greatness of the kingdom under the whole heaven shall be given to the people of the saints of *the Most High*." Nebuchadnezzar, the Assyrian, and Cyrus, the Persian, in some of their proclamations, used a title where the thought is so much the same that it must be regarded as the same title, the God of Heaven. The Persian name for the Deity being Ormazd, this was no more a Persian than a Hebrew title ; and it would seem it must have been older than the divine names peculiar to either country ; a name coming down from the days before the Most High appointed their bounds to the Persian, to the Chaldean, or to the Hebrew ; and its use by Cyrus, in his proclamation, "The Lord God of Heaven hath given me all the kingdoms of the earth, and he hath charged me to build him a house in Jerusalem," * like its use by Moses, proves, that more than any other Name, it conveyed the idea of sovereignty over all the children of men.

---

* Ezra i, 2.

In the New Testament, John the Baptist is called by his father Zacharias, the Prophet, Christ Jesus is called by the angel Gabriel the Son, of the Highest. This name is used by the man possessed with devils, who had his dwelling in the tombs, "And when he saw Jesus afar off, ran and worshiped him, and cried with a loud voice, What have I to do with thee, Jesus, thou Son of the Most High God?" and by the girl at Philippi, in Macedonia, who had a spirit of divination, and followed Paul and those with him, crying, "These men are the servants of the Most High."*

In the ancient Scripture, most closely of all related to the title of the kingdom of Christ, it is said, the King of Babylon dreamed a dream wherewith his spirit was troubled, but it was gone from him ; and he called on his magicians and astrologers to tell him his dream and the interpretation thereof; and they said, There is none other that can show it before the king except the gods whose dwelling is not with the flesh.   Then the king's decree went forth, that they should be slain, and with them Daniel and his fellows. Daniel besought of the King time, and of his companions that they would pray to *the God of Heaven.* Unto Daniel the secret was revealed in a vision of the night ; and he blessed *the God of Heaven,* and said, There is *a God in Heaven* who maketh known unto the King what shall be in the latter days. Thou beheld a great image, its brightness excellent, and the form thereof terrible.   A stone was cut out

---

* See Luke i, 76, and 32, 35.   Mark v, 7.   Luke viii, 28.   Acts xvi, 17.   It is used also in the speech of St. Stephen.   Acts vii, 48.

without hands, which smote the image, and the iron, the brass, the silver, and the gold became like chaff, and the wind carried them away; and the stone that smote the image became a mountain and filled the whole earth. Thou, O King, art this head of gold. After thee shall arise another kingdom; a third, which shall bear rule over all the earth; the fourth kingdom shall be strong as iron; and the *God of Heaven* shall set up a kingdom which shall consume all these, and it shall stand forever. With this should be joined the vision of Daniel himself: Behold, one like the Son of man came with the clouds of heaven, and came to the Ancient of days. And there was given him a kingdom, that all people, and nations, and languages, should serve him: his dominion is an everlasting dominion, and his kingdom shall not be destroyed. (See Dan. ii; vii, 13, 14.)

In the title of the kingdom which he proclaimed the Lord Jesus Christ revived the most ancient and universal of all the Divine Names. He proclaimed the Kingdom of Him whose name on the lips of Melchisedek in the West, of Balaam from the Highlands of the Upper Euphrates, of the Chaldean King of Babylon, and of the Persians, was the God of Heaven; a name that, surviving from the age of the Great Flood, in the remote unchanging East, is still known in the mountains of Thibet, and is heard in the worship of the patriarch-priest-Emperor of China.*

---

* Pekin is the Rome of China. In it are many garden-sanctuaries, with altars in the midst of groves, as, to the Earth, the Sun, the Moon. The most venerated is known as the Temple of Heaven. This is a spacious park, in which are two altars,

Thus viewed in the light of history this Title points
to the Kingdom of all the earth ; viewed in the light

---

raised on triple marble terraces.   Near one of these is a circular building called the Palace of Heaven.   In it there are no
images.   There, in the spring, the Emperor prays for a harvest.
The other altar is a quarter of a mile distant.   There, once a
year, is sacrificial worship of the *God of Heaven*.   In a carriage
drawn by elephants, kept for that ceremony, the emperor comes
and spends the night in the Hall of Penitential Fasting.   Before
the dawn he mounts from terrace to terrace up to the altar ;
where a bullock is sacrificed in a furnace.   The name of the
altar means light-giving.   All the nobility of the court are on
the steps of the terraces.   The light is from the burning sacrifice.   This the emperor, alone, offers to Shang-Ti, Supreme
Lord of Heaven.   This name the missionaries have adopted to
render the word God.   There seems to be no idolatry in this
the most solemn service of the State religion of China.   This
religion is confined to the capital.   It is different from the three
prevailing religions of the empire, the Buddhist, the Confucian,
and the Tauist.   The emperor is the only priest of this State
religion.   It seems a relic of the age after the Great Flood ;
when, every-where, the patriarch-priest of the family or tribe
worshiped the God of Heaven.   The only change seems to
be that at Pekin, the patriarch-priest has become the priest-
Emperor.

In these, and other altars at Pekin, are traces of the old,
mystic science of numbers, spoken of in the Wise Men, p. 75 n.
The ascent to each of the three terraces has 9 steps.   The
pavement on the circular top has 9 circles of marble slabs.
The central circle has 9 slabs, the second 18, and so on, till the
number in the uttermost is 81, the square of nine.   This numer-
ical symbolism runs into the steps, balustrades, rails, and other
parts of the structure.   It is described in official accounts of
these altars.   Odd numbers, as 1, 3, 5, 7, 9, enter into the construction of the Altars to Heaven ; no doubt, as suggesting
something of indefiniteness, and so of infinity.   The numbers
are even in the Altar to the Earth at Pekin.   Its paving bricks
are multiples of 6 and 8.   The Altars to Heaven are circular ;
the Altar to the Earth is square.

of nature, it points to the Kingdom of Him who reveals himself in creation. Viewed in the light of the
Gospel, this world-wide title becomes wider than this
world and points to the dominion over all the worlds,
which the Father gave to the Son after his death on
the Cross, even that of which Christ spake when he
said, All power is given unto Me in heaven and in
earth.

This title, then, whose usual meaning is the Kingdom of Christ on earth, is of manifold meaning.
Through the contrast of the calmness of the heavens
with the turmoil of earth, it gives the idea of a
kingdom of peace; through that of the heavens as
His dwelling-place, of the Kingdom of God; and
when the mind turns from its character to think of
its extent, it hints that each star is a province of
that Kingdom; and its physical glory the complement of its spiritual glory. *This last thought is in
the corresponding phrase also; for universality belongs
as surely as holiness to the Kingdom of God.*

A DIFFICULTY AS TO ALL OF THE BIBLE.

It may be said, You read this Title in the light of
Astronomy; you set forth ideas of the nineteenth
century; the modern thought of the Universe, with
its numberless worlds far greater than the Earth, was
unknown to those Hebrews who heard this Kingdom
proclaimed; how, then, could its Title include them?
Are we not bound to take it as they did?

The answer to these questions *meets with a difficulty as to the whole Bible.* Much of Scripture is
plain beyond any thing else ever written. " Like as

a Father pitieth his children, so the Lord pitieth them that fear him ; for he knoweth our frame, he remembereth that we are dust," are words as plain as they are old. To them " the common pulse of man keeps time." Yet, sometimes, there is a deal of difficulty in fixing the relations of forms of ancient thought in Scripture to forms of modern thought ; as, sometimes, there also is in fixing the relations of its Oriental to Occidental forms of thought, and of translating to Europe the feeling as well as the words of Asia. Fully to do this, as to the former, would be the triumph of interpretation. It is something even to see, that the truths of Scripture, so far as given under the forms of thought, of a Time-Cycle whose course has run, must pass into corresponding forms of thought of a Time-Cycle of wider sweep and fill its utmost compass, while yet unchanged in its essence. If the Bible can thus pass from the Old Time World and fill the New, it is an indestructible thought of the Eternal Mind ; and it will pass unharmed through the future Time-Cycles of this Planet, even when it shall rise from its ashes.

Whether the Bible is to be in the future the acknowledged master of all Thought, much depends on this finding of itself by the Thought of the new Time Cycle in the revelation given in the old Time Cycle. But this is a difficult and great thing. To track the windings of a Thought through the ages ; to identify it, as, like a comet, it appears at different points, in different forms, at different times ; to see it as a star that is seen for an instant and then is hidden in mist and cloud, remaining as a memory and

not as a presence, till the tempest sweeps the face of
heaven and it shines again for the mariner ; to watch
and wait while God hides it in the hollow of his hand,
cherishing and fostering it till it breaks forth in sudden luxuriance of growth ; to see the tomb-buried
seed growing like the cedars on Lebanon ; to trace
in and from the Bible the course of all the rivers
that have silently and invisibly descended from above
the clouds ; to find all the fountains of every Nile ; all
this is not the work of one generation.   And yet any
new Thought may and should find itself in the old
form of Scripture words, and in so doing it will find
*that germ in which is both its principle of Life and
its Law of Growth.*

Here there can be shown only a little of the bearing of this, by answering the questions just asked.
It is said, " the Hebrews did not have the modern
idea of the Universe." What is that idea ? Can the
notions, theories, and facts of any one, or of all the
sciences, be adjusted into any satisfactory answer?
Who can tell what the universe is ?   Who has
stretched the line upon it ?   Who can tell what is in
it ?   Motion and change seem to be conditions of its
being, but who can tell how it comes, or whither it
goes ?   It is said, the astronomical idea is, that the
universe is the creation of the one God : if that be it,
those Hebrews to whom many think the all-wise
Creator of man could have taught little of things
heavenly, because they knew little of things earthly,
knew that much better than some men of science
know it now. How does Astronomy know that ?
As Astronomy it knows it not at all. Its comments

on the fact are new and grand ; but it gets the fact just as the Hebrews got it, however that may have been. It is further said, The astronomical idea of the extent of the universe is more sublime than that of the Hebrews. It may be so ; but it is time that a little tardy justice should be done to the thoughts that were of old.

In lieu of the modern idea of the breadth of the heavens, the Hebrews had an idea of their height quite equal to it in grandeur. It was that three-fold idea of the heavens, of which there is a trace in the words of St. Paul ; of the heavens where the winds blow, the clouds gather, the storms move on ; beyond this, of the heaven of the sun, moon, and stars ; and still beyond, of the heaven of heavens, from whose unutterable height God looked down to behold the things in the lower heavens and in the earth. The old thought could no more measure their height than the new thought can measure their extent. The old thought was lost in the one, as the new is lost in the other. Each passes the picturing power of the mind.

Modern Thought loves to project into the second heavens the spectrum of the first. When some of its nebulous clouds are resolved into the commingling blaze of distant worlds faintly gleaming along the void it feels disappointed, rather liking to get lost in star-mist and to flounder about among forming and dissolving nebulosities like a Parisian balloon escaping in fogs and clouds. The Hebrew picture of the second heavens as calm, untroubled, and silent, may be as near as any to the existing facts ; and yet thought or fancy may play as freely among the second heavens as among the cloud-castles of the first heavens ; may have as much star-mist as it will, and as many world-evolutions ; may repeat, as often as it likes, in the second heavens, the dissolving views of the first ; and all will be well if the soul but say, as Moses said of old, " Behold, the heaven and the heaven of heavens is the Lord's thy God ;" if round all it sweep the immeasurable thought of Solomon at the Great Temple's dedication, " heaven and the heaven of heavens cannot contain Thee."

To the Hebrews the stars were the revolving or fixed lights of the firmament, numberless like the sands of the sea, and declaring the glory of Him " who calleth them all by their names." * As to their distance and size their ideas fell far short of ours, but this quantitative difference is only of degree ; and, essentially, their ideas were so like ours that they might unfold into all that Astronomy has made known.

---

* Another Hebrew idea as to the stars comes out clearly in Job xxxviii, 7 : " When the morning stars sang together, and all the sons of God shouted for joy." Here, as is usual in Hebrew verse, the second clause repeats the thought in the first in such a way as to throw light upon it. The Hebrews thought of the stars as under the watch and ward of angels, and seem in their language almost to identify them ; somewhat in the same way that we sometimes identify the World and Man. In each case the glory and being of either is for the moment wholly thought of as being in the intelligence that presides over it. In this Hebrew thought I find an explanation of words which, till thus explained, may seem to wear an astrological sense : " They fought from heaven ; the stars in their courses fought against Sisera." Judges v, 20.

THE SPACE-EXTENT OF THE TITLE OF THE MESSIAH'S
KINGDOM TO THE SPIRITUAL IN ISRAEL.

But did the Hebrews think the stars were within
the Messiah's kingdom? As to this it is of little
consequence what Caiaphas thought, though he was
of high ecclesiastical rank; or what Gamaliel thought,
able lawyer that he was; or what the people thought,
though they read in the Law that "Christ abideth
forever." Spiritual things are spiritually discerned;
and in this, and all similar inquiries, the thoughts of
the most spiritual are to be sought for, and in their
most spiritual moments, for the search is into the
depths of thoughts which, though human, have in
them something that is divine. That must be for us
the Hebrew interpretation of the space-extent of the
Title of the Messiah's kingdom, which is the highest
possible to men like Joseph of Nazareth, Zacharias,
and Simeon; to women like Elizabeth and Anna.
Saints like these must at times have had such an
idea of the dominion of the Messiah as would include the realm of the universe, wide as that realm
might unfold. Not that they often rose to this
height. Heart answers to heart though ages lie between; and on this their hearts, like ours, could not
take an ever-abiding hold. Their more common
thought must have been of the Lamb of God who
taketh away the sins of the world; yet they read the
divine names of the promised Lord; of the angels
commanded to worship him; of his coming to the
Ancient of Days to receive the investiture of a universal dominion, and at moments they must have

thought of his kingdom as including all things. True it is, and it is evidence of the truth of the Gospels that they declare it openly, they knew not their own idea of the Messiah when vailed in a humiliation they did not understand ; still, their belief in his universal dominion existing before His coming, struggled through this disappointment, till at last they adored in Him the fullness of the Godhead bodily. We have to say this must have been so, rather than it was so ; but it is to be remembered how few are the words that utter their hearts ; and with their Bible open before us, there should be no doubt there were some of the pious in Israel, wise in the Scriptures, whom the Star at His Birth, and the Title of His Kingdom, assured that the rule of the Messiah would be over all there might be in the heavens.

The Interpretation that has here been given of the Title of the Kingdom of Christ disturbs none of the pre-eminent ideas it commonly conveys. It combines with them the idea that the stars are provinces of the Kingdom of Him who was crucified under Pontius Pilate. As to many questions it may awaken it is, of course, silent. And it is not to be inferred from it that Heaven is in the Sun, or in one of the Stars ; for it is written, *Christ hath ascended up far above all heavens.*

THE LAST OF THE THREE SCRIPTURES.

The third, and last, Scripture where the Lord is named with a Star, is almost the close of the Bible and last word of the Lord : " I am the Root and the Offspring of David, and the Bright and Morning Star."

Whenever Scripture cannot be understood by itself alone, other Scripture throws light upon it. In
the first and second Scriptures, where the Lord is
named with a star, one and the same star is spoken
of. In the last, the comparison, implied in the personification, seems to be a specific one. Some one
particular star seems to be the occasion of the figure.
Christ is the Bright and Morning Star. From their
very abruptness the words seem to allude to some
well-known star. One such Star there was, and only
one. Balaam's prophecy had made one Star well
known to the Hebrew Church; its fulfillment had
made it still more so to the Christian Church; and
the presumption is very strong that this Star, foretold and recorded, this familiar Star, gave the occasion for this image. This becomes a certainty when
it is called the Morning Star; for the epithet identifies it. It is the Star of Bethlehem. It is the
Morning Star of the Great Day that opened in the
Eternal Year, when the Word took unto Himself the
Human Form.

Astronomers marked this Star as it appeared amid
the constellations visible to man. Their knowledge
of it passed away. This may have been by some divine decree, lest the Star should be worshiped; but
the Scripture reveals truth of higher worth as to this
Star, and through which it is, perhaps, possible this
lost scientific knowledge may be regained.

Few the words so comprehensive as these, of all
that mortal ear hath heard: "I am the Root and the
Offspring of David, and the Bright and Morning Star."
Dr. South well says of the first clause of this verse:

"Though the Book of Revelations be confessedly a book of mysteries and a system of occult divinity, it can contain nothing more mysterious and stupendous than the mystery wrapped up in the words where we have Christ declaring Himself *the Root and the Off-spring of David.*" These words set forth our Lord's whole relation to man ; and *in comprehensiveness and grandeur the words " and the Bright and Morning Star" must be their counterpart.*

But why above all the stars, is the Star of Bethlehem the emblem of the Lord ? On this light is thrown from the words, " I am the Root of David." Here the thought is more comprehensive than the words ; the thought takes in the human family ; the words are limited to a section of its most living fiber, to a section only of that central line of life which is traced by St. Luke for four thousand years, from Adam to Christ. The thought comprehends the whole family of man, the words are limited to its pre-eminent house, the house of David. Seeing this, and seeing there must be something of correspondence in the two parallel clauses of the verse, " I am the Root and the Offspring of David, and the Bright and Morning Star," there is seen the relation to the universe of the Star with which our Lord identifies Himself.

The stars differ in glory. The planets circle round the sun. Some mysterious movement pervades the deep of worlds ; and these things may hint at some pre-eminent star, holding a central relation to the universe. But here let us think quietly ; the word central, though here convenient, means too much, is too definite, and must be used somewhat figuratively. For the shape of the universe is unknown; and the circling of the planets round the sun, with other facts like this, are partial facts, which may no more point to that form, than its blood-currents, or the play of its atoms, point to the human frame. Nor is it certain that the size of a world would determine its rank; for in the human body the rank of the organs does not correspond to their bulk. It were wiser, then, to avoid any too precise expression as to the rationale of the pre-eminence of this Star; saying generally, its relation to the universe would, if known, be more suggestive of the creative glory than that of any other of the orbs of heaven.

This must be true of the Star of Bethlehem, for it is the divinely-chosen emblem of Him *whose goings forth constitute that Time-world which, all summed up and expressed in the word Day, the Timeless One contrasts with his Eternal Being when he saith, Before the Day I am.* So far as a material emblem could do this, these unutterable facts were symbolized by the Star of Bethlehem, the Bright Star of all the worlds and Morning Star of the Day when the Word, without whom there was not any thing made, took up unto Himself the spirit and the body of man, and visibly made the Universe one in Himself who is its center and its source. Thus, the form of the utterance in the last clause of the verse, I am the Root and the Offspring of David and the Bright and Morning Star, corresponds to the form of the utterance of the thought in the first clause; and the truth in the one equals the truth in the other in comprehensiveness and sublimity.

THE CREATIVE AND REDEEMING WORK, IN ONE VIEW, THE SAME.

Each of the Scriptures consulted give some intimation of the truth that seems clearly to come out from all of them together, that the Kingdom of the Lord Jesus Christ is over the starry worlds; and this continuous, related interpretation is established, when that, which these four Scriptures intimate, other Scriptures plainly reveal. Those other Scriptures seem to set forth the work of the Lord redeeming as the completion of the work of the Lord creating. One of these is the prelude to the Gospel of St. John, which, with an almost legal carefulness and precision in the balancing and repeating of phrases, utters the most luminous, and yet the most profound, thoughts ever written down by mortal hand: " In the beginning was the Word, and the Word was with God. The same was in the beginning with God. All things were made by Him; and without him was not any thing made that was made. In Him was Life; and the Life was the Light of men. And the Light shineth in darkness; and *the darkness overtaketh it not.* There was a man sent from God, whose name was John. The same came for a witness, to bear witness of the Light, that all men through him might believe. He was not that Light, but was sent to bear witness of that Light. That was the True Light, which enlighteneth every man that cometh into the world. He was in the world, and *the World was made by Him*, and the World knew Him not. He came unto his own and his own received Him not. But as many as received Him, to them gave He power to become the sons of God, even to them that believe on his Name; which were born, not of blood, nor of the will of the flesh, nor of the will of man, but of God. And the Word was made flesh, and dwelt among us, (and we beheld his glory, the glory as of the only begotten of the Father,) full of grace and truth."

On first reading this might seem to recite the glory of the Lord creating, to enhance the glory of the Lord redeeming; but, as it is read, and re-read, and meditated upon, there comes the feeling that there is in it deeper meaning; that, in the mind of St. John, the idea of the Lord redeeming was so identified with that of the Lord creating, that what are usually thought to be two offices of the same Divine Being, must, *in some sense, be one.* This impression each one must gain for himself, if at all; yet one word may help toward this: The thought of the Word Creating, that opens this Scripture, may seem to be lost sight of, from the third to the tenth verse, yet it runs unbroken through it all. The apostle, as seen from his first words, had in mind the first chapter of Genesis. From it he took that figure of Light which, throughout these verses, sets forth the Word; and by this figure he meant to keep before the mind the creative office of the Word, the thought of which is the key-note of this prelude to his Gospel. It is heard in the first verse; and, that it may not be forgotten, suddenly it strikes in, loud and clear, in the tenth, "*the world was made by Him.*" It ever should be in our thoughts as from the Word in "the beginning," the apostle leads them on to the Word made flesh and dwelling among us :

"We have redemption through His blood, even the forgiveness of sins; who is the image of the invisible God, the first-born of every creature; for by Him were all things created, that are in heaven, and that are in earth, visible and invisible, whether they be thrones, or dominions, or principalities, or powers : all things were created by Him, and for Him." Here the Apostle Paul reproduces the impression made by the Apostle John. In this Scripture the office of the Word Incarnate is felt to be the same with His office in "the beginning," when by Him "all things were made." It so blends the thought of the Lord creating and of the Lord redeeming, that the distinction between them disappears; and it becomes certain, that *from some point of view* the one may be seen to be the completion of the other. (Col. i, 14.)

THE CROSS, THE FINISHING OF THE REVELATION OF GOD IN THE UNIVERSE.

As the angel who foretold the Birth of Christ to Joseph said, He saves his people from their sins. For man this is the greatest of all facts ; and also for the angels who never sinned, it is the greatest of all facts. For though the expiatory suffering of the Son of God avails for sinners as it need not, and does not, avail for the holy angels, yet the Cross is the finishing of the whole Revelation of the Divine. Well may the angels desire to look into it ; for, in this point of view, its intent and scope is not limited to the World of man. It is the center and height of all Revelation, to all created Intelligence that now is, or is to be, in all Space and Time.

In the purely mechanical study of the Creation, what seem to human thought great difficulties are seen to be overcome; but in Creation there are greater difficulties than these. Revelation is a chief end in Creation, but can the Infinite be revealed to the Finite? The inquiry is heard by the Reason with doubt, and weighed with despair. That which is to be received must be proportioned to the recipient. If so, must not a revelation of the Infinite pre-suppose, what for the want of a better word will be called, self-limitation; and must there not be involved in this what for the same reason will be called, self-renunciation; or something that seems to resemble (though whether it does so is quite beyond our knowing) that which takes place when a man, stooping to converse with a child, holds part of his being in abeyance, so that it is as if it were not?

Without being drawn away to consider how far any revelation of the Infinite to the Finite can fully answer to its name; nor whether the possibility of any revelation must not find its antecedent condition in that mystery, of which the word Trinity is the accepted symbol, our thoughts must here be limited to difficulties shadowed forth in such inquiries as these. In his self-revealing of the Infinite must not the Word of God accept the conditions of an outworking that is to be apprehensible by limited intelligence? Must he not come, so to speak, within the limitations of Space and Time? But what shall measure the recoil of the Omnipresent from Space, of the Eternal from Time? Who can understand how the Unlimited can abide the presence of the Limited? the Perfect of Imperfection? the Infinite One of the Finite World? How shall the All-wise suffer the presence of error? or, mystery or mysteries! how can the Holy Omnipresent God endure to be confronted with sin? In the dim, uncertain light of thoughts shadowed forth in such inquiries as these, something of self-renunciation is seen in all the Divine Self-revealing. It may have been this which the Son of God had in mind when he prayed to the Father that he might be glorified, not with his glory as the Creating Lord before he took to himself the vesture of mortality; not the glory he had in his goings forth when he made the heavens and the earth, but with the glory he had *before the world was;* his thought passing back through all the ages to when the Holy Three, the United One, in themselves were blessed, and there was God alone.

The revelation of the mystery of the Word in all Nature and in all Life is much lost sight of in the Church. And yet, only through the seeing of this mystery in all Nature and in all Life is the power to see all that is revealed in Christ Jesus. And, therefore, St. John in the prelude to his Gospel leads our thoughts on from the wider expression of this mystery in the universe to its highest form. Of this mystery of the Word in all Nature, Hebrew Scripture is full. The thunder is the voice of the Lord. The hoar-frost, so beautiful, and under the microscope so wonderful with its geometrical figures, is "by the Word of the Lord that runneth very swiftly." Of the mystery of the Word in life Hebrew Scripture is full. The tribes of animated Nature are created by the breath of the Lord; and, in later Scripture, it is written, "in Him we live and move and have our being." How this may be it is not given us to know; though after this secret science and philosophy are ever blindly groping. We cannot understand either the making or the upholding of a nature, and therefore cannot understand wherein the difference between them consists. How the Word of God can be in all Nature, and yet Nature be; how He is the upholding ground of Nature, while yet Nature hath a self-hood of her own, her own forces, properties, and laws, her own inevitable cycling from birth, through growth, to decay and change, we cannot tell. Attempts to find this out run clear through all the world's recorded thinking. This is the dream of what is called Philosophy; a dream more vain and wild than that of the Astrologers or the Alchemists. This the philosophy of India tries to find out; this the philosophy of Greece; this the Gnostics in the early Christian ages; this Scotus Erigena in the Middle Ages; this Spinoza, Hegel, and the evolutionists of the passing hour. But here human thought reaches to where it is said, "Thus far but no farther, and here shall thy proud waves be stayed." The Eve-born and curiously persistent soul must at last give over this problem; and then may hear the same voice saying, "Faith is the evidence of things not seen." What is imperfect in the human knowledge is made perfect by Faith. Through faith we understand that the worlds were framed by the Word of God, so that the things which are seen were not made of things that do appear.

The mystery of the Word in Christ none may fathom ; and yet it explains all things, while it is explained of none. The old thought of man as a microcosm, or little world, hath in it ascertained truth ; as well as the suggestion of much which may yet be proved to be true. For science has shown that the body of man is made of the same particles as this, and all the worlds. It is framed after patterns and antetypes in the lower animals, and in him their passions and instincts reappear. Man is akin to the brute and the clod, yet he is akin to the angels. He is as much above the insect that basks in the sunbeam for its hour as he is below Gabriel who stands in the presence of God ; and yet, the ends of the whole orb of created being touch in him. All Life below seems tending upward toward man ; all Life before seems preparing for, and prophesying of, man ; and so, as if one continuous and heightening purpose were in it all, in the Central Place of Man in the Circle of Life, and in his all-comprehensive sympathy, there seems to be a preparing for, and, it may be, a prophesying of, God-Incarnate.

But yet, though toward man, even from the beginning of the world, the lines of the Artificer's wisdom seem tending, Man fails to *re-present* in himself the perfection that seems of him foretold. In touching him, some of those lines so readily bend downward that men often tend to a degradation

lower than all the brutes. Man awakens the thought
that he should hold the Central Place in the Creation,
but he does not hold it ; and, therefore, the religious-
ly scientific mind sees that his state corresponds to
the record of his Creation and his Fall ; and it sees
man, as he was in the thought and purpose of his
Maker, only in Jesus. In him the Divine Wisdom
in the making of man is vindicated. He is man as
made in the beginning in the image of God ; that
man to whom full Dominion over Nature was given ;
and, it seems to me, that some of the marvels Jesus
wrought *may* have been things natural to such a
man. He was that man ; and he was more. He is
Son of man and Son of God ; and so is the Central
Form, not only in the Human World, but in that
Great Circle of Being whose circumference no created
hand may touch. He is the Center of this Circle
and its Circumference ; for the Incarnation of the
Word of God in the Man Christ Jesus is the " finishing " of a mystery that begins with Time and pervades Space. The Universe is a Temple-shrine. In
that Temple visibly and suddenly the God appears.*
And He is the same who built and upholds that
Temple-shrine, and through whom and in whom it
hath unity, meaning, and end. In the thought of
the World-Artificer, His coming in human form was

---

* As promised to the saints of old : " The Lord, whom ye seek
shall suddenly come to his temple." Mal. iii, 1. In Jerusalem
no doubt. But Christ was "greater than the temple," Matt.
xii, 6, "which was a figure for the time then present," Heb.
ix, 9, of " a greater and more perfect tabernacle not made with
hands." Heb. ix, 11.

before the worlds were made, and *may* have been foreshadowed when the Divine Breath was breathed into the body of man, and he became a living soul.

THE LORD'S DOMINION CONSEQUENT UPON HIS DEATH; THEREFORE, THE EFFICACY OF HIS DEATH MUST IN SOME WAY BE UNIVERSAL.

The Word made all things, He upholds all things; in the form of man He took all things unto Himself; and, therefore, it would seem, that the Reason must acknowledge the Man Christ Jesus, in whom was all the fullness of the Godhead bodily, as the Head of the Universe; yet not one nor all of these mysteries (if indeed they be not one and the same mystery in a threefold form) was the immediate efficient cause of the Dominion of the Lord Jesus Christ over all things created. Phil. ii, 8–11, " HE became obedient unto death, even the death on the Cross. *Wherefore* God also hath highly exalted Him, and given Him a name which is above every name: that at the name of Jesus every knee should bow, of things in heaven, and things in earth, and things under the earth; and that every tongue should confess that Jesus Christ is Lord, to the glory of God the Father." This Scripture so clearly reveals that the Dominion of the Man Christ Jesus is over all created beings, that there is no need to cite other Scriptures revealing the same fact. It as clearly makes known that His Dominion is consequent upon His Death; and the almost irresistible inference is, that in some way the efficacy of His Death extends beyond this inferior orb and fallen race. He reigns every-where because He dies; and

it would seem that the space-extent of His Dominion must be the measure of the influence of His
Death ; that the compass of each must be the same ;
that, as the Dominion of the Lord is universal, so, in
some way, must be the efficacy of His Death.   And,
in some way, it is ; for the universality revealed in
express and clear terms as to the one, in terms
equally express and clear is revealed of the other.
In harmony with the impression given by other
Scriptures, that the work of the Lord Creating and
of the Lord Redeeming is, in some true sense, one
and the same, and with the Scriptures declaring that
in Him all things consist, it is written, " It pleased
the Father that in Him should all fullness dwell ;"
which seems to mean, that fullness or completeness
by which all the manifestation of Himself through
his Word, in Time and Space, becomes acceptable
unto Him who inhabiteth Eternity.   This appears
from the next words, which point to what Christ did
for man, and then reach far beyond the human world.
" It pleased the Father . . . having made peace
through the blood of His Cross, to reconcile all
things unto Himself by Him, whether they be things
in earth, or things in heaven." Col. i, 19, 20.

ALL THE DIVINE, PARTICIPANT IN THE SUFFERING ON THE CROSS.

Of his Life Christ said, No man taketh it from me.
His suffering, then, on the Cross was voluntary.
" Being in the form of God, He thought it not robbery
to be equal with God, but made Himself of no reputation ; and being found in fashion as a man, He

humbled Himself, and became obedient unto Death."
His Death, then, reached beyond his human nature.
The denial of this is the denial of this Scripture ; and
yet scholastic theology holds, that only the human
nature of Christ participated in his death. The reason of this may be in the impression made on the
soul through the senses by the phenomena of Death.
What dying is, the living can hardly know. It looks
like a ceasing to be. The eye sees not the departing
ghost. The most thrilling cry hears no answer from
the dead ; and there are moments when the soul can
hardly feel they live any more. It may be, that because this dark feeling darkened thought, scholastic
theology denied this Scripture ; for when the mind,
freeing itself from the impression made by the phenomena of dying, sees in it but a change in the mode
of existence, then, against the fact that God might,
if so He willed, die as a man, nothing can be said
that could not also be said against the possibility
that He could live as a man. The mystery of the
Word living as man lives is incomprehensible ; and
so is the mystery of the Word dying as man dies ;
but the one no more so than the other ; and the possibility of the one involves the possibility of the other.
When the Word became flesh, there was involved in
this assumption of the human nature the antecedent
condition of the possibility of his dying, and the purpose also ; for He became, of his own will, like unto
fallen man, in all points, save sin ; and it is appointed
unto fallen man once to die.

His Death saves his people from their sins. On
this their thoughts have ever been, and ever will be

fixed; but this thought, not taking its place, or in any way changing or disturbing it, may be associated with it: in His giving up of His Life that self-renunciation, which runs through the whole manifestation of God in the universe, reached its foreseen and absolute fullness; the sin of man becoming the occasion, through the Death of Christ, of the perfection of the whole Divine revelation in Space and Time. Everywhere else in the revelation of the Divine, the Word who was with God and who was God, gives and gives up; and while thus in the whole manifestation of the Divine, there is self-renunciation consequent upon the omnipresence of the Word in the universe, whether as originating or as upholding it, this reached its fullness in the Word who became flesh, even in Christ and Him crucified, who is Alpha and Omega, the beginning and the end of Creation and Revelation, these being, *in this point of view*, one and the same.

And yet it is most true, that in this view of the Cross far more is lost than gained, if in the least it hinders the perception of the truth, that in the Passion of the Son of God there is something beyond self-renunciation—in the same line it may be, yet so infinitely beyond it, that nothing before it gives assurance even of its possibility. Self-renunciation may be so generous and free as to be painless; heroic emotion can make it sweet to die; but in the dying of the Son of God there was something beyond the pain of death. To the saint dying is giving up this unreal, unsatisfying world, and waking in a real blessed state. It is dying to Self, it is waking in God. Many have died in Christ's name, saying, " O Death, where

is thy sting? O Grave, where is thy victory?"
What then was that agony of Christ in Gethsemane
when he sweat, as it were, great drops of blood?
What was that agony so great that He would have
died had not the angel strengthened Him?* The
mockery of his trial, the scourge, the nails, touch not
the soul so deeply as this solitary agony. Into that
hour none may look. It is enough to know that "the
chastisement of our peace was on Him," who was truly
God and truly man.

The names Father and Son shadow forth to human
thought some distinction in the Godhead, and reveal
in those thus distinguished, unity of essence. Scholastic theology, fastening upon the difference, has held
that the Father was impassive to the suffering of His
Son; but over against this may be set words warm
from the hearts of the Fathers, of divines of every
age, of all fervent preachers of the Cross, and the
chants and hymns of the Church Holy and Universal.

It dishonors the Father to think he could have
been untouched by the unmerited suffering of Jesus,
even though he had not been his only begotten Son—
whatever those words may mean. If it be the scholastic idea that the Deity is above emotion, this makes
Him below the gods of the heathen. He is perfect,
and therefore unchangeable; but emotion implies no

---

* The Passion of our Lord is sacred and unsearchable; yet,
from his repeating the first line of the Twenty-second Psalm
just as he died, it may be known that with all, and more than
all, that man can know of agony in death, there was hope, and
trust, and assurance of union with God.

change in essence; and, if He is unfeeling, He is neither perfect nor blessed. He is angry with sinners; but is anger a finer emotion than sympathy? does not the one as much imply a change of essence as the other? and is not the one emotion as consistent as the other with blessedness and perfection?

Beginning with the foreshadowing of the Divine expiation of sin, when Isaac gave himself up to death at his father's call, when any one would choose the sharp, short anguish of the young man before the slow life and heart consuming sorrow of the old man —beginning from this ancient parable, the truth of what has been said might be shown from many Scriptures, such as this: "God so loved the world that he sent his only begotten Son into the world, not to condemn the world, but that the world through Him might be saved." Of the Third Person of the Holy Trinity, the one God blessed forever, the same is revealed in these words: "Christ through the Eternal Spirit offered Himself without spot unto God." Heb. ix, 14.

The strange notion which, blindly seeking to enhance the glory of God, in denying Him feeling denies His very being, does not see that where there cannot be emotion in view of what is evil, there cannot be emotion in view of what is good. It confounds things not the same; not seeing that the feeling it calls sorrow outweighs joy. This strange error has often gone so far as to make the Father and the Son antagonists at the Cross. The words Son and Father, revealing unity of essence and unity of love, rebuke this ; words borrowed from the forms of human nature, yet showing the Father and the Son were moved by a common emotion to a common purpose. A minister, troubled at the difficulty of understanding God's giving up His Son for man, conferred with an aged slave about it, but she could not see his difficulty at all, saying, "it was just like God ;" and saying this, she said all that can be said or thought. Behold, then, perfectly manifest the unselfishness of God ! Behold this in the unsearchable sufferings of Gethsemane and of Calvary ! Here opens in cloudless glory the being of God in contrast with the nature of man. Man would have all for himself, God gives up all for others. Self-moved, He makes satisfaction to His own sense of justice, and relieves misery by expiating guilt. Herein is love; not that we loved God, but that God loved us, and sent His only begotten Son to be the propitiation for our sins, and not for ours only, but also for the sins of the whole world. It has well been said : "We have not the least reason to suppose any similar transaction has occurred on the theater of the universe, or will ever occur again in the annals of eternity. It stands amid the lapse of ages and the waste of worlds, a single and solitary monument."

These thoughts end in this : in the Cross of Christ the revelation of the Infinite to finite beings is "finished ;" and in view of this finishing of the whole revelation in the universe, the whole universe was permitted to be. *Short of this*, that revelation would have been imperfect ; and *it being imperfect, creation would not have been.* Because of the Cross, then, the

stars in Orion burn, and the soul of man lives.   The
imperfection of the parts of the manifestation of the
Divine are so made perfect on the Cross in the per-
fecting of the whole to which they belong, that as
parts of that perfected whole, they are acceptable unto
Him who is perfect.   " It pleased the Father that in
Christ Jesus should all fullness dwell."   In Him "all
things consist," that is, stand up together, the Word
in Christ Jesus being Mediator between the Infinite
God and the Finite World, through the perfection of
the revelation made complete in His self-renunciation
and sacrifice, when He who had in Himself all power
and wisdom, unselfishly giving up all things in giving
up Himself to die, not for His friends but for His
enemies, is " the brightness of the Father's glory and
the express image of His Person."

The Cross of Christ * is the center of the manifestation of the Godhead, holding it all in one ; and there
dwells in it that spiritual attraction of which Christ
spake when, signifying what death he should die,
He said, " If I be lifted up I will draw all unto me."
Man, dead in trespasses and sins, looks on His Cross
and lives.   By the expiation on the Cross there is
remission of sins.   But if we would dare so to do,
in vain we try to look through the mystery of Godli-
ness, the center, and depth, and height of which is
the Cross.   At the Cross of Christ knowledge finds
her life in losing it, in rising from knowledge into
adoration.

The Cross of Christ may well be thought of as a
timeless fact, rather than as in the four thousandth

---

* These words being taken as equivalent to His Passion.

year of History. Chronologically, its place is there; but logically, it is before Time was. He was the Lamb slain from the foundation of the world; and for Him all things were made. The Cross is not consequent upon man. It is the cause, as it is the center and the sum, of the whole revelation of the Infinite, in all worlds, angels, or men. The Cross of Christ is the reason for all that is not eternal, for all that exists in birth and change. It is corner-stone and key-stone of the universe.

Since the Creating Word and the Word made flesh are one and the same, *it is in accord with the finest conception of the fitness of things* that the Word Redeeming came attended by the highest symbol of His glory as the Word Creating; that at the Birth of Jesus Christ, the outshining of His Star in the firmament of the human world marked for man the fact, that the seemingly two offices of this Divine Person are, in one point of view, essentially one and the same.

Well might this have been a long predicted Star. When the Conquest of Canaan began, one of those true beginnings of History, in which there ever seems blending something prophetic; when every thing was of a long-continuing, world-wide consequence, and of a typical character, foreshadowing in the march of an earthly kingdom, a kingdom not of this world; when, on the dark mountains that look down so frowningly on the Holy Land, against Israel, powers of earth combined with powers of Hell, well might the Spirit reveal to the apostate Prophet the Sign of the Dominion of Christ the Lord. Since it was the Sign of Universal Dominion, well might this

Prophecy be wrung from the lips of one of His enemies! Well it might be uttered by one not of the
house of Israel! Well might it be an extra-Judean
prophecy, and have an extra-Judean attestation! In
the Bible such correspondencies may every-where be
seen, filling the soul with wonder, yet known only to
the fixed eye and the believing heart.

> Within that awful volume lies
> The mystery of mysteries!
> Happiest they of human race,
> To whom our God has granted grace
> To read, to fear, to hope, to pray,
> To lift the latch and force the way;
> And better had they ne'er been born
> Who read to doubt, or read to scorn.

The Incarnation, through its inseparable connection with the Death of Christ, and thus with His
Universal Dominion, might well be attended with
some foretoken, that, even on the bosom of the
Blessed Mother, the Word made flesh was the appointed heir of all things. The Star of Bethlehem
does more than prophesy of this. It translates the
fact, that the Kingdom of the Lord Jesus Christ is
over the starry worlds, from the realm of faith to the
realm of sight.

CHAPTER VII.

THE ASTRONOMICAL DOUBT AS TO CHRISTIANITY.

MODERN THOUGHT is a phrase sometimes used as an imposing name for that Doubt as to Christianity which rises out of the seeming, or real collision of scientific inquiries, in their many forms, with the science of Theology. In this the science of Theology is mistaken for the system of Christianity. Between the two there is this difference—the one has the wisdom in perfection that belongs to God, the other something of the imperfection and error ever present in man's thinking. When this proper distinction is made, it should be apparent that truth may collide with error and error with truth, as between Science and Theology, from either side, and the system of Christianity not be touched. Yet this collision has given rise to serious questionings, to the partial surrender, or the full denial, of the word of God.

FREE THOUGHT is another well-sounding phrase, sometimes used much in the same way. While this use of the term Modern Thought hints at more than is true, this use of the term Free Thought insinuates that Christianity is not compatible with Freedom. Dogma and usage give occasion for this accusation, and from them I appeal to the Bible. That Great

Charter creates Rights by defining Duties ; and there
Free Thought will be found to be a duty that cannot
be foregone without sin ; for God hath said, " Come. let
us reason together." It is written, " The Truth shall
make you free ; " but how can the soul be free to act,
or free to feel, if it be not free to think ? Intelligence
and freedom are not mere antecedents of Faith; they
are of its essence. In Faith, the soul is clear-seeing
and free. In Faith, with the purest intelligence there
is the most perfect Liberty. The opposite to Liberty
is Lawlessness. There is no freedom in the thinking
of a madman. Lawless thought is not free Thought.
It is power, going forth in conformity with its own
laws and with the nature or laws of that in which
and through which it is put forth, that awakens the
idea or the consciousness of Freedom. Through
union with the Divine, and only through this union,
the Human Spirit so comes into harmony within
itself, that it moves in free obedience to all the laws
of its complex unity of being. To Thought-power
the Spirit gave laws ; and in words having the compass, depth, and manifold meaning of all divine words,
it is written, " Where the Spirit of the Lord is there
is Liberty." Christianity is not responsible for any co-
ercing or enslaving of free thought, for the Word of
God ever addresses the free intelligence. The intellectual rights, alike of those who deny liberty of conscience, and of those who so wrest Science against
Christianity as to make it the vehicle of notions
despised by common sense, abhorred by morality,
and that consist not with civilization, are not to be
denied because of their unrighteousness. Those false

scientific teachings make it none the less a Christian duty to recognize all the truth the Lord has commissioned each and every science to make known. Only thus is the conciliation of Modern Thought to Christianity desirable. For any Science to surrender any truth at the bidding of any ecclesiastical authority is as antichristian, as it is for any ecclesiastical authority to demand it in Christ's name.

Of Modern Thought in this restricted sense, the origin is more directly traceable to Astronomy than to any other of the sciences. It gave the scientific impulse to Doubt : and if the questions raised as to the Bible, by this, the first in order, and perhaps in rank, of those sciences which, since the sixteenth century, seem to be the complement of the new spiritual firmament then dawning on the thought of man, can be answered, it will be felt that what is thus done for one science may be done for all. And in this altered state of feeling many difficulties as to the Bible will almost vanish of themselves.

The measurement of the good or of the evil influence upon Modern Thought, in the widest sense of the phrase, of the discoveries as to the stars, which began in the sixteenth century, would be more difficult than was the measuring or weighing of the planets. Yet, so surely as the good has been great, so surely has the evil been great. The accuracy of astronomy is brought home by the almanac ; it is proved to the common eye by the coming on of an eclipse ; all it says is of common interest ; however astounding, is readily taken on trust ; and somewhat of disastrous effect in its disclosures is widely spread abroad. For ever since the astronomical discoveries of the sixteenth and seventeenth centuries, there has been a growing wonder at what has been thought to be, the silence of Scripture as to the creative glory in the astronomical heavens. There has been a consequent lessening of reverence for the Bible: and some have come to feel, that the place once given by the wisdom and piety of less scientific ages to the Book of God, ought rather to be given to the Book of Nature. Through a confluence of causes this feeling seems to be growing rather than lessening; yet those who are under this delusion are ignorant of

WHAT THE BIBLE IS.

The Written Word is the Book of the Spiritual. The Living Word framed the spiritual and the material into one universe. His Written Word reveals the beginning and the end of material things, and it sends thrills of light through all the natural world: but, in the main, it is a revelation of those spiritual things on which the things material depend; of the unseen behind that which is seen. Through all in space and time, it makes known the infinite and the eternal. It is the spiritual history of man down to the Dispersion of the Nations; and then of one family, tribe, and people. As to them, it draws back the vail of things hidden from human eyes. Inspiration could take to itself the guise of their annals and their literature, because it utters truth, not in the articles of a creed, but in a series of events. It almost seems at times to lose its way amid the multitude of its facts, but it never does. Its chronological, ethnological, genealogical tables, its statistical, legal, biographical records, its pictures of the face of nature, of the thoughts, feelings, and manners of men, are consequent upon that historical form, only in which the historical presence of the Living Word in the human world could be revealed ; and viewing them as a whole, all these things can be seen to be subordinate and subservient to its controlling purpose. Man has lost the sense which discerned the spiritual. Holy Scripture was given by the Holy Spirit, and through it the Holy Spirit gives and preserves to the congregation of those who deal justly, love mercy, and walk humbly with God, that knowledge of the spiritual which, of himself, Man cannot know, or which his eye, clouded by sin, but darkly beholds. The Scriptures utter the eternal Being of Him in whom is the secret of the universe, even of the Word of God ; his creative glory; his presence in all He hath made ; his life on earth in the form of the man Christ Jesus ; who now ruleth over all created things ; and who, in the world of Thought, is the Truth ; and in the worlds of Nature and of Soul, is the Life.

As to the form of such a revelation man can decide little beforehand. What the Bible ought to be is hardly a thing of anticipation, and can be determined only by ascertaining what it is. To ask why this Book, so mysteriously wise, did not teach astronomy, is really to ask much more. For whatever reason be given why it should have taught astronomy holds good for chemistry, botany, machinery, for the compass, the art of printing, the circulation of the blood, the secret of vaccination, the galvanic battery, the

steam-engine, the telegraph. If the Bible should
have done what astronomy has done, then it should
have done what Columbus did, or what Fulton, or
Morse have done. If it should have taught astronomy, then, geography; and, like the Zendavesta, it
should have had treatises on agriculture, on work-
manship of various kinds, on trees, on fishes, on
beasts, on midwifery, and medicine.

But those made infidels by the telescope do not
think that the Bible should have been a school-house,
though their reasoning comes to this, but only that
it should have given some hint of the vastness of the
Divine Dominions. By this restriction, their argument against the Bible seems to gain immensely in
power, and yet is plausible only because it is unjust.
For the earnest declarations of Scripture, that none
by searching can find out the Almighty to perfection,
pass over by open consequence from things spiritual
to things material; and astronomy has only verified
this thought of Scripture in one of many ways. Astronomy gives outwardness to this thought in one
direction far beyond what it ever had before; but
the thought of a vastness that mind cannot compass
in the Divine Dominions, which seems to it a discovery of its own, is anticipated in the Scriptures, in
their own way, through spiritual facts. Astronomy
hints that star-worlds may be the homes of countless
orders of beings. It has not proved this; and there
is no reason to think it ever will. The Scripture does
more than this. That there are intelligent beings
other than those of this planet, which is only an astronomical probability, the Bible makes known as a

fact. The heavens, seen by the naked eye or swept by the telescope, are the lower, material counterpart of higher, spiritual heavens, not made with hands, in describing whose orders of beings the Scriptures exhaust the wealth of language—their thrones, dominions, principalities, and powers, angels and archangels, rising toward the King Invisible, who dwells in unapproachable light, whom none may see and live. It may be said; this is somewhat evasive, for though indeed sublime, this supercelestial world is not the same world that astronomy makes known—but it fairly meets the thought, that the Bible falls short of astronomy in the sublimity of its revelation of the Creator's glory.

The Bible sows broadcast the seeds of truths of all kinds; and the soul oftentimes seems to have as little perception of their origin, as trees and flowers, growing up far away from and knowing nothing of it, have of the plant that grew their seed; and even less than they have of the warmth and light that quickens and nourishes their germ. When Mitchell said, "The Bible utters all the soul of the devout astronomer;" he expressed his own true feeling; and the like is true of so many of the feelings of men, that it is some evidence that the Bible was divinely meant for the Human Family.*

In the same line with what Mitchell said there is a further truth, which those, who think less of the

---

* Of this one other brief illustration may here be given: As the Bible utters all the soul of devout watchers of the stars, so of those who go down to the sea in ships; and yet, the Hebrews were no astronomers, and no sailors.

Bible because of astronomy, or of the other sciences, would do well to consider. It is a truth which opens a glimpse of the power of the Word given in the old Thought-World, to fill out the whole compass of the New. The foundation of the science of astronomy and of all the other physical sciences, the main root from which all their growth is fed, is that belief in the order and unity in nature which comes from a knowledge of the fact, that the one God made the heavens and the earth. Losing this knowledge, the science of the Old World grew decrepit and old; and regaining this, the science of the Modern World has gone on its way shouting like a giant awakened out of sleep, and refreshed with wine. The Bible is full of this thought of a divine order and law in the universe; and with this thought it has filled all thought. Many suppose this to be a discovery of science. They connect it with the names of Kepler and Newton. But its light shines around science from a sphere higher than that of science. It has not been verified by science. Its scientific verification is impossible. For though law and order rule so far as science can see, that which it does see may be little to what it cannot see. It has no warrant for carrying the fact of law and order beyond where it can go itself; has no knowledge that all beyond where it can go is not the reign of " Chaos and old Night;" save in the word, that came of old, saying, " Forever, O Lord, thy law is settled in heaven"—not the heaven of the telescope, but that of which the telescope sees but an inconsiderable fraction.

Through their belief in the one Maker of the

heavens, the Hebrews reached the thought of Law as pervading all celestial space. They knew of the Law, and of its Reason. With them it was not a generalization of facts, not a meaningless abstraction, a name and nothing more, as so often it is with us. With them it was a force obedient unto God. The Hebrew who said, Forever, O Lord, thy word (that is, thy law) is settled in heaven; thou hast established the earth and it abideth; they (that is, the heavens and the earth) continue to this day according to thine ordinances, for all are thy servants, believed this as devoutly (and looking to the quality and not to mere quantity of his intelligence, it must be said, believed this as wisely) as Newton or Kepler did: and had not they, in common with the greatest scientific thinkers, had that belief in the unity of all that is made, which comes from belief in the Divine Unity, Newton and Kepler would never have made known what they did. More than this: all the science that now reads such marvelous new things in the volume of Nature dates from the time when the Bible began to be read by the people in their own tongue. It dwells only in Christendom. It is one of the consequences of the soul's reinvigoration, and of the quickening and guiding of its aspirations to regain its lost dominion over nature by the Holy Ghost. And of His light-giving and life-giving, the Scriptures are among the chief media.

As it has been shown that the belief in order, as commensurate with the universe, which hath sure foundations, comes, and can only come, from revelations of the Most High, it may seem less hopeless to try to point out in the Bible that idea of the almost infinite number of the stars, often thought to be wholly of modern date. The first of Genesis may give a different impression : for, after saying, God made the great lights, it says, "the stars also," as if they were little thought of ; but that chapter describes the making of the World of man, and this naming of the stars is all that should be looked for in such a description.

But more is said as to the stars in Genesis. A father and son consented to crucify their affections : the father an old man's love for his only child, the son a man's love for life, the son doing the father's will in giving himself up for a sacrifice. This they did in the same place where the FATHER AND SON, in like manner, united in the sacrifice that taketh away the sin of the world. A sacrifice which was then foreshadowed, and its spirit equaled, so far as the Human may approach the Divine, by that Father and that Son, through the Spirit of Christ that was in them. Then to that father it was said, "By Myself have I sworn, saith the Lord, for because thou hast done this thing, and hast not withheld thy son, thine only son, in blessing I will bless thee, and in multiplying I will multiply thy seed as the stars of heaven and as the sand which is upon the sea-shore ; and in thy seed shall all the nations of the earth be blessed ; because thou hast obeyed my voice."

If my own experience be that of others, then, not from what the telescope has seen, or the astronomer told, and not from the face of the evening sky, but from these words come our earliest, our most abiding thought of the great multitude of the stars. It is not difficult to count the stars in some small square in the evening sky, and thence to pass to some rough estimate of the whole number. This Scripture goes beyond that. It was just after the old man seemed to have lost his only son, and so was in the mood to hear what the Lord had to say to him of that child's children's children, that he was told, "Multiplying I will multiply thy seed as the stars of the heaven;" these words were uttered in reiteration and confirmation of a promise made many years before, that he should be "the father of many nations;" and in that moment of high-wrought feeling, who can doubt, this comparison gave to Abraham the idea of a multitude whom no man could number? Yet, grouped around or sheltered within the Emir's tents, the tribe of Abraham, his household, or as the Arabs would say, his children, on that very day, equaled in number all the stars that can be seen in the evening sky.* The comparison might then have belittled his hope, had it not been for the parallel comparison, which coming from Him who alone knew the number of the stars, made Abraham feel and know that it equaled that of the sands of the sea-shore. This promise, then, accredited to him, and strengthened that sense of multitude in the stars which the evening sky tends

---

* There are between two and three thousand stars visible to the naked eye. There were three hundred and eighteen men-at-arms in the tents of Sheik Abraham; and on any computation of the others, old and young, women and children, the number of his tribe must then have nearly equaled the number of the stars visible in our hemisphere.

to awaken, by seeming to hide in its depths more than it reveals. Through all the Scriptures runs the chord which begins to vibrate here. " The Lord telleth the number of the stars. He calleth them all by their names. Great is the Lord, his understanding is infinite."

Astronomy, at first, may heighten the glory of this promise ; yet here, as every-where, we at last have to feel, that it baffles all human effort to surpass the wisdom of Scripture. Search as far and wide, find out as much of truth as we may, when we turn to look back to the Scripture it ever seems to look out serenely upon us, with a supreme intelligence that knows all our knowing. As if it were ordained that no thought of man should glory in the presence of Scripture, when Astronomy kindles up the light in the divine promise to Abraham, it so beams forth that in its light that of the science grows pale. For it was the Creator who said, the spiritual children of faithful Abraham would equal in number the stars of heaven. His thought embraced all the worlds, and the astronomer, who has opened to us something more of its breadth, can no more compass it with the telescope than with the naked eye.

Abraham had a vision in his tent before this. (Gen. xv.) Led forth, he is told to look up and see the stars. Afterward the sun went down. Was he not, then, told to look up to the sky in the day-time ? If so, may he not have seen more than the telescope can bring within our vision ? So far as a mortal might, may he not have looked through the starry heavens ? Let each judge for himself. But this is certain : — away back, in that early time, there was revealed that number of the spiritual children of Abraham before which the difficulty in the seemingly slow and as yet partial prevalence of Christianity vanishes. For when Astronomy talks of the stars as so many,that in trying to grasp or to express that number thought breaks down and language fails, *that* is the divine number of the spiritual children of Abraham, and, glory to God! Christ hath not died in vain.

There is reserve in the Bible as to other mansions in the Father's house. But this is like its reserve as to so many of the nations of the earth. The one may seem to differ from the other in this : though it is silent as to many of the nations of the earth, the Bible reveals that God made all men and redeemed all ; but there is no difference here. There was no direct occasion for open mention of other worlds in the Scriptures. It might have perplexed those to whom the word came of old. It might have given aid to idolatry, whose prevailing form was the worship of the starry host, and against which of old the Spirit was contending. The Scripture makes known the higher knowledge of the supercelestial dominions ; there may be unknown reasons for its reserve (for such it really is, rather than silence) as to the other material worlds : and yet it abandons them to the Astronomer only as it abandons to the Geographer the nations of whom it makes no direct mention ; for it reveals that the heavens were made by the Word of God, who dwelt among us, and that the Lord Jesus Christ is Ruler over all that was made. Even were what is said of the stars in the first of Genesis all that is said in the Bible as to the number of the stars, the case would stand thus : Suppose a boy were taught by his father that God made all people, the only people known to the boy being those of his own family, of his own village, and of some small neighboring towns, suppose this boy, grown to a man, and become familiar with capitals, should despise his father's words, because he found New York had a million, and London three millions of people would he not feel, and reason, as do those who think what the Scriptures say of the host of heaven is proved to be inadequate and childish by Modern Science?

WITH the astronomical argument against the Scriptures drawn from the number of the stars, there blends the Thought of the stars as Worlds. In a sense hereafter defined, no doubt they are so : and if it be true, that even one star only, is a world millions of times larger than this world, the silence of Scripture as to this fact might well be perplexing, though other stars were but spangles of light. It is no doubt true, not of one star only, but of stars so many, that "if the world were crumbled to the finest dust and scattered through the universe there would not be an atom of the dust for each star :" * and when this thought meets the feeling (whose justice is here admitted) that the Scriptures give the impression that this world is, *in some sense,* the chief world in the universe, is it a matter of wonder, that some begin to

---

* Nathaniel Hawthorne.

believe that the Bible is an outgrown book which belongs to a Past that is ever receding ? With these
thoughts of the number and magnitude of the star-
worlds, other thoughts, related to or awakened by
these, combine, till they constitute what may be called

The Astronomic Doubt as to Christianity.

This Doubt presents one of the most difficult
problems ever yet offered to the Human Intellect.
It was never more forcibly stated than in these
words: "Though it is not a direct article of the
Christian religion, that the world we inhabit is the
whole of the habitable universe, yet it is so worked
up therewith, that to believe God hath created a
plurality of worlds, at least as numerous as what we
call the stars, renders the Christian system of faith
at once little and ridiculous. The two beliefs cannot
be held together, and he who thinks he believes them
both has thought but little of either. It is a solitary
conceit that the Almighty, who had millions of worlds
equally dependent upon his protection, should come
to die in this world."

This is a clear presentment of a Doubt that widely
prevails in both the scholastic and " the silent yet ever-
inquiring common mind." The spirit of a statement
is as worthy of thought as its logic ; and the sarcastic
assurance of this, its exulting bitterness, reflects the
hope, strong in many to arrogance, that *the system of
the Universe is crushing out the system of Christianity.*
This Doubt, arising in varied forms out of the contrast between the bounded littleness of the world of
man and the immeasurable heavens, and insisting

upon the insignificance of the Christian System as seen from one point of view, and its disproportionate greatness as seen from another, *has more to do with modern unbelief than all the other intellectual elements in it.* They who feel nothing of its power, if any such there be, will hardly understand how it wrings from Christian hearts the imploring, " Lord, increase our faith." It troubles the humblest and the strongest minds. Beneath the words, " Lord, I believe, help Thou mine unbelief," Daniel Webster had this confession of it cut into the rock of his sepulcher : " Argument drawn from the vastness of the universe in comparison with the apparent insignificance of this globe has sometimes shaken my reason for the faith that is in me ; but my heart has always assured and reassured me that the Gospel of Jesus Christ must be a divine reality."

There is great need that, if possible, we should fully comprehend the life that pulsates in all this dubious thinking, pierce clear into the soul that animates it all, and *not merely silence this Doubt, but answer it.*

I. If the mystery of God manifest in the flesh were limited in its influence to the world of man, yet, as man is immortal, it would not be incredible, because the size of this planet is seemingly insignificant in comparison with that of many of the spheres of heaven, nor because its population is infinitesimal to that which *may* people the universe ; for finite mind cannot compute a consequence, which, though supposed to unfold along a comparatively narrow line, unfolds forever ; nor can it set bounds to Infinite mercy. Still there is in this doubt that which is *not thus answered;* and near the end of this chapter this is set forth, and the attempt is there made to answer it.

II. This Doubt takes on several forms, each of which needs to be considered. Rightly presupposing that so great a mystery could only have been in the place most fitting for it in all the universe, this star-born Doubt sometimes comes saying : A world more vast would have been a more suitable place for this manifestation of the Creator of all the Worlds ; it should have been in the grandest star of all. But if there be any thing in such reasoning, can any star be big enough to be in harmony with this manifestation ? a question that looks forward to thoughts hereafter, and should be remembered.

Who can decide even upon the physical conditions of a mystery so utterly beyond the power of the mind to compass ? Is the size of this world in comparison with that of many others too utterly insignificant ? Yet rank is not always, and in every thing, dependent on bulk. The constituent atoms of all the worlds, no doubt, are the same, and so they are in charcoal and diamond ; yet a little diamond outweighs in value tons of uncrystallized carbon.

On the not unreasonable supposition that Death may not have invaded the other worlds, the fact of Death here bears upon the rank of this world as compared with that of the others. For that rank cannot depend on the cubic feet of matter, but on the number of intelligent free beings (here supposed to be in other respects equal) of which each is the homestead ; and a little world whose population is ever vacating

17

and ever filling it again, would in time not only out-rank each other world whose inhabitants, not being subject to the law of death, ever remained the same in number, but would in time be of more account than the collective universe of worlds. This rests upon a conjecture as to that intolerable, hard mystery of death: but with this thought we return to solid ground of fact. In this world of man, twice a thousand millions live and die in less than threescore years and ten, a multitude the mind can no more grasp than it can the multitude of the stars; and granting a sufficient duration for the human race, enough souls made "kings and priests unto God" might here live and die, to rule over or to people all the orbs of heaven.

The worlds may differ in development. It is not probable they all grow at the same rate, one just as fast as another. The few known facts that bear upon this question go to prove the contrary; and there is no such monotony in the growth of other things. The generation of a little world might take up less time in its completion than that of a great one. This may be the only finished world; and if it be so, this would more than counterbalance any pre-eminence based on bulk alone.

As yet this world may be the only world of much account. There are bigger worlds than this, very much bigger; but is there another that is yet peo-pled? Astronomy cannot tell. Conjecture is not knowledge. That the Earth is peopled now does not prove the like of any other world. For that our Earth was not peopled for immeasurable Days, the Scripture said of old: and the same may yet be the case with every star in the heavens.

As we know not our Place in the universe, cannot reckon our latitude or longitude in the ocean of space, nor tell whether we are near center or shore, top or bottom, so we cannot make out our Time in the Universe, whether it be far down toward the end, near the middle, or just at the very beginning. In the universe of worlds intelligent life has begun, for we are of it. It must have begun somewhere in that universe, and perhaps as well in this planet as any-where else. Why not? Why may not the first brightening of free intelligence in the Creation have been right here? right here in old mother Earth? The revelations of which the Earth has been the scene so look. So does the marvel, Man; so does the mystery, Death. In the Creation, Life as high in rank as the human life may have first begun here; and as yet, it may have begun only here. This world may be the only hearthstone on which fire is blazing in the unfinished universe.

This cannot be proved. It may seem incredible; and no doubt the stars are worlds, in a sense thus defined—it is what they are meant to be. They are here supposed to be palaces, though palaces as yet unfinished or unfurnished. With this idea Science has no quarrel. The nearest celestial bodies, the planets, and the sun, hardly seem as yet to furnish the conditions in which intelligent free life can well be supposed to exist; and were it proved that some of the astronomical worlds are now inhabited, still, if all were known, it might appear that the development of those worlds had been keeping time with that of the human race, whose members, by millions on millions, are ever passing out from beyond our vision.

It is hardly probable this question can ever be settled from our post of observation on this planet. But according to the opinion of scientists, all the worlds pass through changes of which the Earth contains, as to itself, some record which may be sufficiently true for the other worlds : and as there have been several stages in the generation of the Earth when, according to Scripture, plant, animal, or human life did not exist, and when Geology, attesting to Scripture, says, in the conditions of the planet they could not have then existed, it is to be presumed that similar stages are common to all the worlds ; and why should it seem impossible, in the nature of things, that the stars have no inhabitants now, to those who hold that such was the fact in some past time ? If this be incredible now, why not always ? Geological times are confessedly indefinite ; let us then say, a million years ago there was no plant, animal, or human life in the universe. Now, if that can be true of a million years ago, or of any other number of years, then it may, perchance, be true now, with the evident exception of this planet, and perhaps of some particles of the unfinished whole !

Yet this theory need not be burdened with any weight that does not belong to it. It does not assume that all the worlds are now empty and silent. Some of them, many of them, and were it not for scientific facts that look as if it could not be so, it might be said, all of them may now be teeming with some kinds of life, the happy homes of multitudes of rejoicing creatures; for the Scriptures say, the Earth was, long before there was breathed into a human body the life-breath of a true human race: and yet, could a man now traverse the starry sphere, it might be, that throughout its whole extent, he would find no living creature, the peer of himself.

It cannot be proved. Yet the completeness of the answer it furnishes to some arguments against the system of Christianity that have a look of power, becomes a kind of evidence for it. With it the first of Genesis may fairly be said to be in harmony; for it seems to contemplate the sun, moon, and stars only in their relations to this world. Much the same seems to be true of all Scripture. Its words are the fitting utterance of the emotions of the devout astronomer. It intimates that the stars are numberless beyond what is seen; it speaks of them as declaring the glory of God; it clothes the heavens with something of a mysterious interest; and beyond this is silent. If what has here been set forth as a conjecture be a fact, that silence is *the silence of intelligence.* How much there is in Scripture of the silence of intelligence may be known from the latent harmony between the Old and the New Testaments; and from the comparison of the intimations of truths in Scripture with those truths as unfolding in Nature and History. The divine silence of Scripture is only less wonderful than its speech, and full of wisdom.

It cannot be proved: what then? it cannot be disproved; and, though only a conjecture, it has full power to countervail what is also only a conjecture, that this orb is so inferior that it could not have been the scene of the mystery in Christ.

III. Another form of the Astronomical Doubt as to the Christian system, wisely presupposing the Revelation on the Cross will nowhere be repeated, wisely presupposing, also, that the knowledge of the Cross must be meant for all the worlds, denies any possibility of this knowledge ever reaching the multitudinous, far-distant orbs of heaven. It paralyzes the imagination by the inconceivable distance of the stars. To meet this, by saying there may be as yet no peopled world save this, is partially in vain. For beyond all question, at some time all the world will be mansions of free intelligence. And it is also in vain to try to meet it by the thought of the varied ways of the Omnipresent, or of the ministry of angels. For if we will here think with the fearless candor becoming so grand a theme, it must be clear that the most fitting instruments would be employed for this purpose, and that these can only be redeemed souls. Herein, this form of the Astronomical Doubt as to the system of Christianity seems to be intuitively wise ; and it will be met, at this point, by a combination of thoughts conformed to its just requirements.

Matter, though its phenomena vary, seems everywhere, so far as it is possible to test this, the same in its essence, general properties, and laws ; and with certainty the like may be said of mind. "Each particular world in the universe may be supposed to have its own botany, its own geology, its own mineralogy, its own natural history ; but a spiritual necessity, a behest of the reason, compels us to say, that in all worlds there must be the same logic, the same grammar or universal laws of language, whether by sounds or signs, the same laws of thinking, the same geometry, the same pure mathematics, the same ultimate rules of taste, the same principles of art, the same æsthetic and moral philosophy. In other words, the good, the beautiful, the true, in themselves must be essentially the same, and cannot be conceived as having a diversity for different parts of the universe."*

What the angels are the redeemed may become. Thought is lost as it travels along this line of limitless aspiration. Yet Christ's humblest child, as the unfolding of his everlasting life goes on, may become the equal of Gabriel, as he stands at this hour in the presence of God. The angels are ministering spirits unto heirs of salvation ; and it is possible that heirs of salvation, made like unto the angels, may make known in other worlds the things done in this.

Even nature hints that man's seclusion from the other worlds may not last forever. Shall this planet have relations with every planet and star, the dust of the earth have earthy relations with far-off worlds, and the spirit of man have no relations with them, now, nor ever ? Such there are even now. The spirit there is in man is touched by planet, sun, and star. Those far-shining orbs allure him. † They awaken the feeling that somehow they belong to his

---

* Tayler Lewis.

† Those isles of light,
So wildly, spiritually bright,

spiritual domain : a feeling perhaps prophetic, an aspiration wherein there may be evidence that it will be gratified.

And that Star of the Incarnation ! that Star of the new morning in the Eternal Year does away with that isolation of the Earth from the great City on high, which paralyzes the imagination, as man looking out into space vainly tries to comprehend the distance to the nearest world. That Star is a sign of some close relation between Christ and the starry worlds, and may foretoken the like for them he calls his brethren.

BACK of all thus far thought of as going to make up the Astronomical Doubt as to Christianity, and intensifying it all, is a feeling that the truths of astronomy are more august and sublime than the revelations of the Bible. We are now coming into full sight of revelations in whose presence any such comparison, not with the disclosures of astronomy alone, but of all the sciences, is vain and idle ; and let it here be said, that not in this case only, but whenever the Bible, of all books the best and the least understood, is in question, the true way to vindicate it is *to bring out the truth there is in it.*

Never reversed will be the relative rank of the volume of Inspiration and of the volume of Nature. As letters to words, as words to language, so are the

---

Who ever gazed upon them shining
And turned to earth without repining,
Nor wished for wings to flee away,
And mix with their eternal ray.

thoughts of Science and Reason to those of the Bible as to things spiritual and eternal. Yet "the invisible things are understood by the things that are made." The all in Space and Time is a manifestation of Him who is in this all, but is neither it, nor of it. What we know not now we shall know hereafter. Yet would the desire might fully awaken to know more of the Divine Presence in Nature, in History, and in every human life! and there seems to be an increasing Divine purpose that in all things the Divine shall more and more be manifest. It may be seen in all the unvailings of knowledge, and even in the times thereof. When the telescope opened to view worlds so numberless that the mind was breaking down under their weight into the feeling that the Great Creator would not concern Himself about such an infinitesimal as a man, and when the wonder of geologic time, with its millions of years, matched the wonder of astronomic space, and the mind was further broken down by the thought that the Eternal would not concern Himself about so evanescent a thing as a man; *then* the eye was turned downward, and the microscope matched the wonders of the telescope, discovering within the ample area of a drop of water a world of beings to whose brief date the duration of threescore years seems eternal, discovering myriad millions of worlds of atomies, fashioned with fitness to all their surroundings, as perfect as that of man or the world of man; and seemingly so much more so as almost to suggest that the Creator gives nicest finishings to humblest things.

What the Hebrews called the finger of God is in this

antithesis and completion of truth, in these contrasted and combining lessons of wonder and adoration, from over our heads and from under our feet: and yet not only these, but all the scientific unvailings of the creative wisdom do but confirm the words, "Canst thou find out the Almighty to perfection? It is high as heaven, what canst thou do? deeper than hell, what canst thou know?" Does Astronomy unroll the heavens, till the soul feels there is no room left for their Creator? of old there came this Voice: "Thus saith the Holy One, Lift up your eyes on high and behold who hath created these, that bringeth out their hosts by number: He calleth them all by their names; by the greatness of his power not one of them faileth." Does Geology unroll the Time of the world till man is hard driven to feel the Ancient of Days would not care for a being so evanescent? there was this Voice of old: "Thus saith the high and lofty One *that inhabiteth Eternity*, I dwell in the high and holy place, with him also that is of a contrite and humble spirit."

Still it is not chiefly, even by utterances such as these, that the Bible counterpoises the down-crushing of the universe. It is the Revelation in Christ Jesus and Him Crucified, that shields against the temptation there is in the overshadowing majesty of Nature for the soul to deny itself, and in denying itself to deny its Creator. And yet, all that may be, cannot be known of the greatness of man, till the Hebrew Scriptures are studied, and studied in the light thrown upon them by the Gospel.

The truth that the Cross will be made known in all the worlds through the redeemed, is involved in

THE REVELATION OF THE DIGNITY AND DESTINY OF
MAN IN THE EIGHTH PSALM.

That brief Psalm is the highest word of Revelation
as to the Destiny of Man. On that brief Psalm is
laid the whole weight of the Universal Dominion
of Christ Jesus over all things created, in this use
of it in the second chapter of the Epistle to the
Hebrews:

"Unto the angels hath he not put in subjection
the world to come, but one in a certain place testified,
saying, What is man, that Thou art mindful of him?
or the Son of man, that Thou visitest him? Thou
madest him a little lower than the angels; Thou
crownedst him with glory and honor, and didst set
him over the works of thy hands: Thou hast put all
things in subjection under his feet. He left nothing
that is not put under him. But now we see not yet
all things put under him. But we see Jesus, who
was made a little lower than the angels for the suffering of death, crowned with glory and honor; that
he by the grace of God should taste death for every
man. For it became him for whom are all things,
and by whom are all things, in bringing many sons
unto glory to make the Captain of their salvation perfect through sufferings. For both he that sanctifieth
and they who are sanctified are all of one, for which
cause he is not ashamed to call them brethren." *

---

* So far as my reading goes, I have not been able to see how
any of those who have written upon the Psalms or the Epistle
make out in this Psalm the truth inspiration declares to be
there, or even how some of them think they make it out; and
I thus set forth the originality of the interpretation of it now to

In the eighth Psalm the Spirit of Him who was "lowly in heart" comes to us wearing a guise that is humble indeed. This word of revelation is given in the form of a little evanescent song, such as, in the stillness of the night, for companionship, the lonely shepherd sings to the answering hills. Some have thought it was a song of the boy David, watching his sheep on the field of Bethlehem. But this is not the song of a boy. It is the Psalm of the old king of Israel, looking out on the skies from the flat roof of his house on Mount Zion.

"O LORD our Lord, how excellent is Thy Name in all the earth! who hast set Thy glory above the heavens.

"Out of the mouth of babes and sucklings hast thou ordained strength because of thine enemies, that Thou mightest still the Enemy and the Avenger. When I consider Thy heavens, the work of Thy fingers, the moon and stars, which Thou hast ordained; what is man, that Thou art mindful of him? and the Son of man, that Thou visitest him! For Thou hast made him *a little lower than God*, to crown him with glory and *worship*. Thou madest him to have dominion over the works of Thy hands. Thou hast put all things under his feet: all sheep and oxen, yea, and the beasts of the field; the fowl of the air, and the fish of the sea, and whatsoever passeth through the paths of the seas. O Lord our Lord, how excellent is thy name in all the Earth!"

be given, that my readers may hear it with the patient conscientious attention of jurors impaneled to render in the verdict as to its truth.

In this Hymn the thoughts are as deep as the words are few. It is a Hymn on the Dignity of Man ; and like man, is little in form, great in spirit. Thus, as man does, it gives occasion for different opinions. To one, a man seems to be a machine of finer action than the spinning jenny ; another, taking less humble tone, esteems himself an ape-evolved brute : and in a man there is a fine machinery that wastes away in running ; in a man there is a life that is common to him and to " the mute creation :"
but to see in a man no more than these, is like seeing in this Psalm only the cunning rhythm and the feelings of the poet. The frame of a man is of the dust ; in him are all the passions of that mute creation of which he is the language-speaking Lord ; yet there is a spirit in a man, a mystery from God, a flame of his kindling, the breath of immortality. So, too, within the human minstrelsy of this little song there is a Divine inbreathing that lives on while races wither from the earth, and will live on when the earth shall pass away. This Hymn is a Voice from God, for whose elucidation there is need of the whole volume alike of History and of Inspiration ; and after all that human thought can do, it will remain as luminous and fathomless as the Destiny of Man.

The Glory of man fills the central circle of this orb of song. Around this sweeps the wider circle of the Glory of God, as round the center of the divinely-

---

* *The mute creation*—this exquisite phrase, so tender and true, should banish from our language the coarser phrase—*the brute creation.* The former was coined by the eloquent advocate, Lord Erskine.

wrought shield of Achilles, whereon the Life of man was pictured, swept the world-surrounding ocean-stream. Yet still the all-encircling thought is of the Lord as *our* Lord, and thus in its widest sphere this Hymn is at one with itself. As it begins so it ends, "O Lord Our Lord, how excellent is thy name in all the Earth!"

Taking a little Child in his arms Christ Jesus said, "Of such is the kingdom of heaven." Some kindred thought was *the germ of this Psalm :* and this thought grew out of something the Psalmist had seen in some child-Samuel, or group of little ones, chanting the hymns of Zion; musing on which, in the night and alone, his heart flowed forth in praise and song. There is, to my mind, confirmation of this idea in the Gospel of St. Matthew. On the day of our Lord's entry into Jerusalem "the multitudes that went before, and that followed, cried, saying, Blessed is he that cometh in the name of the Lord. When the chief priests and scribes saw the children crying in the temple, and saying, Hosanna to the Son of David, they were sore displeased;" and Christ reproved them in the words of the second verse of this Psalm. But whatever may be thought of this : that the fact was as just stated, will be clear to every one who will read the first and second verses of the Psalm, leaving out for the moment the words, *who hast set thy glory above the heavens.* This thought, evidently, was born of the star-lit infinitude, whose presence is felt throughout the Psalm, and over against which is set the Glory of God and then the Glory of man; and, as evidently, the thought in the words, "Out of the mouth of babes and sucklings, Thou hast ordained strength," was not born of the presence of the Night. Before this, there must have been something, musing on which the Psalmist said, "Out of the mouth of babes and sucklings Thou hast ordained strength, because of the Enemy and the Avenger."

Those thoughts and words of the Psalmist are more than his. The outflowing Psalm has a twofold source: the spirit of the aged Prophet, deep-musing on Nature, Man, and God, seeing in humblest things the Eternal Wisdom; and the divine Spirit, amplifying, determining his Thought, making it clear and true, lifting it to heights of truth before unthought of, unknowable by man but for such divine help, giving to it the authority, and making it the medium of universal and everlasting revelation.

The Enemy, no doubt, is the Enemy of the Righteous in the prelude to the Drama of Job, and *the same* who in Eden wrought the ruin of man. But what children are these who are to still this Enemy? and how strange so mighty a thing should be ascribed to babes and sucklings! The Thought that God ordained that babes should conquer His Enemy was a strange thought even to the Psalmist, as shown by the instant passing over of his unexpressed feeling of the weakness of Children into that of the weakness of Man. And in his Psalm, there may be discerned a trace of some previous influence from the Night, that had nearly overpowered him with a sense of human insignificance. Its illusive fires had degraded all, save the children of Abraham, to worship them. They had tempted this Prophet not to

the sin of idolatry, but to the greater and more dangerous sin of *materialism;* that is, to a Denial of
Man such as involved in it the Denial of God. They
had tempted this Prophet, and he had not given in to
this astronomical feeling. They had tempted him
and failed. It were in vain to try to conjecture the
consequence had he yielded to the dark feeling, had
Israel in the person of its great leader fallen back,
in this first outset, before the barriers of materialism ;
but certainly his great victory foretokened, and may
have predetermined, that of the people of God over
that delusion.

Nature had tempted the Prophet but had not prevailed. "When I consider the heavens, the work of
Thy fingers, the moon and stars, which Thou hast
ordained, what is man that Thou art mindful of him ?"
are words betraying that back of them there had been
a struggle in his soul. But that struggle was past.
These are the words of a Faith which rose superior to
Nature ; and because in that Temptation the spirit
of this Prophet did so rise above Nature, he was
fittingly made percipient of truths as to the dignity of man, the highest ever revealed to Prophet or
Apostle.

In this Psalm *there are two revelations.* These two
are quite distinct, though there may be a relationship
between them, as would be natural in so brief an
oracle. The one is, that God, who chooseth the weak
things to confound the mighty, out of the mouth of
babes hath ordained strength that He might still the
enemy ; the other, that *man is to have dominion over
all the works of God's hands*—a dominion whose im-

mensity the Lord made known by Copernicus, Kepler, Newton, and other men of the same God-seeking spirit, and of the same order of science as those of old, who discovered in the heavens the outshining of the Star at His Birth.

Upon *the last* of the two revelations in the Eighth Psalm we must dwell. Light is thrown from afar upon it, even from this Great First Charter of the Rights of Man, all whose Rights are God's gifts: "And God said, Let us make man in our image, after our likeness: and let them have dominion over the fish of the sea, and over the fowl of the air, and over the cattle, and over all the earth, and over every creeping thing that creepeth upon the earth. So God created man in his own image, in the image of God created he him; male and female created he them. And God blessed them, and God said unto them, Be fruitful, and multiply, and replenish the earth, and subdue it: and have dominion over the fish of the sea, and over the fowl of the air, and over every living thing that moveth upon the earth." Gen. i, 26–28. The *historical and precise tone characteristic of all revelation* is heard in this, its oldest utterance; a tone which belongs to it as indestructible fact, as historical in form, and therefore multifarious and exhaustless in its teachings, but yet precise in language. This Charter stands at the head of all legal documents, the first Grant on record, and few have been so clear. The historical narrative is so interwoven with it as to form a part of it; and, taking this instrument as a whole, no father, making a Deed of Gift to a son and a daughter, and meaning to make

18

them equal in the gift, could have been more precise in his terms. The Charter runs first to man to guard the truth of the unity of the human race, then its style changing, it runs to man and woman; granting the dominion it conveys equally to each and all to each. To use the language of the Common Law, it does not make them tenants in common, but joint-tenants; "they have one and the same interest, accruing by one and the same conveyance, commencing at one and the same time, and held by one and the same undivided possession."*

This Document establishes the Equality of Man and Woman on the same basis as every other fact, *on the will of God.* This truth, as inwrought into this Document, was far from being apprehended by the Hebrews. They treated Woman better than the more Eastern nations, or the Greeks, or the Romans, did. Yet this Document seems to have been almost a dead letter, till Christ made it the basis of the Law of Marriage, and thus quickened the germ of the Thought, nowhere as yet come to maturity, of the Equality of Woman and Man. †

This Great Charter, though forfeited by Man and Woman, was afterward partially revived, and our Lord treated its teaching as authoritative. In this Charter,

---

* Blackstone's Commentaries on the Laws of England. Book II, chap. xii.

† In this, as in every thing else, Christendom is so far below Christianity as to prove its religion came from above. Of Woman's Rights the Bible is the title-deed; and if woman, because she has not all her rights, will burn up the Bible, she acts as an heiress, who, because she has not full possession of an estate that of right belongs to her, burns up her title to it.

the purpose that man shall have Dominion over the Earth, follows so closely upon that of his creation as to give the reason for it. For if a king were to say, let us send for a General and give him command of an army, it would be a natural way of saying, he was to be sent for to command the army; and might be preferred, because, while clear as to this reason, it would not exclude others that might enter into the royal purpose. In like manner, the wording of this Charter makes known a relation between the making man in the image of God, and the dominion that was given him.

"So God created man in his own image and said, Have Dominion:"—his dominion then was made known to man through a grant of lordship over the earth. This grant of lordship over all the life in the world carried with it lordship over all there was in the world. Being over what was highest, it carried with it lordship over all that was lower. A grant of absolute sovereignty over the people of a country carries with it sovereignty over all the wealth on the surface, or under ground—all the soil, and all the mines, every thing in the country. So, this grant of lordship over the life of the world *carried with it Dominion over all the powers in Nature.*

Upon man's likeness to God this grant was conditioned.* To Noah, the patriarchal head of the

---

* "In the day that God created man, in the likeness of God made he him." Gen. v, 1. As this was said before, and as it precedes the words, "Adam lived a hundred and thirty years, and begat a son *in his own likeness,*" here is one of the articles of the creeds in historical form; for this restatement marks that

family that survived the judgment of the Flood, " the heir of the righteousness that is by Faith," this grant was confirmed, but in terms that conform to the altered state of man : " The fear of you, and the dread of you, shall be upon every beast of the earth, and upon every fowl of the air, and upon all the fishes of the sea ; into your hand are they delivered." To the Original Charter this grant was annexed : "I have given you every herb bearing seed which is upon the face of all the earth, and every tree in the which is the fruit of a tree yielding seed ; to you it shall be for meat." In the grant to Noah, how great the change from the lordship of man as made in the image of the Creator of every living thing! and musing on it these words come to mind, " The whole creation groaneth, and travaileth in pain together until now. For the earnest expectation of the creature waiteth for the manifestation of the sons of God."*

---

this Child, born after the Fall, was not born in that likeness to God in which man was made. This is the more evident be- cause this child was not the first-born, that murderer, but the pious Seth. Yet, the reason given to Noah for the sacredness of life is, that man is made in the image of God ; and the con- clusion is, the divine likeness is obscured, but not wholly lost. With this the human character and history agree. Men and women are by nature far-gone from righteousness ; yet as they are not angels, so they are not fiends.

* Rom. viii, 19 and 22. Words so clear and yet so dark ! words that reach down into that world without language where we cannot follow them ! and yet in the patient, waiting eye of the ox, in the wistfulness of my dog to speak, I seem to see the earnest expectation of the creature, and know that God will remember the mute creation, on whose sufferings philosophy can throw no light. His mode, his time, how dark ! yet clearly related to the Hereafter of man.

Man keeps something of the divine likeness, has some marred vestiges left of the human beauty; and so, too, of the human dominion. So far as this dominion is still in the human race, it seems to be somewhat in proportion as it is in the divine likeness. In the barbarian this likeness has almost faded out ; he has only of this robe of glory a few shreds left to cover his nakedness. In the semi-civilized peoples the spiritual life, from which came so much as they have of civilization, has hardly more than sufficed to keep it from mouldering away. It is only Christianized man who is regaining the lost dominion over the powers of Nature.

The thoughts of the Eternal Mind as uttered in Nature, in History, or in the Bible, are not uttered in their fullness at once, but in successive times, and to those who are under the law of Time. Yet the human intellect may try to conjoin those instants ; for, though their revealings being successive must be partial, the thoughts of God are timeless, and the thoughts of God are one. Did the Divine Thought, that man should be Lord of the Earth, in part come to naught ? It looks so. But what looks like a defeat of a divine purpose is ever the occasion of the unfolding of a further purpose; and the one that seemed thwarted is a part of this. Hence the failure of man to hold his rank as Lord of the world, Vicegerent of heaven, could have been but the foreknown condition of a purpose of greater scope ; later in its appearing, yet the older ; and so including the other, as a part of itself, that the seeming two are one. The divine thought of Man's Dominion seemed to

fail, and then was first made known that Superior
Thought, ever including in it that seeming failure.
Or, rather, the making this known then began. For
the promise of Him who should destroy the Tempter
who had been suffered to work out the degradation
of man, had not for its sole or its immediate aim to
vindicate the sovereignty that knows of no defeat
and no delay; but was rather meant to console the
bitter human misery of that disastrous hour, and to
awaken its despair into hope. All these things look
as if man would regain his dominion over nature, as
far and as fast, as in Christ he regains the likeness
of his Maker; but whether he will ever reach the
fullness of either in this Cycle of Time, and in the
present condition of this planet, as to this, who can
tell ?

Yet, even if in this Cycle of Time, the Redeemer
should call man back into the divine likeness, and
so re-invest him with full dominion over the world,
the fact of his previous dishonor, and the consequent
long years of sorrow and pain to him and the whole
creation, would still remain as a seeming triumph
of evil. If things were only put back as they were
before, this failure of the scheme, though but for a
time, would be wholly unprepared for. Unless it were
the foreseen occasion of something further, greater,
and higher, this triumph of evil would be more than
a seeming one, for though ended in the present, it
would be real in the past. There can be no such
triumph of evil, no such defeat of the Divine Sovereignty; and this must be more and more manifest,
as the Divine Thoughts so unfold in time, that man

may contemplate more and more of their timeless image.

If there be some Divine thought as to man, superior to that of his Dominion over the Earth, including in it the seeming, partial, and temporary failure of this, and contemplating something further and greater, then, both Thoughts must be in the same line : that is, the end contemplated in each must be of a like character. If so, the one Thought might pass into the other, as a lesser light may be absorbed in a greater, without being lost and without changing its nature. That further and greater Thought as to man is uttered in the Eighth Psalm ; for whose interpretation, as said before, the whole volume both of History and of Revelation is required.

The fullness of the original Grant of Dominion never vested in the fallen children of men ; nor did the Psalmist have them in mind. The pious Hebrews knew that by nature all are alike, even as all are alike under the government of the Most High. They knew that " He beholdeth all the sons of men : He fashioneth their hearts alike." They said, " The Earth is full of the goodness of the Lord ;" " His tender mercies are over all his works ;" " How excellent his loving-kindness ! therefore the children of men put their trust under the shadow of his wings." Even the word of Christ, " He maketh his sun to rise on the evil and on the good, and sendeth rain on the just and on the unjust," is not a clearer statement of the Universal Benevolence than some in the Psalms ; and yet in them is felt the difference marked by Him, between man as born of woman, and man as

born from above. The Psalms witness to the fact,
stated by one of his Apostles with the precision of
science, "If any man be in Christ he is a new creation," and clothed by another with unuttered promise,
when he said, "Now are we the sons of God, and it
doth not yet appear what we shall be." Light was
thrown upon the rationale of the two Races by Him
who is the Light of philosophy as well as morals:
and there was a master in Israel who knew not of
this higher race; but our Lord seemed surprised at
this; and it was strange in one who had read the
Psalms; for the Psalms are the voices of a Life that
is not the human life. The Life we inherit through
Adam is a Life concentered in self and burning
downward. In the Psalms there is a Life where this
selfishness is consuming away, a Life blazing upward.
The masters in Israel tell of some who said "there
is no God;"* of some who held Him to be a Power
as untouched by prayer as the power of gravitation,
saying, "Is there knowledge with the Most High?"†
of some with "no fear of God before their eyes;"‡
of others who through pride would not "seek after"
Him;§ of others satiated with sin, and saying "who
will show us any good:‖—how unlike those voices
of the Race whose life is from Adam, are these of
the new Race, whose life is from Christ! "O, how
great is thy goodness, which Thou hast laid up for
them that fear Thee, which Thou hast wrought for
them that trust in Thee before the sons of men!
Thou shalt hide them in the secret of thy presence

---

* Psa. xiv, 1.   † Psa. lxxiii, 11.   ‡ Psa. xxxvi, 1.
§ Psa. x, 4.   ‖ Psa. iv, 6.

from the pride of man. The Lord is the strength of my life, of whom shall I be afraid? Thy statutes have been my songs in the house of my pilgrimage. As the hart panteth after the water-brooks, so panteth my soul after God. Whom have I in heaven but Thee? and there is none upon earth that I desire beside Thee. I am a stranger in the earth. My heart and my flesh faileth, but God is the strength of my heart, and my portion forever. Though I walk through the valley of the shadow of death, I will fear no evil, for thou art with me. The men of the world have their portion in this life; as for me, I will behold thy face in righteousness; I shall be satisfied when I awake with thy likeness."

To one of these Races the thoughts of this Psalm are given, even as the affections of the Psalmist were. Its opening and its closing words, O Lord, *our* Lord, encircle only them, and he makes himself one with them, as Moses did when he said, "Lord, Thou hast been our dwelling-place in all generations." *

---

* The words, "mindful of him," do not prove the Psalmist was not thinking of the children of Adam, for the Lord "looketh upon all the inhabitants of the earth, He considereth all their works," (Psa. xxxiii, 13–15;) yet His mindfulness of the pious of old was dear to them: "many," they said, "are thy thoughts to usward," (Psa. xl, 5,) and "precious are they." (Psa. cxxxix, 17.) "The eye of the Lord is upon them that hope in his mercy," (Psa. xxxiii, 18,) a looking down to the looking up, thus pictured: "As the eyes of servants look unto the hand of their masters, and as the eyes of a maiden unto the hand of her mistress, so our eyes wait upon the Lord." (Psa. cxxiii, 2.) Thus while the words, "mindful of him," do not prove the Psalmist thought only of the sons of God, they accord with it; and it is proved by the words, "Thou visitest him;" in which the thought is

" *When I consider the heavens, what is Man,*" are words often quoted and often called to mind, as the motto of human insignificance. In doing so, the verse is cleft in twain, half is remembered, the rest forgotten; and thus the Psalmist is made to seem to say, what it is his glory never to have thought. He was thinking of the new Race of children of God, of His regard for such, and *not of their insignificance.* That is, not at the instant of his speaking. Some such thought had tempted him ; but before the instant of the Psalm, it had been repelled, and was gone.

Even for the infancy of this new Race such strength is ordained, that through its babes and sucklings God is to still the Enemy. And when this was revealed to the Psalmist, it was natural that he should then have been led on to those thoughts, whose utterance make this Psalm the highest word of Revelation as to this New Race of Men.

The mind will receive more readily, and the better comprehend that Revelation, if it consider, and with some carefulness and fullness : First, How the king attained to his Thought of the superiority to all the other Divine creations of the kind of man whom he had in mind ; Second : The greatness of the victory in that Thought over Materialism ; Third : The fitness

---

more clear when the line of it is traced on to where Christ says of the man who loves him and keeps his commandments, " My Father will love him and we will come to him and make our abode with him." (John xiv, 23.) A visit from a king is a signal favor. None such is named in Scripture as conferred on the children of men. The Psalmist, then, had in mind only those spoken of by Christ, as *born again.* John iii, 1-21.

of that Thought and that victory to the character of the Prophet.

1. Even in the Scripture, there are few words that so unvail the Divine Nature, so touch the human heart, as these persuasive words, " I love them that love me ; " and few more wonderful chapters than the eighth of Proverbs. It is wonderful for what it is in itself; and wonderful is the way in which other Scripture, like a torch to smouldering fire, resolves it into flame and warmth. The Wisdom, who was "before the works of old, before the mountains, before the earth," is the Word who was "in the beginning."* " In the beginning " when the heavens and the earth were made, Wisdom was there with God, "rejoicing always before him"—not as the English version has it, "like one brought up with him," but, "as the World-builder"—a correction that brings out the harmony of the two Scriptures. What is poetry and figure in the earlier, becomes history and matter of fact in the later Scripture, where it is written of the Word, "all things were made by Him." This Wisdom, "whose instruction is better than silver, whose knowledge than fine gold, with whom all things that are to be desired are not to be compared," in this older Scripture saith, I am understanding : to which, in later Scripture, the parallel is, I am the Truth. By this Wisdom, "kings reign and princes decree justice : " a truth unrolled to the fullest, when it is declared of the Word, " He is the Light that enlight-

---

* This rendering of the Greek, Logos, by Word, cannot be better ; and yet, in the term Wisdom, something that is in the Greek, is more clearly reproduced.

eneth every man." This Wisdom sends forth his
cry "in the places of the paths, at the entry of the
city, at the coming in of the doors; and "in the last
great day of the feast Christ stood and cried, saying,
"Come unto me," and he said, "Behold I stand at the
door and knock." This Wisdom, then, is the Word
who "was with and who was God, who became flesh
and dwelt among us." And as in thinking or speaking of men, we for the most part, think and speak of
the spirit that inhabits and will survive the mortal
frame, somewhat so in view of the highest in that
which constituted his being, it seems to be said of
Christ Jesus, in whom was "all the fullness of the
Godhead bodily," he is "the same yesterday, to-day,
and forever." In that day, when the Queen of the
South came from the uttermost parts of the earth to
hear the wisdom of Solomon, even then it was true
of Christ, "Whoso findeth Him findeth life, but he
that sinneth against Him wrongeth his own soul, and
they that hate Him love death."

As light is thrown on this eighth of Proverbs from
the prelude to the Gospel of St. John, so from this
older Scripture light is thrown back on these oldest
of all Scriptures, " Let us make man," and " In the
beginning Elohim " *—a term translated God, but a

---

* From the plural Elohim, some have tried to make it out
that out of older belief in many gods rose the Hebrew belief in
the One: to this it has been well answered, that history nowhere records the rising of polytheism into a purer faith, that
in the Shemitic languages plural nouns are sometimes joined
to verbs in the singular; and the thought I would bring out is
this: If Scripture was to be consistent with itself, it must find

plural noun with a verb in the singular—" made the heavens and the earth." The eighth chapter of Proverbs and the first of Genesis perfectly agree as to the Love for Man of this Wisdom, who is the World-Artificer. Compare the plural Elohim with the words, " Let us make man," and running the eye along the first page of Genesis, mark how each stage of the world-building is pronounced good, and how in the later Scripture the World-builder, like a cheery carpenter building higher and higher the stories of his house, is "always rejoicing ;" then in the older Scripture how this house of the World is for man, so that when man is made, Elohim rests, and then mark how exactly the eighth of Proverbs tallies with this, the

---

or form some such word as Elohim, or some phrase equivalent to it. In no other way could there be harmony between the first of St. John and the first of Genesis. As the first verse of Genesis is written in Hebrew, there is such ; but as it stands in the English and other versions, there is not the harmony between them which there must be between divine words.

Unity is one of those simple ideas that cannot be analysed, and so cannot be defined ; but surely it is not what it is often assumed to be by those who deny the Trinity on the ground, that it conflicts with the Unity of God. Such mistake the idea of Unity, or else the doctrine ; for in man the idea of the Unity of his being is indestructible ; and yet he says : It seems to me wise, I feel it is right, and will do it ; language as contradictory of Unity of being as those Scriptures where the Trinity appears, such as " Elohim made the heavens," and " Let us make man." Some arguments against the doctrine are as good against the true Philosophy, which in the Unity of the Soul distinguishes the Mind, the Heart, and the Will : but it is not well to reason from the one mystery to the other, as if they were the same, for we neither understand the three-fold Unity within, nor the three-fold Unity around us and above us.

poetry of the one with the history of the other, when *in words not the least instructive of all the words in Holy Writ,* the World-builder says, "my great joy was with the sons of Adam." This double record of the world's building runs up into the same thought of the Divine Love for man ; and this Love, astounding as it may be to some forms of philosophy falsely so called, and even conflicting with some systems of theology, has in all the Bible the same touching, human-like expression as in the words, "I love them that love me." Words uttered so long ago!—yet from them whoever would be loved of God may know how to gain his love ; and whoever will test these words will find out more of himself, and more of his Father in heaven, than man can teach.

Through his consciousness of that Divine Love which said, "I love them that love me ;" of the same individualizing Divine Love that loved Abraham and the disciple John ; the Love through which the soul may become a Temple-shrine wherein the Spirit of God, loving and beloved, may dwell ; that Love of which Christ said, "If a man love me, he will keep my words, and my Father will love him, and we will come and make our abode with him"—through his consciousness of that same Love, the greatness of man became clear to the soul of the Prophet. It is inwrought into the language of his Psalm, that through his consciousness of that Divine Love which came to visit him, he felt that man must be superior to all the other Divine creations. This he then felt as it was never before felt by any man, even among his own people, who kept the ancient idea of the Creator,

while all the world around, and many even of the
Israelites esteeming themselves as nothing in comparison, bowed down in worship of the mountain, the
grove, the river, the moon, the sun, and all the host of
heaven.

In that hour, what before was, and yet was not,
became a new thing in the world of thought. Until
a Thought is thus born, it has at most but a nebulous
being, floating from brain to brain, with such form
and consistency as a cloud may have; but when, suddenly, in some one soul, it is condensed into a star,
thence onward, by its own light, it shines forever.
From the soul, where by the will of God it thus is
born, its light ever tends to kindle up its own light,
and to become common to all kindred souls. When
thus a thought comes clearly within the field of intelligence, the soul so takes hold upon it as never afterward quite to let go its hold. For none of such
things as these are without some divine foreworking,
some gracious ordering of the circumstances, some
lasting decree. God orders these beforehand as a
father, who praying, believing, and arranging all
things, leads on a little child to where it may, perchance, behold some new truth, and in that blessed
moment so lay hold upon it, that it shall never afterward cease to be a part of the moral being of that
dear child. The first demonstration of some new law
or force in Nature is a grand moment in science, because its discovery by one is felt to be its discovery
by all, even though it be foreseen that ages will roll
away before it become such. And so, the moment
when this Thought of the superiority of man in the

Creation was thus born in the soul of the Psalmist, was a grand moment in Religion : for a Truth known to one as this Truth then became known to him, is, in like manner, known to all.

To every one who will think steadily upon it, it must be clear, that before Man could apprehend the Divine manifestation in Christ Jesus, there must have been a prevision of several spiritual truths, of which truths, this, that Man is superior to Nature, is one. Of such truths, the knowledge could not pass away; because of the Record of them given by that Mercy that has done for man all he could not do for himself. The many vain attempts of the Nations show it is difficult to seize hold upon spiritual truths, very difficult to preserve and transmit them pure : and if any one, in spite of this lesson, will still think all recording of such spiritual truths and facts as those might well enough have been intrusted solely to the human faculties, let him consider that it would not have been possible, without especial divine aid, to have so discerned them as to set them forth beforehand, in their historical and logical relations to the Divine manifestation in Christ. And with reference to the portraying of the Life of Christ Jesus, let him further consider that no man can rightly describe another unless he be that man's equal, and so the biographies of Cæsar or Napoleon satisfy no one; that no man, be he ever so wise, can comprehend the soul of another man, be he ever so humble : and then he will hardly fail to see that, if there were to be any just portraiture of that Son of Man and Son of God, of whom men wondering could only say, What manner of man is this?

the Spirit of God must quicken and uphold the human spirit to the achievement. And seeing all this, he will then see how needful is the light of all the truth in Scripture before that in the New Testament, to the full illumination of the portraiture of this pre-existent and wonderful Being.

2. "One morning as I was sitting by the fire, a great cloud came over me, and a Temptation beset me ; and I sat still and it was said, *All things come by Nature,* and the elements and the stars came over me, so that I was in a measure quite clouded with it ; but inasmuch as I sat still under it and let it alone, a lively hope arose in me, and a true voice arose in me which said, There is a living God which made all things ; and the Temptation vanished away, and Life rose over it all, and my heart was glad, and I praised the living God." Like the Psalmist, George Fox was tempted by the Thought of an all-containing, ever coming, ever changing Nature, wherein man is an appearing and vanishing "bubble, lashed from the foam of ages." This is the same Temptation before which the infidels of these times succumb. King David overcame it by the affirmation of God and the affirmation of Man. They yield to it in their denial of God and their denial of Man.

This two-fold denial is the mathematical sum of that many-voiced, vociferous folly of those who deny the Supernatural ; or the possible knowledge of it ; or that it ever intervenes in the course of human events ; who deny Creation and substitute for it endless and meaningless evolution. The field of this philosophy is a wide, flat marsh, where the noisome taint of

death is every-where to be smelt, and for the song of
birds and the pure breath of heaven, is the chant of
the wizard, the sharp scream of unclean poets, and
the dreariness of Milton's hell without its sublimity.
According to this unreason, man is a link in a necessitated endless chain. Nature is all, all is nature ;
and this nature is a passing show. Wisdom and
folly, good and evil, right and wrong, sin and holiness, God and man, are as fabulous as the unicorn,
the phœnix, the fairy, or the ghost. Spiritual realities, grand, solemn, eternal, vanish at the lively crow-
ing of these philosophers over natural facts of whose
deeper meanings they know no more than the barn-
fowl, cackling over the fallen grain, know of the mystery of life and the power of God. These infidels
seek to put their Creator as far away, and as much
out of the way as they can. Multitudes of men do
the like; yet with self-reproach, owning it is wrong,
and hoping at some more convenient season to make
their peace with God : but these illuminati glory in
their sin and shame ; they style it the perfection
of reason ; and try to sneer at those who are mean
enough to believe "it is appointed unto all men once
to die, and after death the judgment." In the place
of OUR FATHER they set up a sort of blind, irrational
fate, that is mighty and ridiculous. The tenor of their
folly is determined by their hatred of their Lawgiver
and Judge, who saith, "Be ye holy: the soul that
sinneth it shall die." Dig down to the intertwisting
roots of this poison-tree, and you will find they are
a base love of wickedness interwoven with the fear of
damnation.

If man the creature be, God the Creator is : and, of course, there goes with this denial of God, a denial of Man. They have to say, that Man is an illusion ; an ever-evolving unreality, necessitated by the circumstances in which and of which it is a part, to think, feel, and act as it does ; and that there is no power within it, and none without it, that can alter this. This ever-evolving phantom can have no real relations with the past, or with the future. It can know nothing of either.

Evolution, as they preach it, is arbitrary, irrational, universal predestination. As to what seem to be living beings, they preach the election of strong, and the reprobation of weak, races. How long their election of strong races may hold, they know not. By their own showing, their science and their philosophy is mere illusion ; yet unhesitatingly and inexorably they decree the annihilation of the strong as well as of the weak ; and this of the human being, as well as the brute. In the stream of nature, ever, for nothing, madly rushing from nowhere, and ever rushing back there, drowned Man is lost. With him all virtue is gone. There is but one moral character to actions : that is, none at all. The dead, whom, looking beyond the visible to the eternal heavens whence Christ shall come again, we buried in faith, are forever dead ; and there is one doom of annihilation for all. The Temptation, then, for a man to degrade himself into a Materialist, is even now a Temptation. And from this glance at the world around, I go far back *to that first recorded hour, when a man trampled this Temptation down in the name of God, and then in the name of the man who is born again of the Spirit of God.*

3. Rising to this great height of faith, through some quickening in what he had just seen in some children of God, probably in some little children, and setting the glory of God and then this glory of man over against and above that might and majesty of Nature which almost overpowered him, the Psalmist had vanquished the dark thought that Nature is all, and his first word is the breath of victory: "O Lord, our Lord, thou hast set thy glory above the heavens." This was a thought of his fathers, an heirloom in the family of Heber. It was inbreathed with the words, In the beginning Elohim made the heavens. But his thought of counterpoising the whole down-crushing of the universe by the Man whom God loves, was a New Thought, then and there born to everlasting human life in the soul of this Prophet.

Of all men this poet, warrior, king, was the man in whom this thought might have been born. Cæsar's will is proverbial; but in David we can hardly say there was more of one manly element than another; more of will than of heart, more of heart than of mind. Solomon had more wisdom, Joshua was a stronger man, Elijah had more of fire, though David had enough; but, to say all in a word, there was more man in him than in any man. He was "the man after God's own heart;" and though pious pedants may call this an orientalism by way of a disguise of ignorance, it is an orientalism not used of Moses, or even of faithful Abraham. It must mean something. It does mean a good deal. It throws some light on the King of the Hebrews, and more on the King of Kings, if, instead of evading its force, we find out its meaning. The materials are ample. The portraiture of David is more full than of any of the old Bible men, as should be that of the man after God's own heart. It is twice drawn ; in his history and in his songs. Unlike most of those who have written about themselves in prose or verse, this poet was as honest as the light, whose nature it is to reveal all and hide nothing. If ever soul was self-revealed, it was his. To this self-portraiture there is no parallel.* Let a man read the Fifty-first Psalm as a voluntary public confession, a lasting testimony to his own sin and shame, given to all his people, by an Eastern king ; let him remember the sacred ministerial character, as well as the despotic power of Oriental monarchs ; let him ask himself, if he has ever known, or has ever read of any man who could have made this confession, the like of which no king had ever made before ; and if he knows, or has heard of any such man; and if he thinks he could have done as well; and thinks that he himself is without sin—no doubt this worthy Pharisee would stone this penitent sinner. All others may find for themselves a lesson in this murder and adultery: not the vulgar lesson taught by so much of history, that lust and murder haunt the palaces of kings, the secure places of irresponsible power ; not even the better lesson that from such depths the soul may rise to the heights

---

* The songs of Burns are more like it than any thing else, though so different, and in so many ways. And there was a good deal of man in Robert Burns.

of penitence and praise ; but the lesson in the words—
the man after God's own heart.

They were said of this man's life as a whole : and
in his life this crime so stands out, that the human
conscience cannot accept these words till the soul
sees what justifies them, even in that course of events
where murder had its part. This murder the Bible
conceals not, defends not, palliates not. Through the
Prophet Nathan it utters condemnation, re-uttered by
every tongue. It must, then, be David's penitence
that approves him the man after God's own heart; and
the words teach that the Father's mercy for those
who rise out of sin is more than his anger at their
falling into it. This, which is the teaching of the
whole Gospel, is taught with great power in the very
words, which the ministers are ashamed of, and the
people hear with uneasy wonder. The king's abhor-
rence of what he had done, shown beyond all doubt
in his willing eagerness to own it for the warning of
his people, the uprising of his soul to a height higher
than where he stood before his crimes, prove those
words not unworthy of the Judge of all, when they
are placed where they belong; which is, after those
dark and terrible events end in confession. Through
those words is then revealed in the Judge of all the
earth, the spirit from which salvation came. For
Christ came into the world to call sinners to repentance. There were no others to call. His call to
repentance, with his promise of pardon and of acceptance with the Father, is the Gospel of the Son of
God ; and to enforce this Gospel, the wailings of
this criminal are heard forever in the songs of Zion :

"Have mercy upon me, O God, according to thy loving-kindness: according to the multitude of thy tender mercies blot out my transgressions. For I acknowledge my transgressions : and my sin is ever before me. Deliver me from blood-guiltiness, O God, thou God of my salvation : and my tongue shall sing aloud of thy righteousness. Thou desirest not sacrifice, else would I give it ; thou delightest not in burnt-offering. The sacrifices of God are a broken spirit : a broken and a contrite heart, O God, thou wilt not despise." In the Bible voice answers unto voice, though ages come between. In all this confession of guilt there is the assurance of mercy ; and were not this thought of mercy whispered from on high it were here presumptuous indeed. Ages pass ; and the thought out-breathing from the heart of this peni- tent sinner, in the low sad tones of his Psalm, is heard loud and clear from the unutterable height : "Thus saith the Lord, The heaven is my throne and the earth is my footstool, for all these things hath mine hand made, but to this man will I look, even to him that is poor, and of a contrite heart, and that trembleth at my word."

By his own heart-portraiture, and by his history, David is better known to us, from boyhood to the hour of his death, than any other man ; and in re- ligion it is a question that leads to unexpected results, what sort of a man was he? As a boy was he the forerunner of the worthy youth often held up to passive, enforced admiration, whose lack of power to make the evil there is in him stand out, is mistaken for something better ? Was he the matter-of-fact

man, self-recollecting and controlled by self, sometimes chosen for a deacon? Was he one of the
sanctimoniously ambitious who plod their politic way
into a high seat in the synagogue? Was he of that
safe sort of stuff of which some think that bishops
ought to be made? Not after their sort his soul of
fire. He was thoroughly alive : and how can a man
dead to any thing but sin, be thoroughly alive to
religion, when religion is every thing? Salvation is
life—that is the root meaning of the word. Christ is
the Life-giver. Christ was David's son and Lord,
and David was the most living of those Hebrew men
who live forever. He was ever in earnest, and he
ever meant what he said. His words are all soul,
and yet he is the most impersonal of all poets.
Though speaking of himself he so forgets self in
feeling and thought that his soul-voice becomes the
voice of every soul, the psalms of David every body's
psalms. A musician, he brought music into the
worship of Zion. A poet, he gave the tone to the
lyric poetry of Israel, which was to be the song of the
universal Church forever.

David was a genius. This does not set him apart
from other men, for man ate not of the tree of knowledge for nothing ; and genius, like sin, is the birth-
fact common to all. How could the Greeks respond
to Homer, the English speaking races to Shakspeare,
and all the world to Beethoven, if there were not in
all something of the same genius there was in Homer,
Shakspeare, and Beethoven? Bonaparte had more of
genius than any of the soldiers of the Army of Italy ;
but the same genius there was in him there was in

them, for only through this in them could they have
sympathized with it in him.   Whether they knew
it as such or not, and though one word cannot describe that wonderful fusion of many elements, yet
it was this immortal fire, more than aught else, which
blazed out till the world saw the light and was
astonished, when this unromantic people, whose feudal castles are at Moyamensing and Sing-Sing, this
unchivalric people, who own no lord but the Lord in
heaven, this trading, mechanical, farming generation,
at the firing on Fort Sumter, rose to arms, that this
land might be free from Slavery forever.   Respect-
ability-seeking hypocrites hate men of genius, as they
do all who any way surpass themselves, yet they
whiten their sepulchers ; and the people honor men
of genius, living or dead, feeling that there is in them
the might of God-given power.   They feel this be·
cause there is the like power in themselves.   But for
this, they could neither rejoice in, nor recognize its
fuller measure in others.

David was a genius ; and it is of great moment for us
to know this, because he was eminent among those
of old, through whom, as types of Him, it was meant
we should be better able to understand David's Son
and Lord.   I will not say of Him he was a man of
genius.   In his presence human language is abashed
and put to silence.   His words and his deeds describe
Him.   We can only, wondering, say, He was Son of
Man and Son of God.   Yet, in his words and deeds
may be seen every characteristic of genius.   This
does not remove Him away from us ; for it is the
genius there is in every soul which, more than any

thing else, individualizes that soul, and makes it real to itself. Genius is often deep buried. Some there are who live only to pile higher and higher the sand on its grave within the soul. But genius is by nature in every one. It is the best thing there is by nature in any one. It is the secret of fine sympathy. It is the spring of noble achievement. Its moments stand for years. Strike its pulses out of the threescore years and ten and they are little worth.

Alive in every feeling, as passionate in friendship as in war, a man of varied genius, musician, poet, soldier, and king, was the man after God's own heart. He was the finest kind of a man ; his varied life, even from a boy, brought out every power of his soul ; and *therefore*, in him of all men, would most naturally be born the highest thought of man. To any other of the great of the Hebrew line, great as they were, and varied in character and life, the Revelation made to him of the Dignity and Destiny of Man would not have been so appropriate. Some of them must have dimly seen some such idea as that of David ; but all great divine truths are born in some one soul out of such a half-conscious existence into fullness of life with preordained fitness of time, place, and circumstance ; and such Thoughts are rounds of the ladder let down from heaven for man to climb above the stars.

In no other place in the Bible does man so fairly confront the Temptation in the thought that all is nature, as here ; and nowhere else does he bid it depart in the name of man. The moment of the Eighth Psalm recalls that when Abraham obeyed the Voice calling him out of heretical Chaldea, and that of the

confession of St. Peter. It does not rank with those
supreme moments: still it was a great moment in Religion, when the old soldier won his victory over the
Goliath of Materialism, and more than matched the
combat of his youth. In that hour his Faith rose
to a height to which the Soul must rise if the Divine
purpose to reclaim man was to go on. He won this
glorious victory through the Spirit of Christ that was
in him. And he won it not for himself alone. He was
our Champion, and stood for us. All these things
make it natural, there should then have followed—
the highest of the revelations as to the Dignity and
the Destiny of Man.

WHEN he had just risen above the Temptation in
the overshadowing mystery in Nature for the soul to
think so meanly of itself in the comparison, as to
deny God in denying itself, and when he was thinking of the Divine regard for the sons of God, then it
was, that, with a boldness suited to that hour, and born
of that triumph, David would know more of what he
had discerned by faith. Then this king in Judah would
know, why in the sight of his all-wise Creator man is
superior to all the works of His hands. At that moment, the king felt that the man whom he had in
mind, was grander than Nature in her grandest show ;
and he boldly prayed to Jehovah that he might know,
What is man?
The desire to know this is so human, that, when
the Thought of man's greatness, as it was in the
mind of David, was once firmly grasped, this desire
was very sure to come out somewhere in the Bible.

For the Bible is the Book of the spirit there is in man, as well as the Book of the Spirit of God. As the Divine is mirrored there, so is the Human.

The quick asking of this question was like David. In the question there was a boldness born of the love that casteth out fear, yet like David, boy and man. And there was a Divine wisdom that doth not err, in his making the Divine visiting of those who are born from above, the sole proof of human greatness. This does prove it of them. For the feeling whence this visiting cometh is not the complacency with which, as said in Genesis, the Creator looks on his inanimate works; not his good will toward the mute creation, of which there are touching instances in the Scriptures; not the same with his pity and kindness for the children of men. It is different from and far beyond all those. It is a personal liking, the thought of which is foolishness to philosophy. It is the love that to our Lord was proof of the immortality of Abraham, of Isaac, and Jacob.

In the Human, as distinguished from the Christian, Race, (meaning by the latter all who before, as since, the Incarnation, have worked righteousness,) in the Human Race there is nothing entirely or truly great. There is nothing entirely or truly great in man as born in the likeness of the fallen Adam,

> In doubt his mind or body to prefer,
> Born but to die, and reasoning but to err,
> Sole judge of truth in endless error hurled,
> The glory, jest, and riddle of the world.

There is nothing in the works of this man that will not perish; and the sophist is alike convincing

whether he declaims of their greatness or their littleness. Hamlet, crying,—" What a piece of work is a
man ! How noble in reason, how infinite in faculties !
in form and motion, how express and admirable ! in
action how like an angel ! in apprehension how like
a god,"—countervailed this truly Shaksperean eloquence, by calling him " the paragon of animals, the
quintessence of dust !" With a latent sarcasm, worthy of Mephistopheles, with a serene unconscious-
ness of how fitly these words picture himself, Goethe,
its grandest impersonation, pointed out to modern
Thought in Hamlet, some strange, foreshadowed
likeness of itself; and, in the sneer with which it
ends, this jeering of the heathen Dane did anticipate
what with some now passes for science.

If it be said; this word-mongering about man is in
keeping with the unsubstantial, theatrical pageant
where stalks the wisely-foolish Hamlet, half feigning
madness and half mad, but that nothing can be more
unfair than such parading of this sickness of the
heart as philosophy or science ; and that true science
is proof of the greatness of Man :—I reply, Such
things are the indirect confession of science and
letters that man is vanity; and that, while true
science is evidence of a greatness in man, it is not
possible in true science to separate the work of the
Human and the Christian Intellects. Its pioneers,
its creators, its masters, its Keplers and Newtons—
to whom such workmen as La Place and Humboldt
are as masons who pile bricks, and plaster in mortar,
to architects—have been devout men ; and the science of Christendom is no evidence of greatness in

man, apart from the spirit of Christ. Man is only great when he dwells in God, and God in him.

Of the man who dwells in God, and God in him, the Psalmist prays to know what that man is; and the soul hushed to stillest expectation listens for the word of reply from heaven. Only irreverent rashness would dare prefashion that answer; but, may it not be frankly said, that when it comes it seems at first not as great as looked for? When the Creator utters his purpose in the original Creation of Man, there is a like feeling—of which it may be some evidence, that no creed repeats that utterance. For a moment let us think of that older and kindred revelation. There is nothing metaphysical about it. As set forth, the purpose is not, as theologians have it, the glory of God, nor, as philanthropists have it, the good of man; though, it may be, that each is included in it. In that Council in Eternity, it is declared, that man is created to have Dominion over the Earth. That is the revelation; and that is the whole of it:—an unexpected, disappointing, yet a thoroughly self-vindicating revelation, when at last it is seen the Divine purpose in the making of man is to confer upon him that, which, more than any thing else, is the Divine Prerogative. This Council in Eternity seems to have been before Time was, or Space; and how its purpose was to come to pass, this all the then future revelation makes known:—a thought which gives a startling glimpse of the unity of the written Word from its beginning.

Through his purpose to share his Dominion with

man, God is indeed revealed! and his Decree is harmonious with itself: *Let us make man in our image,
and let him have Dominion.* This Divine Word
comes ever to look more and more beautiful, as the
Divine ever does. It is accordant with an instinctive
desire implanted in the soul by its Creator, whose
strength may be known from its artless, intense delight in every new achievement that enlarges the
human dominion. This is the feeling that so exults,
when the sleepless pilot of the unknown seas, tired
Columbus, to whom, in a vision long years before,
the Almighty had given the keys of the doors of the
ocean, beholds through the darkness the light moving
on the shore; when Vasco de Gama, fulfilling the
prophecy of Noah, that God should enlarge Japheth,
opens the ocean-road to the ancient East from whence
the sons of Japheth came, as with difficulty his frail
barque rounds that Cape of Storms, ever after to wear
the name of Good Hope; when the thought-worn
Fulton sees the masts and spires of this fair city,
anchored eternal on its tributary floods, retire in the
distance, as his steam-barge slowly stems the current of the Hudson; or when Morse sends the lightning with the message, *What hath God wrought.*
This feeling is in harmony with the Thought of the
Creator in that oldest of his revelations, which makes
known that they who extend man's dominion over the
world work on in the line of His purpose in making
Man. They who are doing this feel they are doing
His will. Deep down beneath every other feeling,
more efficient than every other, this sent Livingstone
to Africa; and when men go on this errand the

heart of Man goes with them. This feeling, rejoicing in hope, now takes possession of the soul, as if the eternal purpose revived. It works with a will ; and, however blended with lower motives, drives home every spike in the railroads that are belting the globe, with a glow of hope which mere love of gain could never awaken :—so does the Divine purpose in man's creation commend itself to man.

As there is nothing metaphysical in the Revelation of the Divine purpose in the Creation of Man, so there is nothing metaphysical in the revelation that answers the question, What can man be that God should think so much of him? though here, even more than in the former revelation, we might look for something of the kind. Here, again, the revelation does not seem, at first, to be the great thing looked for ; and here, as before, the soul at last is filled with unutterable content.

A philosopher might answer the question by an analysis of the faculties of the soul, and if so, we may be sure the Divine answer would come in some other form. Such a philosophical answer would come no nearer to the secret of what man is, than the knife of the anatomist, searching the nerves, muscles, and bones of a dead man, comes to the secret of life ; and man can make such analysis as that for himself. The Divine answer does not attempt to do what all philosophy has always been trying to do, and always for naught.* Its Luciferian, proud curiosity has ever

* " Mystery," said Cousin, " is a word that belongs to religion but not to philosophy. Philosophy is content to offer gently its hand to Christianity, and to aid it in ascending to a higher ele-

had the impossible aim to pierce into the secret of Creation, and this, because there is involved in that, *the secret of the soul.* But the secret of Creation is the Creator's secret. It is incommunicable. For the conceiving of it, man has no faculty. Creating is putting forth a power that pertains only to the Creator, and its secret cannot be known by any created being. That man is, and that God is, can be known; the one fact as certainly as the other; but each are known through the outworking *word* of each, which is all that we can apprehend of either. Thus much is man's, all else is God's. Here, then, the teaching silence of this Revelation gives to the endless toil and vain endeavor of all philosophy a reproof as much needed as it has been little regarded; while its speech gives to the question, What is man? all the answer that in the nature of things can be given. It answers not to the words of its Prayer, but to the soul's desire and need; and it gives to each appropriate and sufficient satisfaction.

To know what man is, passes man's power of knowing; to know what he is to do, which, even as to this life, he never seems to know, and cannot know of the life beyond this, is all that can be revealed to him. The first revelation as to Man is, that he is made to rule over all the earth; the purpose as to Man revealed in and through the Eighth Psalm is similar, yet of almost infinitely greater amplitude: "Thou

---

vation." Thus, false science, profiting nothing by the Christian doctrine of Humility, is still the same as when St. Paul said, "beware lest any man spoil you through philosophy and vain deceit."

hast made him to have dominion over all the works of thy hands. Thou hast put all things under his feet."

These words sound like the breathing of the Prophet's own soul; and from words which soon follow them, some may take them for a high-wrought description of the human dominion then known to the Psalmist as a man. But if this were so, his Psalm would not be merely high-wrought or over-wrought, but incoherent. For in the same breath he speaks of the moon and stars as works of God's fingers; and what dominion over the moon and stars fully answering to the exceeding breadth and force of his words could he have thought that man then had?

It is perfect union of the human spirit with the Divine, which here so gives to the human and Divine thought in the soul of the Prophet so much the form of his own thought, that he seems himself to answer the very prayer he uplifts to the Most High. And thus it also is, that what as yet had hardly begun to be, seems to be spoken of as something that now fully is. This is not wholly because of his perfect assurance of the fulfillment of the decree; but rather, because that in the sublime exaltation of his spirit the Divine decree is, so to speak, not read off to him, but read off by him; and that neither past, present, or to come, are to be predicated of these timeless thoughts of the Eternal Mind.

"Thou hast made Man a little lower than God:" the Hebrew translators of the Bible dared not utter this thought and thus toned it down—Thou hast made Man a little lower than the angels. They seem to have

been driven to make this change in the meaning of
the text by their reverence for the High and lofty
One who stoopeth to behold the things in heaven.
Whence, then, came into the mind of the Hebrew
prophet, his Thought as it is in the Hebrew? It is
not explicable according to the laws of the human
intellect.

"Thou hast given him dominion over all the works
of Thy hands. Thou hast put all things under his
feet." These are the words of one looking out upon
the night; they are uttered in the same breath in
which he speaks of the moon and the stars that were
shining down upon him; and, though the idea of
Asiatic amplitude and exaggeration of speech might
be called in to lessen their compass, if these words
stood alone, or if they could be construed apart from
their context; or, it might be said, this frenzy of poetic
feeling should be translated into the soberness of
prose with largest limitation; yet here these words
of one looking out upon the star-lit sky are so related
to what he has just said of the heavens, that no line,
save one that measures the heavens, can measure
their extent.

But can the Thought in the Psalmist's words be so
enlarged as to compass the astronomical heavens, and
this without substituting another thought in the place
of it? The human form of a Thought of inspiration
has for its bounds those of the human spirit in which
it was born to human life, and the Divine form of the
thought may transcend these to any degree:—as in
two minds there may be essentially the same Thought,
and yet higher, deeper, greater, and every way reach-

ing further in the one than in the other. *Only thus* could the Bible be an everlasting oracle, which the Church may grow more and more to comprehend, but never can outgrow. *Only thus* is intelligible revelation through a Book possible. For the human form of the Thought is the rule by which alone the divine form of the Thought is determinable.*

The Psalmist's words may be enlarged to the compass of the astronomical heavens, if between his thought of the skies and the astronomic thought there is the correspondence which there is between a less and a greater form of the same thought. If so, then Astronomy may open more of the Divine form

---

* Much as the human form of the Thought may and should be enlarged, so that more and more it may correspond with the divine form of it, this must be done with exact conformity to its lesser form ; just as the face in a miniature must be exactly reproduced when it is enlarged to life-size, or else it is not the same face. Precisely to determine the human form of the thought as it was in the mind of the inspired writer, and then to give to it enlargement in right proportion, is what the vast expansion of Thought in the Modern World—the chief cause of which is the Bible itself—now makes so imperative. Unbelief will have done no harm in bringing out so openly the fact that there is a wide and deep chasm between the thoughts of the Bible and those of the Modern World, if it shall drive the Christian intellect earnestly to the work of bridging over that chasm.

But in no case can the idea be resorted to that inspired men knew nothing of the sense even of their profoundest utterances. This degrades inspiration into something magical, and Scripture into something cabalistical. It makes such Scripture a mere useless display. For if they knew nothing of the sense of their words none can know. Their idea of what their words meant is the only ground on which can be placed the ladder that reaches up into the heavens.

of his thought, which is essentially the same with its human form. The compass of the Psalmist's thought of the starry sphere to that of the astronomic thought may have been as is that of its seed to the broad-shading elm ; and yet it was such that the one could open into the other. For, of the thoughts of Astronomy, the only one that need here come into view, is that of a vastness in the heavens which makes them so fitting a symbol of the Divine Infinity; and that the skies were to the Psalmist also, a symbol of that infinity, and that he had an idea of the expanse above him which might enlarge into the compass of the astronomic heavens without changing its nature, are too certain and too plain for argument.

As there was in the Prophet's mind that from which, as from a germ, the Thought of all the orbs of heaven might unfold; so there was that which might, as to man's dominion over them all. The distinctions of past, present, or to come, do not attach to words of ecstasy; yet, for that very reason, they must be as really of the present, as of the future. The words themselves bind down their interpretation to something which was not then entirely in the future, not wholly promised, but then existing. They embrace the heavenly bodies so far as these were known to the Prophet. But could the Prophet have then thought of these as any way under man's dominion? It is impossible that he could have thought of them as wholly so. Absolute dominion belongs to God alone. But there may be a sense of dominion every way different from this, and which is a thing of degrees. One who feels a sense of

superiority to certain objects, one who feels that it
is the will and pleasure of Him who made them
and has absolute dominion over them, that they
should serve him, and who feels that they do serve
him, surely might feel a true sense of dominion
over such objects, even though in some respects he
had no power over them at all. Like to this, and
no more than this, was the feeling of dominion in
the monarch of Israel over the people of Israel. As
that such was the relation of the heavenly hosts to
the Psalmist was a chief part of his knowledge of
them, such may have been his feeling toward them ;
and such it seems to have been at the instant of this
Psalm. The fullness of our astronomical knowledge
of the heavenly bodies would have been in the way
of any such feeling ; and it would have been as
impossible to the heathen of old, as it would be
now to those pseudo-philosophers who hold to the
inviolability and immutability of natural laws. As
the heathen did, they deify nature ; and so bow
down before it, that the idea of man, under God,
as the Lord of nature, can find no entrance into
their souls.

The idea of Man's superiority to Nature carried far
beyond all possibility of his knowing it of himself
constitutes one of the *two* great revelations in the
Eighth Psalm. It is here regarded as a truth partly
wrought out by the Psalmist in his own soul ; and
then as confirmed and unfolded within him to the
utmost by the spirit of Christ. For in this Psalm
there are signs of a wrestling for truth and a seizing
hold upon it, blending with which and rewarding it

with further and higher vision of truth, is the influence of the Divine Spirit : and so it would seem that even inspired Prophets had to work out what they knew of truth with fear and trembling ; it being God who worked in them, and only to those thus working with him, granted knowledge of truth unattainable by the unaided powers of man. Before the Psalmist rose to his Thought of man's superiority to nature, he had to gain an immense victory over thoughts which reigned every-where outside of Israel, and had great power among the Israelites themselves. This victory was his own victory; though it was so conditioned upon all the struggles and experience of the children of God, that, without the light and strength which came down to him from the sacred past, it would have been impossible. Through these he was so ready to meet the Temptation which beset him, that in the hour when its strength was to test the strength of man, there was a man prepared of God to overcome it :—even as there was when a greater Temptation came, and the " power of darkness " tested all the strength there is in man : and in all the temptations of his people recorded by inspiration of old, it was the spirit of Christ which struggled, as really, as in that great Temptation it was the Captain of this host, Christ himself as a man, who at last won the whole battle for man.

It seems difficult almost to the verge of impossibility, for those who have wound themselves in the meshes and tied themselves with the cords of a false science, to rise where a true vision is gained of the superiority of Man to Nature. Yet this could have

been hardly less difficult for the Psalmist in that old
heathen world, in which he may properly be thought
as living ; for it then encompassed Judea, as now a
degrading, heathenish, and false science encompasses
the Church, with a potency of evil which made way
on every side into that inclosed garden of the Lord,
as may be known from the apostasy of his son and
successor, and of most of the subsequent kings of
Judah and Israel.

A bald statement of the difference between his
thought of the heavens and that of the heathen
around him, gives hardly an intimation of the mental
and moral firmness of the grip with which he fastened
upon it and held on to it ; and still less of the boldness of its challenge of all heathenism, through all
time and of whatever name, through its containing
in itself, as it did, the germ of the perfect Divine idea
of Man, when born of the Spirit, as above Nature;
and this as a necessary consequence of his affiliation
with God.   Yet, the briefest and simplest statement
of that difference is all that can here be given.   The
heathen thought the sun, moon, and stars were gods ;
David thought of them as creations of God, and made
by Him for man.   The heathen thought they were
to serve the sun, moon, and stars ; he thought of
them as servants of man.   There may have been
more than this in his thought of them ; and probably
there was ; for his words show something that looks
like the astronomical feeling. But he thought of them
as made for the need and benefit of man as really
as the flocks of the valley or the cedars of Lebanon ;
and this, though not an exhaustive thought, and

probably not supposed by him to be such, was a true thought. Alike, then, as to the grandeur of the skies, and as to the superiority of the soul to the stars, his were germinant Ideas, capable of almost infinite expansion : and Inspiration caused him to utter them in words corresponding to their extent in the Infinite Mind, the Eternal Will.

The compass of his Thought changed with the words, "All sheep and oxen, yea, and the beasts of the field, the fowl of the air, and the fish of the sea, and whatsoever passeth through the paths of the seas." Do these words limit those before them to this planet? No; those words cannot be so limited : and this instantaneous change in the compass of the Thought is comprehensible; the real wonder being the height and expansion of the thoughts before, and not this sudden narrowing of their range. Even if the lowest view of these words be taken, they are the almost human seizing upon visible, humble tokens and confirmations of the truths just uttered. But they may allude to the oracle as to Man's creation ; and some allusion to this is rather to be looked for here. For into the channel of older inspiration later inspiration flows, and together they form that river with far-off fountains, fed from above the skies, whose streams make glad the city of God. Thus, these words may be a prophecy of the return on Earth again of the original Dominion of man over the world: but whether in this, or in some future Time Cycle, who can tell? Even should this be so, there is still an instant narrowing of almost boundless thoughts ; yet, admitting this to the utmost, and holding to the very widest compass of those before, it can be explained. In the twinkling of an eye, the soul can pass from the widest to the narrowest range of related thought. In the boundlessness of the star-lit skies thought may lose itself, and yet, if the glow-worm in the grass attract the eye, the mind may at once link the unseen insect's fitful fire with those far lights as works of the same hand, or through His all-pervading symbol, the *element* Light. Thinking of the Divine Fatherhood over the multitudes of men and angels, the mind can pass in an instant, without the least jar, or violence of turning in its thought, to an earthly father's humbler love, and find in the less an image and confirmation of the greater.

Troubled by the mystic lights on high, oppressed by the grandeur of the awe-inspiring night, the Psalmist put forth a sublime faith in man's superiority to the heavens. In that same instant, and when he was thinking of the heavens as the work of God's fingers, their glory pales in the splendor of his vision of the glory of Man, for it is shown to him that Man is to have dominion over all the works of God's hands. From this super-celestial height the stoop of his thought is sudden, yet not more so than its previous exaltation. Quick as the glance of the eye from heaven to earth are the changes of thought ; but the narrower sweep of vision cannot do away with the higher and wider, from which, like the eagle that has soared above the clouds, it stoops to the ground. If the close of the Psalm so narrows its range that man is to be Lord only of the fowl and the brute, if the higher and wider thought be not in it, the Psalm

is here incoherent, and it contradicts itself. If the
higher thought be there, all is in keeping, all is uni-
fied. It is the same thought, varied only as passing
from a higher and wider to a lower and a lesser circle.

ALMOST infinite expansion is given by the Divine
Spirit to the words of the Psalmist, when, in the
Epistle to the Hebrews, He applies them to the
Second Man, the Lord from heaven. But the Spirit
cannot have brought out of the words what was not
in them, nor have put into the words what was not
before in them. For then they would not be as He
sets them forth to be, the Psalmist's words, but new
and other words from heaven. Therefore, all there
is in the words as applied to the Son of Man was in
the words when they were spoken : and as thus read,
they test the faith of every man in the Bible ; they
show how infinitely beyond all possible disclosures
of science or conjectures of philosophy are its revelations, every way how different, and such as it hath not
entered into the heart of man to conceive of. *For these
words were spoken not of one man, but of a Race of
Men.*
Before, we distinguished between the Human and
the Christian Race ; we must now make a distinction
within the Christian Race. Before, we withdrew the
title man from the Human Race ; we must now with-
hold it in its full, mature sense from the Christian
Race ; for *as yet there is but one True Man, the Man
Christ Jesus.* Man perfect in obedience and love to
God is to have dominion over all the works of God's
hands. In the Son of Man this obedience and love

was perfect. To Him the Spirit applies this prophecy, and then it is written, in close connection with it, " Both He that sanctifieth and they that are sanctified are all of one, for which cause He is not ashamed to call them brethren." The same connection of these two ideas appears when it is written of Christ, in words again taken from the Eighth Psalm, " God hath put all things under his feet, and given Him to be head over all things to the Church."

As yet all things are not put under " the Second man," and there is no man save Him alone. *The age of the True Man is yet to come.* In the light of this fact we can apprehend the first of the two wonderful revelations in this wonderful Psalm; for whose elucidation, though simple its form and few its words, I repeat again, the whole volume is required both of Nature and of Revelation. Out of the mouth of those who are babes in Christ, God, who chooseth the weak things of this world to confound the mighty, ordaineth strength because of His enemies, that He might still the Enemy and the Avenger. This peculiar and very ancient language is in harmony with language of far later Scripture : " I thank Thee, O Father, Lord of heaven and earth, because Thou hast hidden these things from the wise and prudent, and revealed them unto babes."

The prophesied work of these babes and sucklings of the Christian Race goes noiselessly yet surely on ; and the human race works with them, unconsciously against its will, and knowing nothing of what will come from its labor, though it fills the air with many voices and loud clamors. So in the resounding forest, the Tyrians hewed the cedar beams for a Temple they were not to see, and in the set time, without a sound, the goodly house of the Lord rose above the holy mountain :

> No workman's steel, no ponderous axes rung ;
> Like some tall palm the stately fabric sprung.
> Majestic silence !

Of that Race of which, save One, there are but the children not grown to the stature of men, of that Race *who are to rule over all the stars of heaven*, the Psalmist could have had, even as we can have, but the faintest idea ; yet he thought of the race of the children of God, who, born as babes, were to grow to be men. Just glimmers before us the sheen of its future perfect glory. Through what untried vicissitudes of being, in what far off ages the vision shall come true, only God knows. Yet, if our imperfect conception of the True Race of Man admits of expansion into the fullness of the truth, if the light that just gleams before our eyes may go on to noon-tide splendor, that which would be true of this idea, as foretokening the future, would also be true of the Psalmist's. Our conception of it may assume a definiteness beyond that possible to one who lived before the manifestation of the Second Man, the Man Christ Jesus ; it may fill out a wider circle ; yet, like his, it is tentative, ill-defined, imperfect, though germinant, and capable of perfection. Even now, the circle of the truest Humanity is felt to be the circle circumscribed by the Church on the map of the globe ; but this feeling points onward and upward to a truth, the

height of which it does not attain, the truth that man
is truly man, only when he is a son of God.

What is in the future is revealed and unrevealed,
seen and unseen. Will the barbarian perish or be
reclaimed? Will the semi-civilized people be Christianized? Will the children through centuries on
centuries of growth grow up to be Men? or will the
world come quickly to an end? amid some earth-
changing convulsion the dead in Christ arise, those
living in Christ be changed, and a new Race of Men
possess the new Earth?

Here, it matters not how, or when, or where, this
Race shall come to its pre-ordained perfection. Much
in Scripture seems to point to a glorious hereafter of
the Church on this Earth; and any and all the hopes
of this in the hearts of believers, as they have read
the prophecies, may come true; and yet a purpose of
God that the Christian Race, the true race of Men,
shall have Dominion over all the works of His hands,
have its set time in a higher chronology than that of
this planet. The Earth has had its changes. It may
have more to come—but the Earth is mortal, Man is
immortal.

Through all the worlds the Cross will be revealed:
but the time of its universal revelation may be delayed for as long a period, measured on the great dial-
plate of the Universe, as will correspond with the
time the fact itself was delayed, as measured on the
dial-plate of this planet; and this fullness of the
universal time may be beyond the Great Day of the
General Judgment, beyond all the mutations of this
planet, beyond the fated hour when the Earth's frac-

tion of the everlasting duration, Time as measured by days and years, shall be no more.

Are there large spaces in the System of the Universe? over against them are set times of more than corresponding greatness in the System of Christianity. Does man seem too feeble to be put over all the works of God's hands? Man is all contrasts. Weak as he is, in him there is the breath of the Almighty. Made of the earth, he is the imperishable tenant of a perishable world. Long he may cling to his homestead, but Man must quit it at last to become the Pilgrim of Eternity:—a cold thought to flesh and blood, but Eternity, with its many mansions, is his Father's house.

Is it thought incredible that far down in the Ages all created things may be put under the race of Man? All power now is given to the Man seated on the right hand of God; and, if there be those whom he calls his brethren, may he not share with them his dominion? That universal dominion is His, because, being equal with God, he became obedient unto death; and what may he not do for them for whom he has done so much? and God who gave his own Son to die for them, may He not with Him give them all things? Hath not his Spirit written in that mysterious Book, whose Thoughts all may understand and none can fathom, they are "*heirs of God and joint-heirs with Christ?*"

As the star-born Doubt as to Christianity confronts us, wrapped in a benumbing shroud of immensity, it may be righteously confronted with thoughts of more than equal grandeur. Such thoughts have their permitted hour. Yet we may well be thankful all the future is not clearly revealed. The silence of Scripture is full of mercy, as of wisdom. The Lord knoweth our frame, He remembereth that we are dust. Flesh and blood is not strong enough to bear the full burden of this exceeding and eternal weight of glory. More grateful to the wayworn pilgrim, tired with life's weary march, the soothing words of the Spirit, Blessed are the dead who die in the Lord—they may rest from their labors. But let us hear no more of any comparison of the revelations of science with those of the Bible, or that Christianity as a System of Faith is belittled and made ridiculous by the System of the Universe! Let us hear no more that the results of Christ's Death on the Cross are incommensurate with his glory as the only begotten Son of God!

IV. So far from being in hostility to the facts of Christianity, the Astronomical Discovery that Stars are Worlds, brings to light the unknown and unsuspected fact of the correspondence of the size of the World where the Word of God was manifest in form as man, with the humility of the manger, and with all the lowliness of His advent. Three hundred years ago, the discovery of the inferiority of the Earth to the rival spheres of heaven was made; three thousand years ago, the similar fact was foretold, that little Bethlehem of Judea would be the birthplace of the Lord :—a fact that may have tried the faith of the Magi, familiar with the imperial cities of the East. If mere comparative magnitude of place be a condition precedent to the mystery in Christ, ruling all other considerations, then it is incredible that the Son of God was born in Bethlehem. If the Earth, because it is little, could not have been the place of the Advent, Bethlehem could not. For though our mere sense-conception of the vastness of some of the worlds that make up the Universe overpowers the reason till it is lost in wonder, yet the instant that reason reasserts itself, it cannot but see that, if the argument be good in the one case, it is good in the other. Is the Earth smaller than some of the planets? So was Bethlehem smaller than some of its sister villages. Is the Earth smaller than the sun, or the stars? So was Bethlehem smaller than Jerusalem, than Antioch, than Alexandria, or Rome. Is the Earth but a small part of the solar system, and a still less particle of the Universe? the parallel is still exact : Judea was but a small part of the Empire, the Empire of the World.

Unlike the contrast between the vastness of the worlds and the littleness of the globe, the contrast between the ineffable grandeur of the mystery in Christ and the humility of Bethlehem is no modern discovery; nor was it first thought of by man. A thousand years before, the Spirit seems moved even to wonder at the littleness of the birthplace of the Maker of the heavens and the earth, at the contrast between his going forth from Bethlehem, and His goings forth in the Creative Days of the beginning : " Thou, Bethlehem Ephratah, though thou be *least* among the thousands of Israel, yet out of thee shall he come forth unto me that is to be Ruler in Israel ;

whose goings forth have been from of old, from the Days of Eternity."*

The volume of nature runs parallel, so far as may be, with the volume of Revelation, each proceeding from the same Lord; and Reason, illumined by Faith, seeing the comparative littleness of the village birthplace of the Son of God requires the comparative littleness of the Earth, sees that the moral considerations that determined the one must have determined the other. Hence, when we read in the lower volume of nature of the littleness of the Earth, this should be heard, so far as it bears upon the Advent of the Universal Lord to this inferior orb, as a truth known before. We should see the parallel in the size of the village where the Lord was born, as compared with the cities of the Earth, and the size of the Earth in comparison with the worlds of the Universe; should mark that each fact is the counterpart of the other; and apply to this Orb the twofold thought of the Prophecy: Thou Earth art both *little and great* among the thousands of the Universe, for out of thee goeth forth the Ruler, whose goings forth have been from of old, from Everlasting.

V. YET this untiring Doubt still says: Even though the contrast of the humility of the Birthplace of the Son of God with his creative glory was foretold, and though the events of which it has been the scene, and the destiny of the Redeemed, make it not the least among the thousands of the universe, even as Beth-

---

* Micah v, 2. See marginal reading.

lehem was not least among the thousands of Israel, and though the Earth may be the oldest, or the only peopled world, and though the Cross should be known through all the worlds for the instruction and blessing of the whole intelligent creation, even though all these things be so, I am not satisfied : I still feel that in the one indivisible universe the Advent of God cannot have been a thing so separate and alone as it seems to be in view of the isolation of the Earth. *In this feeling throbs the very life and soul of the Astronomical Doubt as to Christianity.* The replies as yet given to it, though all bearing directly upon it, do in fact rather *silence than answer it.* It cannot be satisfied unless there be something from *" the beginning"* pervading all the indivisible universe, which, in some sense, is one with the mystery of the Incarnation. Nothing short of this can satisfy the feeling, that by the Advent of God the Earth not only becomes the pre-eminent world, against which reason can allege nothing, but a world so apart and alone that the indivisibility of the spiritual, and of course of its correlative, the material universe, is broken up by the appearing within its common conditions of space and time of something apart from, and not truly related to the whole, *and that the unity of the Creation of the One God is clean gone forever.* This is a very subtle feeling ; it was long before I was so conscious of it, that I could drag it to the light to find in it that which, undiscovered before in the searching of years, had hindered my mind from resting content with the several answers to this Doubt already given. It is a truly rational feeling, and one that can be met only by what the Bible reveals of the mystery of the Word of God, in all Nature and in all Life.

This is a secret hidden in all created being, toward which science has not made even infinitesimal progress; though in its investigation of natural laws sometimes startled by a feeling that the universe is no machine, no corpse for the knife of the anatomist, and is informed with a life, the intimations of whose nearness fill it with a momentary awe, but into the chamber of whose secrecy it can never come.

The Presence of the Word in the universe is something that even revelation hints at, rather than reveals; as if man had no faculty for conceiving of it. It is seen in flashes of intelligence that leave the soul in darkness. It is a vision that tarries for no question. We cannot touch the hem of its garment.

The Creation is no illusion, and yet exists in and through the Word of God ever present therein; and may not this mysterious presence of Himself with what He hath made, be thought of as His Advent in the Creation, "finished" in His Death on the Cross? Thus, the mystery of the Incarnation, though in this world rising to a height not seen or prophesied elsewhere, has a wider field than this planet, even the one indivisible universe. It fills all Time, all Space— its center the Cross, its circumference every-where.

CHAPTER VIII.

THE WORSHIP OF CHRIST BY THE MAGI.

THE outshining of the Bright and Morning Star at the Birth of the Redeeming Lord was the symbol of His glory as the Creating Lord. Its Guiding ended the long procession of the miracles of old. It prophesied of that guiding by the Spirit which marks the new Age. In the framing together of the Time-worlds made by the goings forth of the Eternal Word, this star was the Evening Star of a day then setting, and the Morning Star of a new Dayspring from on high.

The outshining and guiding of this star so prove themselves to the Christian Reason as to prove the history of the Wise men; for the proof of its greater facts proves the less. Yet thought may well be here given to some of those lesser facts. For St. Matthew's words, and his method, ceasing to be well understood, there gathered around the Wise men an air of mystery. Their story seemed to have neither prelude nor conclusion. Unthought of and suddenly those strangers came, and they went as suddenly. There was not a word about them afterward, and who they were no one knew. They almost seemed like beings from another world. They appeared, no one knew whence; they told a wonderful story, and they vanished. In this state of things some called the second chapter of St. Matthew the first Legend of Christianity, and with a show of reason; for difficulties thickened with every line, alike as to the facts, and as to the truths interwoven with them, until the supernatural in the history seemed to them incredible, and the historical fabulous.

TWO MINOR DIFFICULTIES AS TO THIS CHAPTER.

Two of the minor facts in this history thus came to look unhistorical—the boldness of the Wise men; and the Tyrant's welcome to strangers bringing such unwelcome news. But these facts look reasonable when it is known who these Pilgrims were; and when that which befell them at Herod's court is read with the knowledge of the time and its usages, which St. Matthew assumes. For religious dignitaries of the dreaded Parthians, coming under the safe conduct of their Generals on the Upper Euphrates, or of their King himself in Ctesiphon, were as sure of honor from Herod, and as safe from harm, as religious dignitaries of the Russian Empire would once have been from Hanover, Hesse-Cassel, or any of those petty German rulers, whose names so lately passed from the roll of kings. The bearing of these strangers accords with the high rank of chiefs of the Parthian Magi. In calling them kings, the Middle Ages showed a historical insight which was keen and true, compared with that which has seen in them only beggarly fortune-tellers, of questionable character and wandering habits. These Eastern Magi act like men unaccustomed to have their actions questioned. They make no secret of their mission. All Jerusalem knows why they came. Apparently, they go straight to the palace: and St. Matthew would have thought it needless expressly to state this; for to whom else should strangers, of such rank that for them the Council of the kingdom is called together, report themselves but to the King in person? The bloody tragedy in Bethlehem makes their boldness strange: and yet it was natural with their religious ideas of Him they sought; and Herod's conduct agrees with that of Pilate. Jesus told this officer of Tiberius, that jealous Emperor, I am a King; yet Pilate said to the Jews, I find no fault in him; and surely Herod might distinguish between a spiritual and a political claim, as well as this Roman Governor. But the Jews did not understand that the Messiah's kingdom was not of this world; and for that quick, warlike, and oppressed people to believe the Messiah was born was of dangerous import, because to them it was a political as well as a religious fact. To the Magi it was purely a religious fact; and their inquiry set forth that they were seeking a spiritual Lord. They came to find a babe whose Birth was signified to them from heaven. They styled him King of the Jews, but took this Title from the Prophecy of Daniel the Magian; and it must have been clear to all that they used it in a religious sense, for they said, they came to worship Him. Other strangers in Judea nailed this Title to the Cross of Christ. The Wise Men used it in reverence, Pilate in scorn; but it had with each only a religious meaning.

Otherwise, the course of the Wise Men in Jerusalem, high as was their rank, would have been in

open disregard of the requirements of prudence and
common sense. Nor could they have thought the
Messiah was a descendant of Herod. For had they
started from the furthest bound of Parthia, wholly
ignorant of the politics of Judea, before they had
come so far into Herod's country, they must have
heard his children were grown up, and that he was
old. Nor would they have asked, Where is he that is
born? had they thought him a son or a grandson of
Herod. They seem to have made their inquiry of
Herod himself; and if so, could have had no idea
that it would kindle his jealousy. A European king
might have treated such singular visitors quite dif-
ferently; but Herod's bearing suits the traditionary
policy of Oriental kings, which has ever led them to
pay a popular show of respect to all forms of religious
faith or delusion. Ignoring its political bearings, he
treated their inquiry as if it were of spiritual import
only. He sought the confidence of the Magi in a
bold, thorough, kingly style; and he gave to their
coming most public recognition, meaning to deceive
his own people also. In a measure, this was forced
upon him by the rank of the Magi; and yet it accords
with the adroit but fearless character of Herod, who
was one of those few men who have made themselves
kings by craft and courage. He trusted to the ignorance of those foreigners as to the state of things
around them, to the charm of regal courtesy, to the
credulity of the pious when listening to pious words
from politicians, and to his own well-trained power
of dissembling. He thought to play with the Magi
till the Holy Child was found; and for this he thought

they would be his best, and meant they should be his willing instruments.

Policy that fails seems poor policy; but that of Herod was shrewd, if there be included in our estimate of it one thing, which St. Matthew may have thought too plain to mention, but lost sight of in losing sight of the rank of Herod's guests. Herod meant that a guard should attend these Parthian noblesse, who were journeying in his country to do honor to a Child in whom he professed to feel a religious interest. If he wished no great publicity given to this journey, a few trusty soldiers would have been enough; but less honor than this would have been unusual and uncourteous. The quickness of the Magi thwarted the king. The Session of the Sanhedrim and their private audience must have taken up the day ; yet they left Jerusalem before its gates were shut for the night ; and even the sagacity of Herod could not foresee that guests so courteously treated would hurry from his capital.

Their haste may be accounted for in two ways. Some Israelite may have warned them not to trust Herod. Their keen eyes may have detected trouble and alarm in the Sanhedrim. Around the Tyrant there was an atmosphere of dread. The astuteness of priests matches the craft of kings. " The Persians are, of all nations, the quickest to read character." It may have been, that the Wise Men distrusted the perilous honor of a guard, and meant to prevent it by their instant departure. On the other hand, it is not likely they met with the Sanhedrim; or that any warning could have reached strangers of rank in a palace, and who were watched all the time by spies of the king. Enthusiasts are easily beguiled; and Herod, by pointing from his palace-windows to the Temple he had magnificently rebuilt, could seem to prove to those strangers that he took a great interest in religious things. He could readily give a sanctimonious coloring to his really strong desire to find the Child. The wily old politician's show of cordiality must have been a masterpiece of polite dissembling; and it was a success, for the Wise Men meant to come back to him.

There is another explanation of their hasting away, which is even better suited to their character. The quality of these men was of the best. In their hasting from Jerusalem undoubting faith instantly passed into corresponding action; showing they were of a kind of men whom, from Abraham to Paul, God seems greatly to prize. Such strong souls finish their course. Irresolute, double-minded men, an Apostle saith, receive nothing of the Lord; and the Lord himself said, the violent take the Kingdom of Heaven by force. When the Wise Men had learned where the child of their desire must be, their need of rest, the honors of the court, converse with the wise, even the services of the Temple, could not stay their pressing on. Theirs, the resolution our Lord so often enjoins. Theirs, the hope his Apostles so earnestly commend, that runs to win. Theirs, the true spirit of the Christian race, as they pressed on to the mark of the prize of their high calling of God in Christ Jesus. This is one of the Lessons of their history; and it accords with the beauty of the whole ordering of the Kingdom of Grace, that the first of the nations who sought the Lord, set this high example of earnest resolve.

Their faith was born of his oracles. They believed in his Scriptures; and this, too, is one of the Lessons, as it is one of the evidences, of their history. If it be inquired, How could Persians have believed in Hebrew Scripture? the answer, elsewhere more fully given,* is this: they believed in the God of Israel, as did their King Darius; they believed in Hebrew Scripture, as did Cyrus, the High Priest, and Founder of their nation. The Temple which met their eyes in Jerusalem was built by his decree, and it attested to his faith in Hebrew prophecy. Thus, in Scripture, one event answers to another. Its great facts tower above long intervening wastes of time, like the far-severed yet kindred peaks of a mountain range.

A DIFFICULTY NOT HERETOFORE CONSIDERED.

How consistent the intervention of the Supernatural with the natural when the Pilgrims went forth from what was to them the Holy City but in name, how accordant their Guiding with their virtue and need, how appropriate to the opening of the kingdom of all nations, and how prophetic of the Age that then began—has been shown. The reasoning against it, that errs in opposing the astronomical to the natural idea of the heavens, has been answered. For a theory as to the mode of that miracle that makes it almost incredible, there has been substituted

---

* See The Wise Men, chap. iii, pp. 90, 91.

another, against which rationalism, save that it would deny all things, can allege nothing ; and having set aside these and other objections to the history of the Wise Men, I would now offer one, that through its answer, one fact in that history, which is far too little thought of, may stand out in bolder relief.

St. Peter's Confession of the Divinity of the Lord Jesus, from which time the Church began,* with a Life, the same in essence with that in the old Dispensation but so much higher in degree, that the least in the new is greater than the greatest prophet in the old,†—a Confession in the worship of these Persians like unto his, proves them partakers in the same life with the Apostle. The proof that they had this life is this : our Lord said, " He that believeth in Me hath Life," and they believed in Him. This belief appears simultaneously with the Life. The one is the vital breath, the other its breathing.

These Persians, then, were born before the time into the Kingdom of Heaven. It may seem strange to say this, when the kingdom of heaven seems not then to have begun to be ; but in both the kingdom of Nature and the kingdom of Grace, there are facts which, in a time point of view, are similar. To speak paradoxically, there are in each, beginnings before the beginning. In both worlds the Word of God exults in type and prophecy. In one cycle of time

---

* Matt. xvi, 13–20.

† Matt. xi, 11 : " Verily I say unto you, Among them that are born of women there hath not risen a greater than John the Baptist : notwithstanding he that is least in the kingdom of heaven is greater than he."

and life the naturalist sees the appearing of what
seems to belong to a later time and higher cycle of
being; and the like may be seen in the spiritual
world. In each cycle of life, whether natural or
spiritual, fore-intimations are given of higher life.
In the spiritual cycle, this higher stage of life is
through the quickening of the same life-giving Spirit
by whom what was before was so made, that the
new might thus be quickened within the old. Such
changes come about at great epochs wherein old
things give place to new. And, before these, there
are premonitions and foretokens of the coming
change; and, highest prophecy thereof, the fact that
is to be, itself appears. One clear illustration of
this in the Kingdom of Grace, is the Resurrection of
many saints in Jerusalem, on the Day of the Crucifixion, before our Lord's Resurrection, a prophetic
fact, and sign of the Resurrection of all saints. Another is this: the Descent of the Third Person of
the Holy Trinity was on the Day of Pentecost, yet
before that day our Lord breathed on his disciples
and said, Receive ye the Holy Ghost.

Facts, such as these, make it probable that the
Life in the Soul, higher in degree in the new Dispensation than in the old, may have appeared in the
Old when the time of its end drew nigh, as sign and
evidence of the spiritual unity of the new and the
old. This typical, prophetic quickening of the New
Life could only have been in some few who were the
flower and crown of the old religion. Only in such
could its types and prophecies of a higher spiritual
life have passed over into the fact itself. It is diffi-

cult to believe this could have been even in Israel;
and if the New Life appeared in any of the heathen,
it would seem that it must have been inbreathed into
their souls by the Holy Spirit through the contact
of their spirits with some in Israel in whom there
was the breath of this New Life. For the Christian
Reason can no more do without the cardinal fact of
the oneness of the spiritual being of the children of
God from the beginning to the end of the world,
constituting them all one race, than the Scientific
Reason can do without the cardinal fact of the oneness of all Life in nature. If the connection in
these chains of related being be severed anywhere,
for one instant, in one minutest link, the kingdom of God is no longer his kingdom, and never
could have been his kingdom at all, for every-where
and at all times his kingdom is one. The Christian
Reason denies there can be any break in the chains
of being, whether in the realms of nature, life, or
grace; yet here, in the highest of these realms in
whose indivisible trinity is the unity of the universe,
this seems to appear in the Worship of the Lord by
the Wise Men in Bethlehem.

The explanation elsewhere given of that Worship,
combined their Oriental, Persian idea of a king as
God's representative on earth, their ancient patriarchal traditions, the teaching of Hebrew prophets
in the Far East, and the Miracle of the Guiding; yet
is there given only as its partial explanation. It is
too outward. It does not reach far enough. It does
not touch the heart of the mystery. All those things
prepared for that worship, they tended toward and

were in harmony with it ; but they were not in contact with it.   Its immediate, efficient, only cause was
the Holy Spirit ; and it would seem that the medium
of His influence which imparted a new Life to their
souls could only have been some soul or souls in
Israel to whom this new life had been given before.
That new Life from which came the Worship of
Christ by the Magi could not have been inbreathed
into their souls through contact with the Church
they found in Jerusalem, for it had but a name to
live and was dead.   Here, then, is a fault in the chain
of spiritual being ; and this argument against the fact
that the Magi worshiped Christ is here presented in
order to secure a hearing for the only interpretation
of this part of the history of the Wise Men that can
give to it an answer.

THE WORSHIP OF CHRIST BY THE MAGI CONSEQUENT UPON THE FAITH OF THE BLESSED MOTHER.

As the spiritual children of Abraham were ever
distinct from Abraham's race, so, distinct in spirit
from that Church in Jerusalem, which knew not the
Messiah was born, which learned it with alarm from
strangers, and which crucified the Lord—distinct
in spirit from that dead Church, there was a living
Church in Israel.   The silence of Scripture seems to
make it certain that with this living Church the Magi
were not in contact in Jerusalem.   Whether or not
they clearly understood this, they must have felt it ;
for the hardest trial of souls seeking Christ is, to find
a Church that is dead, to touch what is thought to
be the Lord's body, and to touch a corpse.   How

this tried their faith, and how marvelous their faith, is known when Nature was made to give them the guidance man should have given and did not give.

By the guiding of His star they found the Lord outwardly, even as the soldiers of Herod would have found Him had they gone with them ; but this could not have been that spiritual finding of Him of which their worship is sign and evidence. Their true finding of Him was in their own souls. His Life in them recognized its source in Him, and adored his uncreate, essential Deity. This Life in them must have been inbreathed through communion with his Church in Israel ; and without the fact of such communion their history would be imperfect, and being so, could not be sacred history.

By these words the sacred history is made perfect : " And when they were come into the house, they saw the young Child with Mary his Mother, and fell down, and worshiped Him." This naming of the presence of the Blessed Mother at the instant of their worship reveals that there was some relation between that worship of her Son and Her who is named in such close connection with it. Here the form of the statement is of the substance of the truth conveyed. *It is not written*—When they saw the young Child they fell down and worshiped Him. The Holy Spirit gives the facts in this form : " They saw the young Child *with Mary his Mother*, and fell down, and worshiped *Him*." In this naming of the Blessed Mother there is the record of the fact that seemed wanting on the sacred page.

To this Worship all this history tends. It gives

unity and highest meaning to all before. For this the Star was seen in the distant East at its first shining into these heavens. For this the Star was made to guide the Magi to that house where they beheld Him of whom the heavens had prophesied. In describing this worship the Holy Spirit speaks of their beholding Him "with his mother" before their falling down and worshiping Him is told; and He thus reveals that the Blessed Mother was the human cause of that worship, whose Divine cause was the Holy Ghost.

Trains of events converged to that hour from the birth of time. Events in history, from when the Prophet, suborned by kings to curse the Prince of the House of David in the person of his people, was made to predict the Star of the Lord, from when Daniel interpreted to Cyrus words of the God of Heaven commanding him to rebuild His house in Jerusalem while consenting Magi wondered and approved, the Star in the sky above, and faith in the hearts of men below, all met together in that central hour in honor of Christ. But the Spirit of God marks only that She was there, the Blessed Mother. For Her, as one of its ends, had been the election of Israel, that in the family of Abraham, the house of David, should be born the Woman worthy to nurture the Holy Child—the Woman predicted in the hour of man's ruin—the Woman who is in the place of the Woman who fell—the Woman who, as the Mother of Jesus, is the Mother of all the Living. In the Blessed Mother the Representatives of the Nations found the Church they did not find in Jerusalem. To the

22

Blessed Mary those strangers were known in their true relation to the ancient prophecy of a stranger, and in them the Mother of our Lord welcomed the Nations to her Son. Through her lips the Holy Spirit may have opened to them the Scriptures. But the Evangelist, who must have received his knowledge of this hour from the Blessed Mother, was not permitted to record her words of salutation, nor theirs of reply. His silence seems to reveal, that when the Holy Child was shown no word was spoken. There is a soul-like speech of the eye, perhaps a fore-gleaming of the language of seraphs reading in and through the eye the thoughts of seraphs, and may not that moment of the Epiphany have been too spiritual and holy for other language?

In a lonely dwelling those Pilgrims, familiar with the palaces of earthly kings, saw a little, helpless, speechless babe, but with Him they saw His Mother. In her, that religion which the Word of God from the hour of the fall of man had instituted for all was incarnate. The light of its burning types and prophecies was in her eyes. When the Blessed Mother showed to the Magi her Son, the love and adoration of those eyes may have met the eyes of the Pilgrims, the first of an endless succession, and through that look of Hers, the Eternal Spirit may, in that instant, have so kindled their faith, that sinking to the earth they worshiped him as the Eternal God. The manner of her influence is unrevealed, but the fact is there on the Record. This spiritual miracle, this prophetic miracle at the opening of the new age, this great miracle, higher in degree than that of the Star, was wrought through Her Faith, whom all nations shall call Blessed.

NOTE.—Exceptions are often taken to the manner of the presentation of truth which hinder its reception, even though they do not touch the substance of the truth presented. What here is of the substance is, 1. The spiritual miracle in the worship of the Magi: (as to the greatness of this, see chap. iii, pp. 149–151.) 2. The revelation that the Blessed Mother was instrumental in their worship of her Son. To some of the opinions set forth above, others may be preferred, without its really touching these great and sure facts. Possibly, in the East, or in the Far East, the Magi may have met with some of Israel, like Simeon or Anna ; or even in Jerusalem. The silence of Scripture makes strongly against the probability of the latter supposition. But if either were the case, and if the Magi thus became participant in that New Life, which then could only have been most rare, and only in the highest spiritual conditions, while this would, in some respects, change what is written above, it would not change those two great facts.

It may be said, that as the Magi came " to worship the King of the Jews," they only carried out their previous intent in Bethlehem, and so the Blessed Mother could have had nothing to do with their worship. But, while the word which is rendered worship is in both cases the same, it may have had a higher religious significance on the lips of the Evangelist than on those of the Magi in Jerusalem. Its meaning, as used by him, is determined by this use of it in the last chapter of his Gospel, 17, 18: " Then the eleven disciples went away into Galilee, into a mountain where Jesus had appointed them, and when they saw Him they *worshiped* Him, but some doubted."

My opinion is firmly held, that in Bethlehem the Magi recognized the true Divinity of Christ, as did the eleven disciples (that is, as most of them did) on that mountain in Galilee ; but even if their worship reached not so far, the two great facts remain. The religious honor given to the Lord by those not of the house of Israel, and after the faith of those strangers had been so tried in Jerusalem, is still a great and (as they were the Representatives of the Nations) a prophetic spiritual fact.

That even to the lower form of faith in her Son the presence of the Blessed Mother may have been helpful, will be readily admitted by those who remember St. Peter's paroxysm of doubt as he walked on the water. The human spirit has often faltered in the moment of the decisive act, that very moment to which it had long been going forward with scarce a doubt, and then at a look, or word of cheer and faith from another, has cleared what else it would seem it could not pass. How many death-beds have shown all that!

The minds of the Magi were high-wrought by the miracle outside of the house—how natural a reaction, how sudden may have been a sinking of their hearts at the instant when they lost sight of the Star within that poor little, humble room! Would this have been more strange, would it not have been quite as natural as Elijah's running away, after the sight of the miracle on Mount Carmel, into the desert and lying down to die? The poverty of the place may have frightened them. But the woman there! She enriched the room. She made them feel it was the house of God, the very gate of heaven. To the lower view of their worship she may then have been indispensable. To the higher view of it she must have been. Take either view of their worship, yet the fact that she then was indispensable to it appears on the Record. On her faith, in her reply to the annunciation by the angel, (Luke i, 38,) the Incarnation followed; on her faith, at the marriage in Cana of Galilee (John iii, 5) followed the first miracle wrought by her Son; and in Bethlehem the worship of Him by those who were the first fruits of the Nations. Whatever the worship of the Magi, whatever their need, and however the aid of the Blessed Mother was given to their worship, whether by word, or look, or prayer, or all combined, or by some act of Hers worshiping Him, the fact is revealed that of their worship, She was the immediate human cause. Not thus to honor the faith of His Blessed Mother is not to do fitting honor to her Son, who is "the author and finisher of Faith."

CHAPTER IX.

THE LESSON TO MEN OF SCIENCE.

NOW that the cloud around the pilgrimage to Bethlehem is dissolved in light, Men of Science may read the lesson, set for them to learn, in the evangel of the Magi. But as the culture of the Eastern world was all represented by the Magi, the compass of the phrase, Men of Science, must here be enlarged to the breadth of this fact. It must here include all men of letters and of art. To the poet, sculptor, painter, to the philosopher and the historian, to the chemist, to the physician, to each and all of the students of nature, as well as to the astronomer, the lesson in this Gospel is addressed.

The Magi believed there was more in Nature than the natural, more in human affairs than the human. " Conversant with His works, they searched for God diligently." * It was this God-seeking spirit in them which God honored, when they made the greatest of astronomical discoveries ; when the scientific finding of the secret of the universe was prefigured as Nature led them to the house in which was the Lord ; and when the Magi, unconsciously prophesying of the future of science, worshiped Christ as God. The lesson in their history reveals the spirit in which the greatest discoveries in nature are made ; and that

---

* Wisdom of Solomon, chap. xiii, 7.

*the highest office of Nature is to guide to Christ, the
true end of Science, the worship of the Lord.*

Faith in the Divine Unity was early broken up
into a worship of many gods. Yet some lingering
reminiscence of the One Supreme Being long gave
aspiration and impulse to Science, which in the
earliest historic ages seems every-where to have
been religious. It must be confessed, by all who are
willing to do justice to great men whose works are
their only records, that the achievements of the men
of ancient Science go far to equal those of the men
of modern Science—due regard being had to the
novelty and difficulty of the problems they solved;
and if belief in the one God, though rapidly degen-
erating, so quickened and so upheld their Science, it
might seem that the full belief of this truth might
suffice to stimulate and encourage the scientific spirit
to the utmost and forever.

But there is a Divine lesson in modern History
that teaches otherwise. God rent the orb of civilization in twain. He gave the southern half to Deism,
the northern half to Christianity. He made the contrast between the two religions sharp, the struggle
between them well-balanced and severe; and the lesson of it plain. The religion of Islam drew from the
patriarchal religion traditions traceable in the Koran,
and resembling those in Genesis, but independently
preserved in the memory of the desert; it owed much
to the Hebrew, a little to the Christian religion;
and was truth in comparison with Arabian idolatry.
Its central idea of the unity of God kindled in de-
generate Ishmael the genius of science and art; and

for a time Deism grew a civilization better than that
of Christian countries. Humanizing barbarians, it
built in the Ottoman Empire hospitals of charity and
mercy, solid, immense structures which, though now
uncared for and empty, yet more than the chambers
of the Alhambra, attest to the ennobling power of
Deism. But this quick and brilliant spring of Mohammedan civilization ripened into no summer. By
its aspiration and impulse Deism carried civilization
to a certain height; and then it helplessly and hope-
lessly curved downward. The minarets of the once
Christian cities, Constantinople, Alexandria, and Jerusalem, still send forth the call to prayer, "God is
great;" yet well the Moslem forbodes the coming
end of the long historical experiment that proves the
inferiority of Deism to Christianity.

Is it said, that if the Thought of God, the grandest
of all thoughts, cannot uphold man in any thing it is
well for him to do, there is none that can? it is true
only when said of the Father as revealed by the Son:
for it is written, no man knoweth the Father but the
Son, and he to whom the Son shall reveal him. The
grand old Patriarchal Idea of God was but the gateway to the Mystery of Redemption ; and so it is but
the gateway to the Mystery of Nature. The Patriarchs sought to look into Redemption, the sages of
old to look into Nature ; but even the Prophets could
not then clearly behold the Lord, through whom
alone is manifest all that can be known of nature.
The science of these last days has clearer vision of
God, and therefore is wiser and firmer in purpose
than the science of old ; but more than Deism is

needed by science. The work of the Lord redeeming
is one with His work creating; and Science must
trace in Nature the purposes, and carry out the work
of the redeeming Lord, or at last her sight and her
strength will fail, and her path will end.

The Earth seems but a poor home for women and
children when storms are wide-raging on the sea, and

            — Like a drop of rain
Man sinks into its depths, with bubbling groan,
Without a grave, unknelled, uncoffined, and unknown;

when earthquakes, like that of Lima, crush and
drown twenty thousand, or that of Lisbon sixty thousand, human beings; or when the pestilence walks
in darkness and wastes at noon-day. Horrors like
these have ever kindled the doubt whether there be
not a lack of power, or of wisdom, in the Maker of
the world; or whether, if not merciless, He be not
at least careless of his creatures. These doubts were
ever rebuked by manifold tokens of benevolence in
all the Divine works; yet the heathen world, at its
best estate, has ever been full of such dark and troub-
ling thoughts, as it is now. Even to Christians, there
has ever been, and there still is, much in this world
that is very dark—as the sufferings of the mute
creation, and the death of infants. All this darkness
seems to have been meant to drive man to faith, to
make him look beyond this changing scene of men
and things. But there has been and is so much on
the earth that is strange and fearful; since the Christian era the problem of sin has grown so much greater
and more intense, through many iniquities unknown
before, such as the burning to death by the Inquisi-

tion in Spain of twenty thousand persons for their
religious belief, that faith such as the patriarchs had
could hardly continue in the earth, were it not for
the light ever more and more shining forth from the
Cross upon this increasing darkness.

But, withdrawing our thoughts from spiritual and
moral guilt, and limiting them to those physical evils
against which Christ has set science to contend ;—
even from their presence, science can bring no full
relief.   There seems to be no hope that science will
free the world of poverty, old age, and death.   And,
so far from being a sufficient Teacher of religious
truths, a purely Deistic science culminates in the
experimental verification of seemingly immutable
laws. These, though awe-inspiring symbols, reveal a
Being on whom the heart can take so little hold, that
at length the Deism of science tends to congeal into
Atheism.

That which was known of God in the patriarchal
ages must open into the fullness of the Divine manifestation in Christ Jesus, or it cannot completely and
forever so satisfy the Heart, as forever more and more
to quicken the Mind.   Only in Christ and him crucified is the Divine Mercy and Love for man beyond
all doubt.   Only when it is known that, by its seeming imperfection, the Creating Word conformed the
world to his foreseen work as the Redeeming Word,
is the ever-increasing darkness of the world touched
and dissolved with light.   A perfect world might
have done for angels ; this imperfect world is suited
to men.   It is perfect in this, that it perfectly answers its moral ends.   It is the fit dwelling-place for

an apostate race, whom the Lord Jesus would bring back to God, alike by restraint and freedom, by sorrow and gladness, by fear and gratitude, by punishment and mercy. Believing that in Nature the justice of the Judge of all the earth is every-where tempered by his love and mercy, believing that the Lord in the making of the world every-where thought of man, and pre-fashioned the powers in Nature to the human powers, Science in his name can evoke them from their hiding places, in full assurance of faith, that they must do her bidding.

What is the finding of Christ by Men of Science? It is the being filled with his Spirit. What is the worship of the Lord by Men of Science? It is the working with Him in his great work of redeeming the world from sorrow and pain, the correlative of his greater work of redeeming it from sin. Through this worship of Christ by Men of Science, the wilderness and the solitary place shall be glad for them, and the desert shall rejoice and blossom like the rose. It shall blossom abundantly, and rejoice with joy and singing.

Faith is the life of Science, and losing this it would soon turn to corruption and pass into nothingness. Only by faith in the Redeeming Lord can science be firmly and forever held to the severe task of subduing Nature. Without the thought of the unity of all Nature, and of great purposes that run through all time and all worlds, which science receives from Christ, even her rich rewards and worldly honors would not long lead on her toilsome march, nor preserve her past acquisitions. Those rewards never had much to do with the efforts of men of science. The Divine Thought that Man is to have dominion over the powers of Nature overmasters their souls. They seem to feel as if the set time for this drew nigh. Their sympathies seem to be with the humble rather than with the great. They seem to see that the Star of our Lord points not to kings' houses, but to the manger and the babe. To soften the lot of labor they have labored, and to help the poor they have been poor. They have cheered life with comforts, adorned it with elegancies, in which their own share has been small. They have realized the wild dreams of the Alchemist and the Magician: but not for themselves. They have enriched others. How much of Christ-like work they have done, lessening labor and pain! How much of this with a martyr-like zeal, sacrificing to it every other hope, and with little or no wish save that of doing this for man! often hardly conscious of their best motive, yet sustained by it through unrequited years! How many of these direct and simple men have done these things and not known for Whom! When the Son of Man shall come in his glory, He will say to some: "I was an hungered, and ye gave me meat: I was thirsty, and ye gave me drink: I was naked, and ye clothed me: I was sick, and ye visited me." And, surely there will be men of Science among those bewildered by His words and saying, "Lord, when saw we Thee an hungered, and fed Thee? or thirsty, and gave Thee drink? when saw we Thee naked, and clothed Thee? when saw we Thee sick, and came unto Thee? And the King shall answer and say unto them, Inasmuch as ye did it unto one of the least of these, ye did it unto ME."

Science has too little known Christ, who is her guide. She has been led by Him in ways she dimly knew. She is not in cordial, intelligent accord with Faith. In the main she has wrought for Christ, yet sometimes has fought hard against Him. *Where is her path, and what her bourne?* There are those who fear that Science is passing into Atheism. The reason seems to be this: a purely Deistic Science must report that inflexible, remorseless Law is all that it can discern; when it tries to pronounce the Word of God as the sum of Nature's teaching, it cannot reconcile all the word now suggests with what it sees; and so Deism, its first utterance changed on the lips of the astronomer La Place, and Humboldt the naturalist, into Atheism.

Is Atheism, then, to be the teaching of Nature and the end of Science? No. Look again into the evangel of the Magi, and there see Nature guiding men of Science to Christ. From time to time the Lord holds out to all students of Nature signs and symbols of his presence, which He alone can interpret to the reason, and these He interprets through his written word and by his Church. Thus in new ways and forms, the opening of the evangel of his Star ever repeats itself. It is so in Astronomy; it is so in History, in Medicine; it is so in Music and Art. With its facts in part interpreted by means of religious ideas and traditions, Science comes to what claims to be the Church, to know more. In the parable of the Wise Men of old a king is troubled, and all his city with him, at their news of the discovery of a divine signal in the realm of Nature. King and priest have to take cognizance of the wonderful tidings. A politic encouragement is given to those men of Science. With an honorable pretense, with a purpose which is deceitful and deadly, they are told to go and find out more, to return and report what they find. A Divine dream warns them not to return to Herod, and Science no more goes back to Jerusalem.

The Church in Jerusalem had failed to do her full office. The Lord had come very nigh, but she knew it not till she was thus strangely told, and she was then filled with alarm. Then her office to guide men seeking in Nature for more than the natural, seeking in the Human for the Divine, was given to Nature. In this there seems prefigured what has been and is. Science has been to Jerusalem. She has there conferred with king and priest, and she has turned her back upon them. To them she joins herself no more.* She is following a light in Nature. The awe of the supernatural is upon her. She is led by Nature, but it is Nature controlled and made to guide her from on high. Whither she is going she knows not. The night is around her and she is alone. She follows the moving light, but knows not what it is. She is seeking she knows not what, even as the Magi

---

* Science put the musket into the hands of the common man. The first ball that pierced the plate-armor of a knight shivered the feudalism of the Middle Ages. Then the day of the King was done. Science put the printed Bible into the hands of the people, for them to read it. Then the day of the Priest was done.

knew not what they were seeking. The natural, supernatural light pointed the Magi to a house, and they rejoiced with exceeding great joy. That house was a Temple. It was a figure of the Temple of the universe. There the Guiding of Nature ended. The Magi came into the presence of Christ. The thing that has been is the thing that shall be, and there is nothing new under the sun. What was thus pre-figured has come, and will come to pass. It was a sure word of prophecy, when at the opening of His universal kingdom, His own Star led to Christ men who represented the Science of the world; and thus runs on this prophecy: " When they saw the young Child and his Mother, they fell down and worshiped Him ; *and when they had opened their treasures, they presented unto Him gifts.*"

CHAPTER X.

THE HOLY INNOCENTS.

THE Holy Spirit, and the holy angels, move the soul in ways which are conformed to the soul's estate. As star-gazers, the Magi were led by a Star; as dreamers, they were led by a Dream.

DREAMS OF THE MAGI AND OF JOSEPH.

In the New Testament six dreams are told; and all in the Gospel by St. Matthew. For telling these, some of those infidel scholars, whose show of acuteness and learning is but a show, have called the writer of that Gospel a credulous man, bending a listening ear to legendary tales. Here, as usual, they evidently have not looked into the facts with that closeness of observation which the facts in Scripture, like those in nature, ever reward. Matthew naturally thought much of the dream of the wife of the Roman Governor of Jerusalem, because he himself had been in the service of Rome; and this warning dream, which came on the night before the Crucifixion to Claudia Procula, Pilate's wife, and was told to Pilate in the Judgment-hall, meant too much, and the word she sent with it meant too much, for them to pass unrecorded.

In the common dreaming that comes of light or broken slumbers, the half-awake soul is no fit recipient of supernatural influences; but there is a deep repose, a seeming death of all but organic life, in which, if the soul awake to full consciousness, it may be in a most fitting state to hold converse with the invisible powers. This is so peculiar a state, that its repetition in the same person would be probable ; and, so, the temperament of Joseph, the Dreamer, which may have determined the form of his first spiritual visitation, as naturally may have determined the form of the second, the third, and the fourth. This goes some way to make the recital of his four dreams but as the recital of one.

Five of the six dreams were caused by questions so arising out of supernatural interventions as to call for supernatural answers. The Magi meant to go back to Jerusalem ; but that may naturally have come up again at Bethlehem. There, for the first time, perhaps, they seriously began to consider it. A word or start of alarm from Joseph at their coming, and what they could not but have seen in the face of old Herod, double-faced as he was, or have heard of his history, little as they may have understood the politics of his kingdom, would have been enough, when they saw that poor and defenseless Family, to set them thinking. Viewed on its human side, their dreaming shows they passed, with this trouble on their minds, into that land of shadows, where they were warned not to go back to Herod.

It was a glorious, yet a troubled night. To Joseph, troubled by the publicity which the coming of the Magi gave to the birth and dwelling-place of the child, there came the angel, who told him to go down into Egypt. But for this, Joseph could no more have

known what he ought to do than the Magi, of themselves, could have known what they ought to do. It
was too much for him to decide to take the Holy
Child out of the Holy Land. The City and Temple
of God were there, and there it must have seemed
to him that the Holy Family should dwell. That he
took the Holy Child away from the Holy Land was
so strange, that the Evangelist, as if it were hard to
believe, points to Israel sojourning in Egypt; thus
revealing, that as many in Israel were, so was Israel
itself, a type of Christ.

To the Magians a dream appeared; to the child
of Jacob, in a dream, the angel of the Lord. Thus,
these supernatural visitings were every way suited to
those to whom they came; and from the agreement
in one minutest particular, of the dream of the Magi
with the last dream of Joseph, may be drawn important conclusions, which throw some new light on one
of the most difficult questions as to the harmony of
the Gospels. The troubled Magi, warned not to go
back to Herod, went, of course, to their own country.
Their warning, and that in the last dream of Joseph,
furnish evidence of what has been said before:—that,
while in Nature there is that which looks like waste,
a thousand acorns falling and one oak growing, Supernatural power runs not even to seeming profusion.
The higher up in the world of grace the more simple
seem the means, the greater the economy of power:
—something as in this world, where the rich, the
strong, the wise, proportion the means to the end,
while the poor, the weak, and the foolish are improvi-
dent and wasteful. The Holy Family were on a

journey at the time when Jesus was born; their home
was at Nazareth, within the old limits of the land of
Israel. In Egypt Joseph was told to take the young
Child and go into the land of Israel. It would seem
then, that, when he came up out of Egypt he would
have known where to go. But as all Jews then felt
that Judea was exclusively the Holy Land, no doubt
Joseph thought he must take the Holy Child back to
the town or city of David. No doubt he was going
to one of these, but—probably after he had crossed
the desert into the settled plain along the sea, where
the Judean highlands could be seen along the eastern
horizon—such unlooked for bad news met him from
Jerusalem that he was afraid to go up into Judea,
and *he knew not where to go.* Then, divinely told,
just as the Magi were, where not to go *and nothing
more*, he gladly hastened* to cross the border line
of Galilee; and then naturally turned aside to his
old home, and dwelt in Nazareth.† Galilee was then
very much a heathen country. Part of it was called
Galilee of the heathen. It had passed into a proverb,
that from Galilee no prophet came. It was as thick-
ly studded with towns and villages as Belgium is
now; and among those towns Nazareth had a well-

---

* All this seems to be in the Greek αναχωρησεν.

† Skeptics have said that the Evangelists Matthew and Luke
contradict each other as to the home of the Holy Family, and
that St. Matthew did not know that Joseph had before lived in
Nazareth. Yet here is evidence that he did—of a peculiar kind
no doubt, yet to my mind good evidence of it. I think the reasons can be given why St. Matthew was silent as to what was
afterward told by St. Luke, but the full consideration of this is
reserved for a book of Thoughts on the Gospel of St. Matthew.

known evil reputation.* The knowledge of the reason of this has passed away, but the fact appears in
the Gospel. That so thoughtful a man as Joseph
brought up the Holy Child in one of the wickedest
towns † in that wicked Galilean country, never could
be accounted for from St. Matthew's Gospel only.
St. Luke tells us how it came about. God had appointed this town to Joseph as his home, before that
through the decree of Cæsar Augustus, he sent him
on his journey to Bethlehem. Hence, when it was
made known to Joseph that the Holy Child need
not be brought up in the Holy Judea, his road to
Nazareth was as clear as theirs to the Magi, when
they went to their own country. Thus, the fulfilling
of what all prophecy had prophesied of Christ—that
He should be despised of men—was, as naturally as
it was unconsciously brought about by Joseph, so far
as this—the manifestation of Christ unto Israel was
from a town so bad that it was enough to ruin a
man's reputation to have lived there.

AFTER the Wise Men left the village of Bethlehem
no more is known of them; and here we might take
leave of their history had not the murder of the boys
of Bethlehem been consequent upon their Pilgrimage.
The gold of the Magi came in good time for the flight
of the Holy Family; and Joseph, the blessed Mother,
and the Holy Child, were on their way down into
Egypt, and the Magi on their way to Persia, before
Herod, perhaps, knew the Magi had left his guarded
town. When he knew they had left his country he

---

* John i, 46.   † Luke iv, 28, 29.

was exceeding wroth. In wrath, in madness even, there was a quick cunning in Herod, and knowing that such pretenders to the throne of his house would be most dangerous, he did not try to single out the One, but meant to be rid of all the boys to whom the coming of the Magi might in future afford a pretext for appealing to the Star. His murder of all the boys of Bethlehem suits his well-known sagacity and thoroughness. It was so effectual, that no political adventurer of the next generation in Judea connected his birth with the Pilgrimage to the town of David. A thrice-repeated swiftness, not to have been fore-seen, baffled the king. He failed, as man must fail when Heaven opposes. In his youth the wrath of Herod was the wrath of a king ; in his old age he was at times little better than a madman ; and the wonder of certain critics at his order to slay all the boys in Bethlehem of two years old is reasonless.

But this is a great wonder! how this cruel wrong could ever have been suffered to be! The first-born of the girlish Jewish wife and her graceful husband, the youngest born, the fond delight of doating grand-parents, the sweet babes of Bethlehem, in whose cradles were hopes more precious than all the gold of the Temple, were murdered, and the quiet hills resounded with wailing. Their mothers looked up to the skies and cursed the king. Herod dies. Yet how strange the consequences of the Witness of the Wise to the Son of God! the exile of Jesus, the death of those boys! In the first lines of life, the Holy One is subject to more than the common lot. The infant Redeemer seems to be the destruction of those born with Him. In all the darkness of human life, what is there so dark as the death of an infant? yet here it seems a consequence of the Birth of the Life Himself! And then it is so strange, that the murder of those boys should have been consequent upon the Pilgrimage of heaven-guided worthies, that he who believes and yet inquires may reverently ask, Might it not have been as well had their little bodies been buried out of sight, this horror forgotten?—a question that leads on to a great truth which is revealed through the massacre of the Innocents of Bethlehem.

THE HISTORICAL FORM OF THE WRITTEN WORD.

Though the Globe endure for a time proportioned to the long ages of its growth, there will ever come to light in the Bible more and more of the wisdom it brings nigh to man, not in abstract forms, but inwrought into human lives and trains of events, which through the essential sameness of all human things are everlasting parables. Though Christianity is often said to be a system of truths, even its most mysterious truths are facts. In the Written Word truths are not usually set forth in the form of principles, but embodied in facts; and the seeming exceptions to its historical way of presenting truths are, in most cases, more seeming than real. Through the facts in Scripture the soul receives the clearest and highest form of a truth it can at once receive; and the study of the facts, more and more brings out that truth which dwells in them. The final reason for the historical form of the Written Revelation may be this : the Infinite reveals Himself through the forthgoings of his

Word ; only through history can these be portrayed, for the soul can form no picture of these goings-forth in themselves ; words are but pictures of thoughts, and the Written Word must conform to the limitations of the soul and of its language.

The visible things are so fashioned as to help the soul's thinking of the things invisible. As seen from this, that all names of things spiritual were originally names of visible things, bearing some fancied or real resemblance to the spiritual things of which they are supposed to be pictures, though in truth they are little or nothing more than symbols. Thus, in many languages, breath, the original meaning of the word spirit, became the name for the immaterial essence there is in man, because it seemed the best picture-symbol of itself the soul could find. This picture-like stage of words tends to pass away, and their symbolic meaning fades out. Thus they change into mere names that stand directly for thoughts. In this change in speech something of freshness, of clearness, and wisdom, passes from thoughts, as well as from words. Thus, languages grow old ; and had not languages, other than the one before common to all the living, been called out at Babel, so that different tongues might act and interact upon each other, and had not some of these been providentially renovated, Language, the great instrument of thought, would have worn out with using.

Of each spiritual thing we may know that it is ; we can name it from some symbolic thing, and trace its effects, though we know not what, or how, it is. Philosophy tries to find out things in their essence ;

but in that direction there is a barrier to knowledge, while its field opens wide in another direction. Take that of which the word Life is the picture-symbol, and then the name :—all attempts to find out what Life is in itself end in calling it a form of matter, or a form of God ; and these materialistic and pantheistic speculations, old as recorded thought, and ever recurring in new forms with nothing new but the form, show such attempts are vain. But in the direction of its conditions, effects, and laws, what endless fields Life opens ! what difficult, useful, delightful Sciences, boundless enough for all human desire and effort !

The mode of the Written Word may, perhaps, be illustrated by the way all that can be known of Life is known. For Life is the consequence of the forth-goings of the Living Word. It is written, "That which was made in Him was Life."* In Life in this high, deep, and broad sense of the term ; in Life as running clear down through all things, in Life as expressing the material as well as the spiritual creation, in Life in this universal sense, the Word of God glasses Himself, so that from it His image is thrown back, as the image of the sky from the mirror of a lake. The lake-mirror is real, the sky is real, the image is neither the one nor the other : so, the Living Universe is not the Word of God, nor is it his image. It is the mirror from which his reflected image meets the eye of the soul ; and the clearness of the reflection will be as the polish of the mirror, and the purity of the eye.

The self-revealing of the Living Word follows in

---

* This seems to be the meaning in John i, 3.

the Written Word the same mode as in all Space and Time. With no vain effort to set forth the Infinite One in words, with none of those grotesque or horrible genealogies of the Creator that provoke our wonder in the mythologies of the nations, the ravings of the Gnostics; with no attempt at the impossible elucidation of how it was done, as in the Indian dreams of Spinoza and Hegel; it is written; God created the heavens and the earth. Then follows the recital of six goings forth of the Eternal Word, with divine compression of the facts, tracing the continuous line of these in nature up to the creation of man. The ongoings of the Word are then, for the most part, revealed in the central family of the human race, until this portraiture of Him completes itself in Christ Jesus and Him Crucified, and in the vision of his universal and everlasting kingdom.

The Bible is a compend of the whole Revelation of God in Space and Time ; and, if man will take the Bible for his guide and light, he can make all nature and all history like unto the Bible in reflecting his glory. *For not the history of the Jews only, but all history, is a mirror that reflects the image of the Word of God.* The Bible itself is the proof of this. For it begins where Time began, it draws its line to where Time shall end, and it includes all Time between. In bringing to light the Presence of the Word with one people, it does not mean to deny it with others, *but to illustrate it.* If the history of other nations had been divinely written, the reflection of His Presence from their history might have been far less spiritually instructive, but would have been no less real than from that of the Jews. In its recital of the history of one people, the Bible makes the history of all intelligible, by disclosing the spiritual forces, ideas, and aims that fashion all history; by throwing light on the character and destiny of man, and on the being, purpose, and mode of working of the Word of God; and by prophetic light that suffuses all the future, awaking and guiding thought, even where it can hardly be said to illuminate it. It never contemplates other than the whole world. In presenting the central line of the world's life, how could the Word of God lose sight of the other lines, when to do this would be to lose sight of His own workings? and every-where in the Scripture are clear intimations of the Spirit, that he never does lose sight of these. St. Matthew opens his Gospel with a genealogy of Christ that has a narrow, Jewish look; but he grandly alters all the impression of this by the Coming from afar of the Witnesses of the Nations to the Lord. To the Birth of the Lord he gives a few verses, to this a chapter. By this brevity in the one case, (whatever other reasons for it he may have had,) and by this fullness in the other, he at once gave to his Evangel universality; and to his Lord his true place as the center of all humanity. Marking this, turn to the end of his Evangel, and see how its opening and its close agree. Turn then to the other Evangels: the Gospel according to St. Luke traces the genealogy of Christ to Adam; in the opening of the Gospel according to St. Mark there is no note of the family or nation of Christ Jesus, He is the Son of God; in the opening of the Gospel according to St. John He is the Maker of all things, through whom and in whom Life is in nature, Light is in the soul.

The upholding Presence of the Word in Nature and in Life, while yet they have a real existence, a true and proper selfhood, is the Great Mystery that explains all things, and is explained of none. By his mysterious presence therein the volume of Nature and the volume of History have everlasting significance. In those books of secrecy, it may be, that little can be made out of the spiritual meaning; but there is good hope of doing this as to the facts He chose, fashioned, and recorded for the instruction of man; and whose meaning ever grows more clear, because he guides and orders events to this end. Through its presentment of these facts the Bible *re-presents* the Word of God; and this it does in all the Scripture before His coming in the Form of man as in all afterwards; all being historical in spirit or in form, till, at its close, Prophecy takes the place of History in a vision of His ongoings to the end of Time and the World. Thus the whole Bible is the perfect mirror of his uncomprehended Deity. The Old Testament, like the New, is incorruptible and full of his glory. It was of the Old Testament that the Lord himself said, " In the Volume of the Book it is written of ME."

OF THE TRUTH EMBODIED IN THE GOSPEL OF THE INNOCENTS.

These general ideas as to Scripture compel me to presuppose, that *some truth of great moment is revealed through its history of the Massacre of the Innocents*

Its very strangeness and horror the more compel me to presuppose, that the open secret of the Almighty's permission of a murder so confounding to all preconceived ideas of the blessings the Holy Child would diffuse around Him, seemingly so out of keeping with the hallowed place and time, must be in some Lesson commensurate with the wide significance of those surpassing events with which it belongs.

What, it would seem must here be the fact, may be illustrated by what is written of the Death of our Lord: let us suppose the Evangel of His Life was before us for the first time and all at once; the prophecies which foretold, the wonders that attested his birth; how Nature and Death obeyed Him; till at last, nailed to the cross, he died. We should feel, we could not but feel, this was no common dying; that such a view of it was out of all fitness to the preceding life; that some great truth must be shrouded in that darkness, which, if seen, would enshrine that pale form in a brightness above that of the sun; that the whole history of the man Christ Jesus was incoherent and impossible, unless there were some Divine Mystery in the Cross.

Even· thus, when the death of the infants in Bethlehem is joined to that train of preceding events with which it belongs, we feel—with all of the certainty there is in the truth that Divine Wisdom ordereth in the affairs of men we know, this tragedy closed this grand procession with some Lesson of commanding moment. To the eye of sense how pitiable, that a Pilgrimage ordained before the heavens, led on by miracle, finding the Eternal Word manifest in the flesh, should leave as its monument in the town of David only the mound where lie the little associates of Jesus in the Mystery of Birth ! It cannot be, unless some treasure is buried in that grave. It cannot be, unless there cometh from that mound a voice which vindicates that sepulcher, unless the Gospel of these murdered Innocents reveals some truth that makes this strange thing harmonious with the whole of these events in manifesting the Divine glory. With any just idea of how truth is embodied in the facts of Scripture, we cannot but believe that the record of this massacre teaches more than the well known cruelty of man, or the sudden and bitter disappointment of tenderest and holiest hopes ; we must believe it reveals some truth grandly consonant with the intent of all Scripture to bring to light the hidden things of the Kingdom of the Lord.

OF THE REVELATION OF THE BLESSEDNESS OF THESE CHILDREN.

It is reasonable to think this truth is related to the revelation in this Scripture, that those children are in Paradise. It does not reveal this in terms ; and to have done so would have broken the law of silence as to the dead, which runs through all Scripture ; but it gives this impression, and even as to the first martyr, Revelation gives no more. In the Bible, as in life, when the eye would follow the dying saints, a cloud receives them out of sight.

Let us try to see how St. Matthew gives this impression ; for if the attempt should fail the fact will remain. Though fully to analyze a painting may

pass our skill, yet the further we look into his working toward the effect he produces, the more sure we
are that we feel as the painter would have us feel.
With less than a divine courage, St. Matthew might
have feared to put the Massacre of the Innocents into
a chapter whose design is to set forth the glory of
the Lord ; but far from trying to disjoin his Birth
from the Murder, he joined them as closely as he
could. The foundation fact of his Gospel is named
only in the story of this Pilgrimage : " Now when
Jesus was born in Bethlehem of Judea, there came
to Jerusalem Wise Men, saying, Where is He that
is born King of the Jews, for we have come to worship Him." This single, this incidental mention of
His birth is indeed remarkable ; and though it cannot be the only reason for this, yet assuredly one of
its reasons was, to join closely to the Birth, the Pilgrimage. Just so closely he joins to the Pilgrimage,
the Murder : " Now when Herod saw he was mocked
of the Wise Men, he was exceeding wroth, and sent
forth and slew all the boys in Bethlehem and the
coasts thereof." The flight of the Magi was the occasion of this decree, but they fled because they were
told from heaven to fly. The Magi, not knowing
what would come of their flight, were innocent of
blood ; and may it not reverently be said, that in
commanding their act, God, in some sense, took upon
himself this consequence of it. Thus, from his first
line throughout, the Evangelist so writes that all
shall feel that if Christ had not been born, those
children had not died ; that as truly as their murder
followed the wrath of Herod, and this the flight of

the Magi, so truly it entered into the determinate counsel of heaven. This calm boldness, that so thoughtfully and clearly points out the Birth of the Lord and the Divine warning as the superhuman antecedents of an event so black and terrible on its human side, shows how fully the Holy Spirit made St. Matthew feel that Death is the minister of God, doing his bidding.

Yet the Evangelist's tone is not cold. He brings out all the wonder and pity of the death of these infants, by the figure of the long-buried Rachel weeping for her children; by this striking image he makes the strangeness of the murder felt, while with this he combines the thought that these infants are not motherless where they are gone. The Wife of Israel throws her arms around them. She claims these little ones. They are all safe in Rachel's bosom.

Misled by the fact that Rachel's tomb was nigh to Bethlehem, some have said, that St. Matthew here used the words of Jeremias by poetic license; but he himself says, that he applies them to an event within their prophetic significance. How it was so included is seen when the old prophet's image, which is something quite apart from other prophecy, is understood. It is one of those grand images where the Spirit of the Lord molds, not of lifeless clay but of living beings, prophetic forms that approve him the archetypal artist of painting, sculpture, and poetry. Rachel, sought so long and loved so well, the wife of the last of the Patriarchs, the happy wife, the unhappy mother, dying as she gave birth to the youngest of the Twelve Fathers of the Tribes, the beautiful, the sorrowing Rachel, is transfigured by the Spirit of Prophecy into the sorrowing Angel of her Nation, ever watching and mourning as her people mourn, and never forsaking them in the miseries that befall them because of their sins.

The prophecy embodied in this image is for all time. In the world of the imagination, Rachel is the wakeful mother on whose ear falls every cry of weeping Israel. As that cry is heard, by the rivers of Babylon, in the persecution of Antiochus, when Jerusalem fell, or in the massacres of the Jews in the Middle Ages, ever the voice of the weeping Rachel is heard in Ramah mourning for her children, and refusing to be comforted because they are not. Of old, the Lord said to this mourning Rachel, Refrain from thy weeping, thy children shall come again. This voice of comfort is for all time. Ever when Rachel is disquieted in her grave, the Lord quiets her with this assurance that her children shall come again. The image and the voice abide till Jerusalem is no "more trodden down," till what was typified when the midwife said to the dying mother, Thou shalt have this child also, doth come to pass. To readers familiar with this prophecy, St. Matthew needed but to quote its opening to assure them, that those murdered boys of Bethlehem were safe with the Angel of their nation.

By making the death of the Innocents part of a narrative whose burden is the glory of the Lord, and through the image of Rachel, the Evangelist taught that, truly as the Lord's birth was the occasion of the death of these children, so truly was He their salvation.   He thus revealed, that these flowrets were by Him transplanted from the bleak hills of Palestine to the garden of Paradise : * a truth, no doubt, divinely whispered to the souls of their parents, who tried to believe in God against such seeming cause of unbelief.

OUTLINES OF ECCLESIASTICAL TEACHING AS TO THE HEREAFTER OF INFANTS WHO DIE.

Whenever any Scripture, historical in form, everywhere and at all times gives one and the same impression, it would seem that the impression thus given must be the very truth it was designed to give.   The Christian heart has ever felt on reading the second chapter of St. Matthew, that the Innocents who died in Bethlehem were blessed.   Revealing this, it reveals much more.   It reveals that infants are immortal, and that their salvation is possible ; truths that many will think need no revelation, yet as to which there has been much strange discussion ; and when this Scripture is conjoined with other Scripture, it reveals, that *so surely as those infants slain in Bethlehem were saved, so surely are all infants saved that have ever died.*

The time was, when this assertion would have been

---

* Here a latent correspondence comes to light between the history of Balaam and that of the Magi, in whose history it is not visionary to see somewhat of a contrast, counterpart, and complement to his.   As in the former, so in the latter, the man born in the house of Jacob is Lord alike of the material and the spiritual world, Lord of the starry hosts, and of those whom, unwisely, we call *the dead.*

condemned as heresy: and a brief sketch of some of the facts of the doctrine as to the damnation of Infants, may well precede my argument from the Gospel of the Innocents in connection with other Scripture, in proof that *all infants who die are saved.* Till the fourth Christian century, the doctrine of the damnation of infants dying unbaptized was nowhere affirmed in the Christian Church. It became a dogma of the Western or Catholic Churches, in the fifth century, in the Pelagian controversy. Thence onward to the middle of the ninth century, it was there *universally* held, so far as records show.

Neander's opinion as to the date of this doctrine may be gleaned from these words: " The doctrine of infant damnation, which even from the time of Cyprian had become predominant in the North African Church, appeared to the Pelagians revolting." * Yet even the Pelagian believed, the infants, though free from guilt, could only be translated into the Christian nature by baptism, and dying unbaptized, " though exempt from punishment, were still excluded from that higher state of being, and attained only to a certain intermediate state." If this were not an unimaginative sequence of their denial of a part of the common creed, then, of those beings whom the Pelagians thought of as going to people the spiritual spheres, unstained with guilt, yet incapable of attaining to the life in Christ, there is a felicitous

---

* Dr. Neander's History of the Christian Religion and Church. Translated by Professor Joseph Torrey, of the University of Vermont. Bohn's London edition, vol. iv, p. 433,

picture in the description which the White Lady of
Avenel gives of herself, as—

> Something that neither stood nor fell,
> Something betwixt heaven and hell;
> Neither substance quite, nor shadow,
> Haunting lonely moor and meadow,
> Dancing by the haunted spring,
> Riding on the whirlwind's wing;
> Aping, in fantastic fashion,
> Every change of human passion;
> While o'er our frozen minds they pass,
> Like shadows from the mirrored glass.

Had Sir Walter Scott availed himself of the old
Pelagian notion, and made the apparition an unbaptized daughter of the Founder of the house of Avenel,
the unreality and weakness of the tie that binds the
Spirit to the fortunes of Avenel would not be felt;
and no change would be required to adapt to this her
words on Good-Friday:

> This is the day when the fairy kind
>   Sit weeping alone for their hapless lot,
> And the wood-maiden sighs to the sighing wind,
>   And the mer-maiden weeps in her crystal grot:
> For *this* was the day that a deed was wrought
>   In which *we have neither part nor share;*
> For the children of clay was salvation bought,
>   But not for the forms of sea and air.

Thus, in ways unthought of by itself, genius helps
to interpret Thought. But this fine creation of "the
Ariosto of the North" found as little favor with the
culture of the time of George IV. as did the Pelagian fancy with the Numidian Saints. Those hard
thoughts, that gained for St. Augustine this title—

Durus infantum Pater—the Father so hard upon children, carried the day It was a *hard time.* The vandal was on his war-path; there was fear in Carthage then; and Rome herself with bowed head awaited the inevitable barbarian. Few were the Christians then who could have cared much for the future blessedness of those whom they heartily wished had never been born at all, those savages who were then rifling the shrines of the holy martyrs, burning towers, and murdering priests. Their own children were baptized, and what became in death of the offspring of such, was a matter that could have made no strong appeal to their sympathies at a time when the heathen were ravaging the Christian countries, and the great Augustine lay dead in a town besieged by the Vandals.

I do not mean that at any time after the rite of infant baptism was established, (whenever that may have been,) that it was not much thought of. Even with the newly converted peoples baptism was ever of prime importance.* Of this the best of all evi-

---

* As may be seen from a preface to some of the manuscripts of the Salic Laws, the oldest code of the French ; from which, as given by M. Guizot, in his History of Civilization in France, I quote here and there, not from the lack of earlier evidence of this, but because it is so curious a monument: " The nation of the Franks, illustrious, mighty in arms, noble and healthy in body, of a singular fairness and beauty, bold, active, and fierce in fight, lately converted to the Catholic faith and free from heresy, the Salic Law was dictated by the chiefs of their nation : afterward when Chlodwig, the long-haired, the beautiful, the illustrious king of the Franks, had first received the Catholic *baptism*, every thing in this that was unfitting was amended.

dence is in the fact, that in extreme cases, where no priest could be had, any one might baptize. No consecrated place, no laying on of hands, was then requisite to the validity of the sacrament. Though baptized from the bloody brook by the hands of a slave or a woman, in the ages of Faith often ranking no higher than a slave, the mysterious efficacy of Baptism, whatever it might be, was all believed to pass to the wounded soldier dying in the forest, as permanently and as well, as if the rite had been administered with water fetched from the Jordan in a vase of gold, in the sacred fane, with lighted tapers, the burning of incense, and by priest, or bishop, archbishop or cardinal.

Such, with unimportant exceptions, has ever been, from early Christian times to the present hour, the Christian usage ; and this historical, providential fact, fairly interpreted, is of this high consequence : whatever the efficacy of the ordinance may be, the power to administer it inheres in each and in all of the congregation. It would seem that this fact must at length drive those who call themselves High Churchmen to modify their idea of the intent and efficacy of Baptism, or to confess the Priesthood of all the People. For if their teaching as to Baptism be right, then the Christian Church hath ever declared and

---

"Ionor to Christ who loves the Franks ! May he preserve their :ingdom ! May he protect their army ! For this is the nation which, small in numbers, but valorous and powerful, shook from its head the hard yoke of the Romans, and which, *after having recognized the sacredness of baptism*, sumptuously adorned with gold and precious stones the bodies of the holy martyrs."

affirmed full powers in each one and in all of its People to unlock the doors of the Kingdom of Heaven. In this cheering fact, the finger of God seems to point to a future when all errors as to the rite of Baptism will share the same fate already befalling that dogma of Infant damnation, which is one of the most curious of the many chapters in the long annals of Human Error.

And a dreary chapter it is. For even the Pelagians were almost ashamed of their charitable feelings toward unbaptized infants. This comes out in these words of Neander—where, for the sake of the argument to be presented hereafter, I would have my readers mark the clear intimation of the most learned of the historians of the Christian Church, that his own opinion is, that *Scripture is silent* as to the salvation of dead children: "Pelagius himself shrunk from expressing any opinion as to unbaptized infants: he affirmed that of one thing he was sure, they could not suffer punishment consistently with the divine justice, but what became of them was more than he knew;* doubtless because he was of the opinion, that no distinct declaration on this point could be found in the sacred Scriptures."

The Pelagian controversy covered a good deal of ground; and in it the decision of the question as to infants was incidental to and contingent upon the decision of other questions. Yet the dream of an intermediate state for infants dying unbaptized was

---

* He quotes these words of Pelagius: "Quo non eant scio, quo eant nescio"—Into what they go not, that I do know; into what they do go, that I know not.—*Neander*, vol. iv, p. 434.

anathematized at Carthage, A. D. 418, by a Council of more than common authority, though not a General Council: "The Council of Carthage, in its second Canon, condemned the doctrine of an intermediate state for unbaptized children, on the ground that nothing could be conceived as existing between the Kingdom of God and perdition; but then, too, according to this Council, the eternal perdition of all unbaptized infants was expressly affirmed. It is worthy of note, however, that this particular passage of the Canon is wanting in a portion of the manuscripts."* There can be little doubt this matter then came up; hardly a doubt how it was decided, if decided at all; and as to this, Neander evidently thought the positive evidence outweighed the negative. However this may be, these words of infallible Pope Gregory prove that in A. D. 600 the dogma of infant damnation was received in all the Western Churches: "Some are taken from this present life before they come to have any good or ill deserts by their own deeds, and not having the sacrament of sal-

---

* Comparing statements of M. Guizot, I find, that at a Council not long before at Carthage, and concerning the same matters, there were sixty-eight Bishops present; at this one, two hundred and three. In the interim, Pope Innocent had condemned the Pelagians; and his successor Zosimus had granted them a rehearing, and had written to the African Churches that he was satisfied with their explanations. This did not satisfy the Council. At its instigation the Emperor Honorius issued an edict against the Pelagians as heretics. Zosimus then convened a new assembly; the Pelagians were condemned; and eighteen Italian Bishops, who held with them, were banished from Italy.

vation for their deliverance from original sin, though they have done nothing of their own here, yet they come *ad tormenta*, to torments."* In a Latin Treatise, *De Fide*, On Faith, which from the sixth century down near to the time of the Reformation, (that is, for a period of eight or nine hundred years, and in a time when books were so few that a book might be a more trustworthy monument of opinion than it can well be now,) passed current among the clergy as a convenient and authoritative compend of the faith, there is this spiritual direction: "Most firmly hold, and doubt not in the least, that the little ones quickened to life, whether still-born or born alive, if they pass from this world without the holy sacrament of Baptism are punished with the everlasting punishment of eternal fire."†

Yet, on the other hand, while from deference to the authority of St. Augustine and other of the Latin Fathers, the Schoolmen would not disavow this dogma, they softened it in a way that has been ridiculed by some, who have not caught their meaning. With their characteristic subtilty of thought, the Schoolmen described that fire where these infants

---

* The History of Baptism. By William Wall. Oxford, 1844. Vol. ii, p. 206.

† Milman's Latin Christianity, book iii, chap. x, gives this sentence from *De Fide*, as quoted by Vossius, Hist. Pelag., p. 257. In translating, I have softened the Latin in the third line, the rest is literal: " Firmissime tene et nullatenus dubites, parvulos, sive in uteris matrum vivere incipiunt et ibi moriuntur, sive cum de matribus nati, sine sacramento sancto baptismatis de hoc seculo transeunt ignis aeterni sempiterno supplicio puniendos."

were, as a dark fire that would not burn. From this we should learn that they thought of hell-fire not as a material flame, but as the burning anger of God ; and that such infants were deprived of the light and warmth of his countenance. Yet all mothers felt it was hard for little children to be shut up forever in a dark place. Even this milder exposition of the doctrine contradicted the mercy of the human heart as flatly as it seemed to contradict the nature of fire. Ever the ecclesiastical dogma of infant damnation was undermined by human feeling and common sense : and in the Council of Trent there was some disposition to anathematize those who held that the human *nature* deserved damnation ; an opinion of St. Augustine and the Latin Fathers, revived in all its original sternness by the Reformed ; and of which the doctrine of the damnation of infants has seemed to many a logical consequence.*

---

* "The Orthodox" asserted that, "*without* baptism, none could be saved. It was allowed, indeed, by the Schoolmen, that the wish (*votum*) to receive baptism might avail, in a case of impediment to the actual reception of it. The blood of martyrdom, too, was supposed to flow with regenerating efficacy. For thus had the Holy Innocents been baptized in blood : the sword of the murderer consecrating them to the Saviour, for whom they unconsciously suffered. But, as no wish or vow of receiving the rite could be conceived by the infant, it was impossible that dying unbaptized—humanity may shrink at the recital of such a tenet—it could not escape the punishment due to Original Sin."

In the above, Bishop Hampden (" The Scholastic Philosophy," lec. vii, p. 328) speaks first of the time of the Pelagian controversy, but the citation covers the whole period that has here passed in review. It is noteworthy as giving the curious evasion of the difficulty in the way of the salvation of the Inno-

Luther was a monk of the Augustinian order, the Reformers were not as well read in the Greek as in the Latin Fathers, and they shaped their philosophy of the human nature not so much in accordance with the earlier teachings of the former, as with those that, after the Fourth Century, and through the mind and will of St. Jerome and St. Augustine, prevailed in the West. Under Luther's direction, Melanchthon drew up a Confession of Faith presented to the Emperor Charles V. at a Diet, holden in 1530, in the old town of Augsburg. This was the model of the creeds of the Reformed. It is substantially that of the Lutheran and Moravian Churches now. It teaches that "After the fall of Adam all men descended one from another after a natural manner," that is, all save Christ Jesus "have original sin; and we mean by original sin, that which the holy fathers do so call, namely, that guilt whereby all that come into the world are, through Adam's fall, subject to God's wrath and eternal death. This original blot is sin indeed, bringing eternal death upon them that are

---

cents of Bethlehem by those who, forgetting that the Apostles and Prophets and Patriarchs were not baptized, hold that without baptism there can be no salvation. The learned Bishop in the last sentence could not but have had in mind some of his own communion who had recently asserted the damnation of unbaptized infants; and, perhaps, some high Churchmen, who, malignant in error, and ignorant of Church history, had denied the validity of baptism by Dissenters;—the case being then recent, of charges against an Episcopal minister for suffering a child to be buried in consecrated ground who had been baptized by a Methodist minister, brought in the ecclesiastical courts, where the validity of the administration of the ordinance was, of course, sustained, and the suit dismissed.

not born again by baptism and the Holy Ghost." This the source from which the Ninth Article in the Creed of the Church of England is derived. That Article, adopted in 1801 by the English Churches in the United States, declares, "that original sin in every person born into this world deserveth damnation." In 1643 Parliament convened the Assembly of Divines who drew up the Westminster Confession; this was approved by Act of Parliament in 1645: also by the General Assembly of the Church of Scotland, and is now the Confession of the Scottish Churches in the United States. It declares that original sin "doth in its own nature bring guilt upon the sinner, whereby he is bound over to the wrath of God and curse of the law, and so made subject to death with all miseries spiritual, temporal, and eternal." The Savoy Confession, drawn up by the Congregational Churches in London in 1658, approved by those in Massachusetts, at Boston, in 1680, and by those in Connecticut, at Saybrook, in 1708, has the same words. The Confession of the Seven Baptist Churches of London, in 1646, holds "that in consequence of the fall of Adam his posterity are now conceived in sin, are by nature the children of wrath, the servants of sin, the subjects of death and other miseries, unless Christ doth set them free." The Confession of Belgium and Holland, published in 1563, in French and in Dutch, runs thus, in almost the very words of the treatise *De Fide:* "We believe that through the disobedience of Adam the sin called original hath been spread through all mankind. It is an hereditary evil wherewith even the very infants in their mothers' wombs are polluted, and it is alone sufficient for the condemnation of all." The Confession of the Reformed in France, drawn up at a Synod in Paris, in 1566, and presented to Francis II., declares, "We believe that all the offspring of Adam is infected with the contagion which is called original sin : this is indeed sin, because it maketh every man, not so much as those little ones excepted, which as yet lie hid in their mother's womb, guilty of eternal death." The Confession of the Swiss Reformed, in 1566, approved by the Reformed of Savoy, Poland, and Hungary, declares "that man was in the beginning created in righteousness, but falling from goodness became subject to sin, death, and divers calamities : and such as he became by his fall, are all his offspring ; by death, we understand, not only bodily death, but also everlasting punishments due to our corruptions and to our sins." The Synod of Dort was convened in 1618–19 by the States General of Holland. James I. of England, as the head of the English Churches, by his embassador and by letters urged its convocation. By invitation of the States General, some eighty eminent theologians from other countries were present. Among them were an English Bishop, and two Presidents of Colleges of the English University of Cambridge ; these three signed the Article of this Synod declaring, "that all men sinned in Adam and became exposed to eternal death ; that God would have done no injustice to any one had he determined to condemn them ;" and anathematizing all who teach that no one on account of original sin is liable to be damned.

THOUGHTS AS TO THE DOCTRINE OF ORIGINAL SIN.

That birth-fault whereby all partake of the common misery of a nature inclined to evil, and incapable of holiness, without the help of some power from without, working within and abiding in the soul, is the fact which theologians set forth by the name of Original Sin :—a name not now to be changed for another. The explanations that have been offered of the fact, together with the consequences deduced from it as so explained, are things quite different from the fact itself. It is possible to reject most, or all of those explanations, and to deny some of those consequences, and yet to hold firmly to the fact. Its affirmation, as truly as any other, is the article of a standing or a falling Church. To yield it is, in the end, to yield every other distinctively Christian fact. As to this fact, all experience is at one with the Scripture. It seems to have been the Divine Will that all history should proclaim it ; and if something of burden and misery is about to be lifted from the world, (of which there seem to be omens,) it may have been sufficiently taught by the sin and misery of all the past. As to the reality of the fact, no language can be too strong; and the social consequences of holding to this truth are only less momentous than the religious consequences.

But against the way in which this fact was long explained, and against some conclusions that have been drawn from it, the Christian reason now reacts so powerfully as to warp its perception of the fact itself. Let us then relieve it of the odium of the name—Total Depravity, as now used. This is a close rendering into English of a Latin phrase used by the Schoolmen ; and yet it now means something quite different from what it meant in the Latin. Its current meaning is, that man is as bad as he can be, which would seem to do away with the difference between men and devils. But this was not at all the meaning of the Latin phrase. It affirmed that all alike, the mighty and the mean, the Chatelain in her castle, the Crusader bound for Palestine, the King at his coronation, the Judge in his ermine, the Priest at the sacrament, were stained with the same human guilt ; that none were born free from a depravity *total in this sense*, that there was no one whose nature needed not the healing of the blood of Christ. *It embodied the truth through which the Spirit of the Lord protested against the military and priestly aristocracy of the Middle Ages.*

In this sense it was uttered by many, who, could they have foreseen them, would have little desired the changes it was to bring about. For the human conscience, touched by the Spirit, at last made true response to this truth. It was long seemingly inoperative as a social power, yet when its appointed time was come, it began to change, and it is now changing, the face of the world. Though kings and nobles remembered not the nakedness of their birth ; and denied the dishonor of the grave ; with heraldic blazonries, and banners drooping above their tombs, in death affirming they were knightly and noble ; yet at the bidding of this truth the barbaric vaunt of social and ecclesiastical Feudalism slowly, but for-

ever, retired; and through this truth Christ called
the People into Being—a creation which resembles
the creation of Man in this, that man was created in
the Age of mighty and great Beasts, who were to
pass away from the earth before him.

•It is true, that His calling the People into being
is to be ascribed to His whole ordering of the affairs
of men, clear back through all time, and was not
brought about by any one truth, but rather by all
of His truth; that the sum of all this is the Cross,
and only in the light diffused from it can that sick-
ened estate of man by nature be clearly seen, the
seeing of which is a condition precedent of soul-
health, which is the root-meaning of the word salvation; and true, that man's pride will hardly suffer
him to confess the sin-sickness of his soul till pride
is given up at the foot of the Cross; and yet it is
also true, that while all Christian truths combine
their power, each Christian truth has a sphere, and a
work, and a history of its own.

This is very often such as the foresight of man
could never foreknow. For a Christian truth sown in
human hearts is like a seed planted in the mould,
which puts forth the life that is quick within it, and
though its germination may be imperceptible, difficult, and long, draws to itself the means of its growth,
till at last there is a tree wonderfully different from
any thing which it seemed could grow from out the
seed. From the Truth of the evil estate of man by
birth, it looks as if there might come the humility of
the individual; but who could ever have foreseen that
from it would grow the mighty tree of Liberty, under

whose overshadowing branches the nations are to repose? Yet so it is. For in all the other facts of human
life, in all save what Byron calls "the hard decree,
the ineradicable taint of sin," there may be occasion
for a feeling of difference among men; and the entire
reasonableness of equality before the Law, without
which there can be no perfect Christian society, is
clear to the heart only when, feeling its evil by nature,
it knows that all are alike in the sin that is born with
us; a truth before which the boast of heraldry is
dumb, and kings and nobles are the relics of the un-
christian past.

The silently gathering experience of ages becomes
a mighty enduring power, when some divine decree
embodies it in multitudes of men. Coming thus, it
comes to stay. In the fullness of its appointed time,
at the close of the Feudal Ages, the truth those
Ages were commissioned to teach as to the evil
there is in man, a truth for whose evidence there was
needed this Christian experience in addition to all
heathen experience, was embodied in the People. A
sense of their long suffering in the past, mingled with
the sense of their present suffering, till the miseries
of starving serfs, of prisoners without trial tortured
to death in dungeons underground, all the before
voiceless wrongs of a thousand unhallowed, lawless,
guilty years, then came forth in a cry that deepened
into the thunders of battle.

Democracy was not born of the assertion of rights,
but of the Christian denial that by any law of birth
any human being can inherit rights not common to
all human beings. With a due sense of the birth-sin

of all, no one would assert these for himself, or suffer their assertion by Bonaparte or Bourbon to the common harm. Democracy denies that any hereditary and personal right can inhere in kings, nobles, or priests, because they are men. Yet that democratic feeling which was born of the doctrine of original sin is utterly hostile to anarchy, is easily content to accept governments that are monarchical in form, if they derive their powers from the common assent, and wield them for the common good ; for its humble sense of the human infirmity makes it grateful for human good conduct, and wisely tolerant of imperfection and error. When feudal power would give no hope of the redress of intolerable wrongs, when it avowed it would hold its slaves forever, only then has this democratic sentiment, by a divinely irresistible impulse, been transformed into belligerent force. When Philip of Spain, in violating the right to worship according to the conscience, forbade religion on pain of death, *then* his patient vassals, the long-enduring, slow-moulded Dutch, broke down their dykes. It was only when Charles Stuart denied to the peaceful, law-abiding Puritan the rights he valued as the bulwarks of liberty of conscience, that the Puritan no longer on his knees supplicated corrupt priests conspiring with licentious nobles, rose to his feet, drew his sword, and, affirming he was " noble by the right of an earlier creation, priest by the imposition of a mightier hand," appealed to the Lord of Hosts ; and prelates and princes became as the storm-scattered chaff of the threshing-floor, when the Lord answered the Puritan out of the whirlwind of battle.

The doctrine of Original Sin, like all other Christian doctrines, is of social as well as of religious power; and where it is thoroughly taught and learned, those changes which nothing can stay will be beneficial; but where it is not taught and not learned, there the inevitable ascendency of the working-class is fraught with inevitable destruction. Born of this doctrine, Democracy must be nurtured upon it, or it will become death unto death. They who think the world would get on without Christianity, would do well to consider the difference between a people who, in humility receiving and profiting by this doctrine, honor God by works of mercy, justice, and love as they are taught to do in the Gospel of Christ, and those peoples whose souls are poisoned and maddened by the conceits of infidelity. As a Parisian truly said, It was not petroleum that set fire to Paris, but materialism.

The historical origin of the explanations which St. Augustine gave of Original Sin, and which as introduced by him were generally and long held, the consequences deduced from the doctrine as thus explained, the revival of those ancient theories at the Reformation, and the silent changes of thought since that epoch, which, almost without open argument, have altered some of those opinions, although they still hold a place in the Creeds and Confessions handed down from that period, open wide and inviting fields of inquiry, where much yet remains to be learned. They cannot now be traversed. Apart from all supposed explanations of it, and from a single point of view, somewhat of the importance of a common belief in the evil there is in the human nature has been set forth, that the fact itself—known from experience, from observation, and from Scripture—might not seem to be denied or under-rated in the following

ARGUMENT IN PROOF OF THE SALVATION OF ALL INFANTS WHO DIE.

We call that man dead who is alive no more to generous impulse or noble feeling, from whose soul all higher, better life is gone, on whom there seems to have passed what, in the fearful language of the Written Word, is called *the second death.* From his lower plane of feeling and thought, and in the fierce delirium of his passions, such a man, losing sight and memory of the higher life that once was his, may seem to himself more alive than ever; while the friends of his youth, remembering what he was, think of him as dead :—so, remembering Adam as made in the holy, divine image, the Bible speaks of that lower darkened life, into which his children are born, as death. Of this birth-fault of all of the human race, the Scriptures plainly teach that the sin of Adam is more than the antecedent. But, on the questions touching the relation between them, much of the speculation has been merely the audacious running out of one line of thought to farthest extremes; the sole fact that human nature is the same as that of Adam,* after his fall being taken as its point of starting. Such narrow thinking is wholly inadequate to

* See note on page 233.

compass this relation and the consequences that depend upon it.

It was said to Adam and Eve, "In the day thou eatest of the forbidden fruit thou shalt surely die ;" yet they lived, as to their bodily life, for many years after their transgression. No children were born to them before their fall, and so on this suspension of the full force of the edict the whole relation between the birth-state of the human family and the sin of Adam depended. Adam and Eve seem first to have known that the death of their bodily life would not be an immediate consequence of their sin, from these words to their Tempter: "I will put enmity between thee and the woman, between thy seed and her seed ; it shall bruise thy head, and thou shalt bruise his heel." Such seems to have been the fact, so far as the record goes to show ; and as to this, its silence is to be considered as well as its speech. Thus in the sacred hieroglyph of what took place in the Garden of Eden, the suspension of the full force of the edict of death is revealed in the prophecy of the Son of the Virgin ; and, to a mind open to the way in which, in the Scriptures, truth is embodied in facts, the plain teaching is, that had not the Incarnation entered into the divine foreknowledge, Adam and Eve would then have died, and there would have been no human race. On the Life of the Lord, therefore, depended the living of the children of Adam.

One man may now, in some degree, determine the condition of another. By one man poverty, or disease, or dishonor may come to another man without his knowledge ; and even death may come without his will. This seems very hard, and yet none will deny the fact. It is a universal sweep of this elsewhere partial law, that certain evils of our mortal state are consequent upon Adam's transgression. Yet, on the face of the record it seems to be clear that these consequences would not have been permitted ; it seems to be clear that Adam and Eve without children would have died, body and soul, at the time of their transgression, had it not been for Him, foretold as " the Seed of the woman "—a hope-inspiring oracle, darkly clear, yet never cleared up, till Christ was born of the Virgin. Hence, it would seem that *there would have been no infants, born but to die*, had not God predetermined to send his Son into the world. Our birth-fault, then, the common calamity of the race of man, that which theologians call Original Sin, would not have been, irrespective of the common mercy in Christ Jesus.

Does this view of these facts prevent the common mercy of God in Christ Jesus, which it sets over against the common calamity, from being a free gift ? Does it change this grace into a thing of right ? Undoubtedly it does, if you place the divine purpose after the birth of Cain ; but not, if you place it where it belongs, before man or the world was made. For whether such beings as men were to be born, depended on the purpose of the Father, and of the Son, and of the Holy Ghost, to offer to them all, life in their death. It depended on the divine determination of the Holy Trinity to offer them salvation from their lost and evil estate through the agony of Gethsemane, the blood of the Cross; which purpose must be held to be wholly of grace, as it is to be regarded as antecedent to the existence of the children of Adam, and as their existence depended wholly on the divine will.

That the state in which all the children of Adam are born is really more hopeful, and in this sense better, than that in which Adam was made, would seem to be a true inference from the facts, that sinning once, he suffered the penalty, while his children, though sinning many times, may yet lay hold on the hope set before them in Christ. And if it be said, this does not meet the case, because only part of the children of Adam have the Gospel, the reply is, in this full sense of the word, patriarchs and prophets knew it not; and if their imperfect knowledge of it sufficed for their salvation, how dare we so limit the power of the Creator of man, as to say that a knowledge of so much of His mercy as may avail to give life to the soul that is born with us, may not be given to every one? Who hath so read the Divine, or even the human breast, that he can intelligently affirm, that even with God this cannot be? Who shall dare to say the Almighty cannot graduate down his truth, retaining the essential life-giving, to the heart of a savage, or a child? Is it not uttered in the same breath that reveals the pre-existent eternal Being of Christ, is it not written on the same page that declares His universal creative glory, He is the true light which lighteth every man that cometh into the world?

The true explanation (which is almost purely historical) of the once common Doctrine, that the birth-fault of the children of Adam is their punishment because they sinned in him, together with the various modifications of it, cannot here be given. All that can here be said of this philosophizing is, that in trying to look into the permission, reason, or explanation of this birth-fault, it does not sufficiently regard the most important of all the facts in Scripture which are related to it; namely, that had the birth-estate of the human family been that of the righteous, unfallen Adam, there could not have been that manifestation of the Divine Nature into whose mystery of Grace the angels desire to look. It is written, " The Scripture hath concluded all under sin, that the promise by faith of Jesus Christ might be given to them that believe." *

Limiting now our view of these great matters to the bearing of the facts that have been made prominent, on the fate of Infants who die before they sin " after the similitude of Adam's transgression," there is seen the same relation between them and the Life of the Lord, that was seen between the children in Bethlehem and his Life. The certainty and the reason of the salvation of the children in Bethlehem is in the relation of the Life of the Lord to their living but to die. Because of his Life those few lived but to die. So did the many. The relation, then, of the deaths of all children to the Life of the Lord is the same as that of the deaths of the children in Bethlehem. If, then, those children were saved, all children that die are saved ; and as those children were saved, all the children who have ever died must also have

---

* Gal. iii, 22.

been saved. As surely, then, as those boys in Bethlehem are in Paradise, so surely all dead children are
now in Paradise.

The fact, then, in Bethlehem was permitted to be,
and the Divine Record of it preserved, that through
this Wonder and Sign in connection with other
Scripture, there might be a certain knowledge that
all children who die are saved ; a clear and certain
knowledge that all such children are now with Christ
the Lord, whether children of Seth or of Cain, whether of Jew or of Gentile. The conclusion to be drawn
from this Scripture is broad as the fact of death in
childhood. Had there been among those boys slain
in Bethlehem some boy of Egyptian, or Chaldean, or
Scythian blood, could there have been any doubt of
his salvation ? They were Jew boys, slain by the
sword of a Jewish king, seeking among them to murder the Prince of the House of David ; yet back of
this, the occasion of their murder was the act of the
Representatives of the Nations. Here the breadth of
meaning in this tragedy begins to open. All partial
ideas as to Israel, all narrowness of thought as to
Christian paternity and baptism, are rebuked by the
spirit of this chapter, which throughout is that of
universality. Its scope is unlimited as that of the
universe. It pertains not to Judea, but to the world ;
not to Abraham's children, but to the human race.
It is one page from the unrevealed history of the
grace of God to all nations. Its lessons are pre-
eminently lessons for the whole race of man.

Back of the sword of Herod was the flight of the
Magi, and back of this the Divine Command telling

them to fly. The Evangelist holds back the veil, and the Almighty is seen altering the course of human events so that the death of these children shall come to pass. Antecedent to the cruel purpose of the king, he makes known the counsel of Him who, through the laws He hath pre-ordained, and through His ordering of all human affairs, worketh all things after His own will ; the determinate wisdom of Him who said to Cyrus, the Persian, "I create evil." God put an end to the lives of the children in Bethlehem by the sword of Herod ; and by agencies such as He saw fit to use—by the earthquake, by pestilence or war, as well as by the diseases of which so many children die—He has done the like in the case of the greater number of all the children ever born ; and since, in the case of the death of the child who dies by fire or water, by the rage of man or brute, by carelessness or ignorance, by accident or disease, the Lord's life is the divinely foreseen condition without which they had not lived but to die, it follows as surely as in the case of those children to whose lives God put an end by the sword of Herod, that "where sin did abound, grace much more abounding," God, for Christ's sake, gives to all such children life ever-lasting, life which is life indeed, for this death in temptation, sin, and sorrow.

> Hosanna to the Prince of Light !
> Who clothed Himself in clay,
> Entered the iron gates of Death,
> And tore the bars away !

One of the causes of the fact, that the salvation of all who have died in infancy has not been an article in the creeds of the Christian Churches, may have been in some lack, heretofore, of clearness of insight into the way in which doctrines are interwoven with the facts of Scripture. The reason why Infant Salvation was not revealed in such express and clear terms that it must have been an article in those Creeds, may have been that, in a world so full of sin and misery as this has been, such a revelation must have tended to infanticide. The Living Word, who in framing the human heart there set strong safeguards of infant life, would hardly have formed the Written Word so as to tempt to their breaking down. It might be that He would not permit the silence of his oracle to break into speech till the time had come when the truth, as to the salvation of all infants who die, might be harmlessly uttered. There are terrible household crimes in Christendom that awaken the doubt whether that set time even yet has come ; but if not, the discovery, here made known, will abide till in some happier, holier future, it take hold on the Christian mind. The light of the Divine Revelation to man is ever miraculously graduated to the human eye and the human need. The Divine Spirit presides over this, alike, in the case of individuals and of generations. There is ever shining from His Scripture into the world of man all the light that man can bear. Of this there is evidence in the fact, that while its revelation of this truth has never before been verified to the Christian intellect, it has ever been sufficiently clear to the Christian heart. This fact foreseen may have been one of the reasons why it was not uttered in unmistakable words. For the

Christian feeling as to the salvation of infants has heretofore met the wants of the Christian heart, and with no evil attendant upon it. In despite of erroneous philosophizing, the Christian heart, touched by the tenderness of Christ's words as to children, has ever known that when God takes children out of the world he takes them in mercy. It may not have thought to extend this to all the infants who have died, but within the scope of its own experience it has ever felt this. And the individual Christian heart can hardly do more than this, in the way of verifying to itself many of the world-wide truths of Scripture. Thus, if in the all of history, or even in any important period of history, it tries to discern the Divine mercy, or even the Divine will, it may only bewilder itself in the darkness of seeming confusion rather than rejoice in the light of order; and yet within the sphere of its own experience it may be able to see what it cannot trace out in the world-wide plan. What it thus feels is true of its own little circle, it may still feel must be true throughout all time and all space, though it cannot think this out. The very attempt to do this may rather tend to overpower the feeling; and yet in this feeling there is true wisdom, and, essentially, all the knowledge of this truth that ever will be known. In the like manner, the heart of the mother who feels that her own infant, lost to her, is with the Lord, may feel that other lost infants are safe with Him, even though her mind may have been schooled into a seeming acceptance of the doctrine that by the Will of Him, whose tender mercies are over all the works of His hands, all dying heathen infants pass out of misery into misery. The horror of infant damnation, as thus urged upon her, may bewilder and trouble her; yet the Grace that, through her sense of the tenderness of the Lord toward little children, quieted her sorrow for her own child, quiets this in the same way; or else calls her mind back from it, and forbids her thinking of it at all.

What her heart thus teaches the Christian mother beside the lifeless body of her little child, seems to have been the feeling of the Hebrew as well as of the Christian heart. For King David must have believed in the salvation of his dead infant when he said, " I shall go to him." *   The words of our Lord, " Suffer little children to come unto me, and forbid them not, for of such is the kingdom of heaven," † have ever encouraged and cherished that same feeling toward dying children, which made the royal penitent put away from him all signs of sorrow when his child had passed away : and whatever of error may have clouded the Christian intellect in this matter, the Christian heart has ever affirmed the truth that has just been shown in Holy Scripture.

That there is divine wisdom in the reserve of the Bible and in the gradual outshining of more and more of its exhaustless light, is beyond all doubt. It is equally beyond all doubt, that the Word of God to man will ever give sufficient answers to all proper questions touching His government; and give to all human sorrow its appropriate consolation. This is taking very high ground as to the Bible. But this is

---

* 2 Sam. xii, 15–23. † Matt. xix, 14; Mark x, 14.

the ground that all true Christians have always taken, which they always will take, and which they can defend.   If this be so, then assuredly the Bible is the everlasting oracle of the human family.

Its assurance of the salvation of all infants who die, clears up much of the darkness that broods over the past and over the present world.   As at least one half of all those that have ever been born have died in childhood, more than half of all those that have ever been born are now in Paradise ; and this is the fact, although in all past ages the heathen have been, even as they now are, the great majority of the children of Adam.

In the sayings of our Lord there are depths on depths of knowledge.   All see something of what his words mean, but who can see all that his words meant to Him?   When He took little children in his arms, when he blessed them, and said, " Suffer little children to come unto me, and forbid them not, for of such is the kingdom of heaven," all must see his love and tenderness ; all may see that He recognized in them traits that would mark his disciples ; but it required the experience of ages to see that He may have thought also of the fact, that they who would come to him in childhood were ever to be the greater number, even in His Church on the earth ; and it required the full comparison of all the language of Scripture to see that He may also have thought of the fact, that of children not grown to the stature of men, his kingdom on earth would be, till some great cycle of that kingdom had rolled away ; and it may be He then also thought, that of such

little ones as he held in his arms were the greater
number of those whom He himself, passing as a conqueror through the Gates of Death, was soon to visit
in Paradise.

AS TO THE SECOND CHAPTER OF ST. MATTHEW, IN CONCLUSION.

The revelation of the Salvation of the greater number of those born into this world of sin and sorrow is
most appropriately inwrought into the Evangel of the
Wise Men, because they were the Representatives
of the Grace of God to all nations. Their office
gives great antecedent probability to the idea that
world-historic signs would be wrought before them,
and great truths come to light in their history. For
those Magi of Persia were not only the Representatives of the Grace of the Lord to all nations, but they
were also the Witnesses of his Grace for all the nations. As from time to time this idea of the office
of those Wise Men has risen before us, it may have
seemed to some that while their Representative
office may be readily accepted, those men who, unthought of, come to Judea and suddenly depart, leaving no trace of themselves in the known history of
their own generation, and with no record save a few
lines by St. Matthew in the next generation, cannot
be called Witnesses for the nations; yet in this same
thing their history is in accordance with the ways of
God. It is written, the Kingdom of Heaven cometh
not with observation, or, as better translated, is not
ushered in with parade. This secresy of their Witness at the first, in the little village, the lowly dwell-

ing, the depths of the night, is in harmony with the
ways of Him whose glory it is to conceal a thing,
that the soul of man may search it out.

Divinest things often seem very small and faint in
their beginnings; but at length the Divine Word
cometh forth out of Darkness into Light that Darkness overtakes no more. As from the cloud the lightning shines from east to west suddenly, so before the
end of the first Christian century the Witness of the
Wise Men shone from beyond the Euphrates to the
shores of Spain. We cannot fail to be struck with
its permanence of interest, as well as its universality.
While the Church was converting Europe to Christianity, it told of nothing, save the Cross, that took
more ready hold on the nations. It raised them from
idolatrous prostration before the host of heaven. It
seemed a personal pledge of the tender interest of
the Lord in far-off wanderers in the night of heathenism; and in many ways the deep impression made
by this history on the mind and heart of Europe may
be seen down to the end of the Middle Ages. At
that world-changing epoch, the whole idea of the
heavens was so changed that it might be said, the
old heavens passed away. Did the interest of the
history of the Wise Men pass away? It had fired to
ecstasy the devotion of ages that beheld the heavens
of old; but when the new astronomical heavens
were seen, then only could be known the highest
glory of the fact to which the Magi witnessed for all
coming time. This higher glory will suffer no dim-
inution, no change, save that of increase, so long as
the heavens shall endure.

WHAT THINK YE OF CHRIST? is a question very near to the heart of the present age. Its thought turns to Him as the Son of man with more appreciating earnestness of consideration than ever before. The Religious Thought of this century seems absorbed in the wonder of His Humanity, as that of the fourth century was in the wonder of His Divinity; but a true idea of His Humanity is impossible without a true idea of His Divinity. We cannot attain to a true idea of the Redeeming Lord until He is known as one and the same with the Creating Lord, the great Truth symbolized at His Birth in the Bright and Morning Star.

INDEX.

ANALYTICAL AND EXPLANATORY.

———————◆———————

ABEL AND CAIN. Representatives of True and False Religion, 44.

ABRAHAM. A New Time Cycle began with him, 15, 48. Date of his Call, 17, 20. See Gen. xii, 1–4. His Religion the same as that of Melchizedek, 19. Battle at the Springs of the Jordan, 24. Offering of Isaac, 194, 208. Misrepresentation of, in Lange, 5. His Seed as the Stars in number, 208–211. See also Gen. xii, 1–4 ; xiii, 14–16 ; xv, 1–18 ; xvii, 15–22 ; xxii, 1–18.

AMMONITES. Joined with the Moabites in the calling in of Balaam, 7.

AMORITES. Their defeat by the Israelites, 30, may have led to this policy, 7.

ANACHARSIS CLOOTZ. Referred to, xxxviii. A profane eccentric Prussian, who took for his surname that of an old, wandering Scythian philosopher ; styled himself "the orator of the human race ;" figured in Paris in the opening scenes of the Revolution ; elected member of the National Convention in 1792 ; guillotined in 1794.

ARABIA. Sometimes used as the name for the deserts adjacent to Palestine, 6, 7.

APOSTLES. Chosen as Witnesses to the Life of Christ, they complete the volume of Inspiration, 97.

ASTROLOGY. The Art of Divination by the Stars. Belief in, universal in Asia even now, 81. Example of, in Europe, at the birth of Louis XIV. of France, (A.D. 1638,) 82.

ASTRONOMICAL DOUBTS AS TO CHRISTIANITY. Statement of, 213. See Table of Contents, Chap. VII.

ATHEISM. Atheism and Pantheism come to much the same thing, 121. Atheism the only alternative for Christianity, xxx, xxxi. Evanescence of the present forms of Scientific Atheism, xxvi.

BALAAM. Unwillingness of some that his history should be interpreted to the people, 8. References to, by Philo and by Josephus, 8 ; by Stanley, 8 ; see also 48, 49. Error as to the derivation of his name, 5. The date of this reaches back to the Targums, but they avoid the objection stated by saying his birth-name was Laban—for this there is no Scripture warrant, and see, 59, line 11, n. Boundaries of his World, 16. Of Shemitic race and language, 17. His religion and that of Moses, the same in origin, 26. A prophet, in the Oriental sense of the word, 21. From the Sacred East—this one of the causes of his influence in the West, 20, 34. He is, however, called in Josh. xiii, 22, a Soothsayer, a term nearly equivalent to Wizard, and compare Num. xxii, 7. His knowledge of the history and religion of Israel, 20-32. Worship of Jehovah, 26. The conditioning of his prophetic upon his human intelligence, 35. Relation of his prophesying, to the end of his Cycle of Time, 32-36. His Definition of Religion, 43. His mission, 38. Character, 45–48. Of the writing of his Oracles, 59. How they may have come into the hands of Moses, 59, 60. His death, 58,60. Allusions to Balaam in the New Testament, 75. In the Old Testament, there are, or may be, allusions to his words in Judges xi, 25 ; 1 Sam. xv, 29, 1 Sam. xiv, 47, 48, compared with Num. xxiv, 18 ; 2 Sam. xxiii, 1, and Prov. xxx, 1, with Num. xxii, 24 ; Hab. i, 13, with Num. xxiii, 20 ; Obad. 3, 4, 17–19, and especially, Jer. xlviii, 45, with Num. xxiv, 17. See essays by E. C. Robbins, Bibliotheca Sacra, May and November, 1846. See, also, Oracles of Balaam.

BIBLE. With it is, 202, 203. Reasons for its historical form, 315–320. Its revelation of the World-Plan : early example of this in the Oracles of Balaam, 51, 52. Inspiration includes Revelation as one of its elements, 95–98. The Gift of the Sacred Writers only, 96, xxxviii. In the Bible a Divine Inbreathing xxxiv, xxxv. How communing with the Written Word may be communing with God, 95. Of the Human and the Divine element in the Book, whereby it is an intelligible and an everlasting Oracle, 265, 266. Of the universality of its tone, 205. With it there is Superhuman Power, xli. One of the media of the influences of the Holy Spirit, 207. Our Lord ascribed to words of Hebrew Scripture the same power to bind the conscience as to its own, 97. The Bible reveals glimpses of scientific truths, xx–xxiii, and teaches social as well as religious truth, xl, xli. It sows broadcast seeds of truth of many kinds, whose origin is often unthought of, 205. See, also, 172, 173. The foundation truth of all natural science sure only from the Bible, 205, 207. Of the Truth in the Old Testament, as indispensable to the full and true portraiture of the Word of God, as "made flesh and dwelling among us," 246, 247. A Translation the most perfect of all comments on the original Scriptures, 63–65.

and the Pantheistic. Its causes, a pride of knowledge which aspires beyond all possibility, and a dislike to the thought of the Maker of the World, the Father of man, before whom the Human creature must bow in adoration. See 121–125, compared with 262, 263, and 185, 186 and 247–250.

HEROD. The secret of his policy in making the Wise Men his agents in finding the Child, lost, in losing sight of their rank, 287.

INFANTS. Outline of Ecclesiastical teaching as to the Hereafter of those who die, 326–337. Argument in proof of the Salvation of all Infants who die, 344–355.

INNOCENTS OF BETHLEHEM. Herod's decree putting those to death, 315, reached to male children only. There could hardly have been more than 5,000 people in the bounds it specified, and the number of Boys slain, hardly more than 50. Yet, Milman states, the "Greek Church canonized 14,000 Innocents; even later Jeremy Taylor, in his Life of Christ, (A.D. 1651,) admits the 14,000 without thought." For the Reasons for the Silence of Josephus as to this murder and other facts in the Gospel History, see "The Church and Science." Andover, 1860, pp. 278–279.

INSPIRATION. A word of wider meaning than Revelation. The gift of the Sacred Writers only, 95–98. Dangerous use of this word in any other sense, xxxviii, See also, 95. Thoughts on Language and Inspiration, 91–101.

JOHN. The prelude to his Gospel, 181–183. A different rendering of its third verse, 317. This changes the pointing only : it joins the last three words of the third verse, namely, *that was made*, to the next verse. As those words now stand in the English version, they seem to be superfluous.

JORDAN. Grotto-sanctuary at its fountain, sacred to the heathen god Pan, 3.

JOSHUA. The Greek form of this Hebrew name is Jesus ; hence the name, 156, line 1, compare, 4. On the day of the battle of Bethhoron (or of Gibeon) when the sun stood still, the greatest sign, not in the heavens, but in the man, 131–134.

KINGDOM OF HEAVEN. This Title, official, 162; found in St. Matthew only, 161, in the other Gospels, translated, as it were, by Kingdom of God ; probable reason for this, 161. The Heavens a comment on this Title, 163–165. Its relation to the oldest of the Divine Names, 165–169. Its space-extent, to the spiritual in Israel, 176, 177.

KORAN. A witness to some few facts of early Scripture as preserved in the memory of the Desert, and interwoven by Mohammed (A.D. 570–632) into the Koran, 25.

this people and that by turns." Whether so or not, the Moabites and the Midianites (all akin and of one language) were then in close alliance ; and, so far as the wandering tribes recognized such authority, Balak was king over them all. These facts go to show what might have been the military effect had Balaam been suffered to lay the Israelites under a religious *interdict*, and of themselves are sufficient to justify what is said, note 38.

MIRACLES. The Divine Supernatural may act through and in conformity with the laws of the natural, 309, and use their help, 310, 110. This may, in some degree, have been the fact even in Prophecy and Inspiration, 99, 100, and 240, line 15, and 256, compared with 268, 269, also 33-36. Economy of power one of the characteristics of miracles, 110, 111 ; 12, 312, line 16. Three Great Classes of Miracles, 128, 129. Allusions to that of the Flood (Gen. vi, vii, viii), 9, 10: The Confusion of Tongues (Gen. xi,) 10-14: Of the Sun (Josh. x,), 131-133, also 111. At the Red Sea (Exod. xiv), 110, 131, 26 : The Destruction of the Assyrian army, (2 Kings xix) 135-140: The Sun-Dial of Ahaz, 2 Kings xx) 111 : Darkness over the land of Judea (Luke xxiii, 44, 45), 111. At Cana of Galilee (John ii,) 298.

MOABITES. Some of their characteristics, 30, also 27, 28.

MOTHER OF OUR LORD. The Worship of Christ by the Magi consequent upon Her Faith, 293-298, and the Miracle at Cana of Galilee, 298. See also, 87, 103.

NAMES. The most ancient and universal of the Divine names revived by Christ Jesus in the title of the Kingdom which He proclaimed ; which, supplying the ellipses, would read—The Kingdom of the King of the Heavens. This, found only in St. Matthew's Gospel, should be compared with the equivalent Title in the other Gospels—The Kingdom of God, 165-169.

NATURE-WORSHIP. Its two forms ; prevalence and power ; the Divine purpose to do away with it, 119-128.

OG. Legend of this giant in the Targum of Palestine, 7.

ORACLE OF BALAAM. The term rendered *parable* in the English Version, Num. xxiii, 7, might, perhaps, have there as well been rendered—oracle. It is used for the speech of Job, xxix, 1, for Proverbs, and in other places, as Psa. xlix, 4, but not for the writings of the Hebrew Prophets. Possibly, a Moabite term, that came into the Hebrew from its use in Numbers. As to the Star, the meaning of Balaam's oracle must, in certain respects at least, be the same to us that it was to those who heard it, 63-66 ; how that meaning can now be ascertained, 66-70; interpreted by the Jews as predicting a Star, 70, 71 :—See Star of Our Lord. It was

my mind this is settled by this fact. It is the feller of the Sacred Cedars who is dead, and this was Sennacherib. He was murdered in the temple at Nineveh by two of his sons. 2 Kings xix, 37 ; Isa. xxxvii, 38. See 135–140. In this book the bearing of only one fact upon the *fitness* of this miracle has been pointed out ; much more would need be said to bring out all there is in Scripture by which this might be illustrated.

STARS. Hebrew idea of the heavens and the stars, 171, 175. Explanation of Judges v, 20. "They fought from heaven ; the stars in their courses fought against Sisera," 175.

STAR OF OUR LORD. Foretold, chap. 11. One of the stars of heaven, chap. 111 : argument to prove this, from the word, Star, 78, 79 ; from its use by the Evangelist, 87 ; bearing of his method on this, 83–87. Error, that it was a conjunction of planets, see this Title ; error, that it guided the Magi from the East, 79 ; error, that it was not seen after they left the East, till they went to Bethlehem, 80–87. Its disappearing—of evil omen, 82. The rejoicing of the Magi not because the Star unexpectedly reappeared, 89–107. Its Guiding not inconsistent with its being a Star, 107-111. Its Creation, 158, 159. This Star, the occasion of the personification, see (177, 178,) I am the Bright and Morning Star, Rev. xxii, 16. Its place in the universe, 179, 180. Significance of its appearing, 160, 197. The regaining of the lost knowledge of this Star, perhaps, possible, 188. The loss of this knowledge is an argument against the fact that the Magi beheld a Star, but is not one of much weight. The Magi, as astrologers, were as familiar with the face of the starry sky as astronomers now are. Otherwise they would hardly have felt sure that what they discovered was in fact a new star—unless, indeed, it came out close to one of the planets or to one of the few well-known stars, such as the Polar Star. Had such been its place, they might have identified it to others, so that its place would have been easily and long remembered. But, if an astronomer now points out some one star, not in a place such as has just been named, is it probable that the person to whom it is so pointed out can single it out again, on the next night?

TARGUM. The Captive Jews were among those whose speech was so like their own, that they learned it, yet, so unlike, that their own Scripture ceased to be understood ; and as it was read in the synagogues, a word-of-mouth interpretation of it was given. This was known as—THE TARGUM. It dates back to Ezra's time, but was written out some two hundred years after Christ. This unwritten, *memoriter*, oral Scripture is important as bearing on a like oral

Gospel. See 145, 146. On Moses, the Targums are, that—of
Onkelos ; of Jonathan, or of Palestine ; and of Jerusalem :—the
two last may not have been distinct works. The Targums on the
rest of Scripture are not of equal antiquity. That of Onkelos is
a close translation ; the others are paraphrases, in which are in-
woven legends and fancies of the Jews :—see 7, and, Rod of Moses.
Substantially, these three give the interpretation of Moses, in
Judea, in the Apostles' day. They were translated (1862) by the
late J. W. Etheridge, an English scholar of the Wesleyan persuasion. 1. As to Balaam, they say—"secret mysteries hidden from
the prophets were revealed to him :" compare 8. 2. Where the
Hebrew says, Amalek was first of the nations, 5, they go on to
say—who made war on Israel? This mere conjecture, like some
in later criticism, obscures a fact of value. For that the Amalekites
once held the rank given them by Balaam (who speaks of the past)
is probable enough in itself, and the fact bears on the antiquity of
the power of Egypt. See, also, 23, where a like fact is noted.
3. All the Targums *conceal the Star*, though they bring out the Messianic meaning of the Oracle : as thus :—"Meshiha, the Power—
Sceptre of Israel, will bring to nothing all the children of Sheth."
This may seem to conflict with 70, 71 as to the meaning of the
Oracle to Jews of St. Matthew's day ; but may not this *conceal-
ing* of the Star have been caused by the Second Jewish war (see
70, note) and by the effect of the Second of St. Matthew on the
spread of Christianity? See 141–143. 4. As Etheridge proves
in pages of much value, an idea of the Word of God, like that in
St. John, runs through the Targums. So, too, through the
writings of Philo-Judæus, contemporary with St. John. He said,—
" The eternal Word of the everlasting God—from the center to
the extremities, and from the utmost limit to the midst, pervades
the long range of nature, binding together all its parts. For
the Father who begat Him hath made Him the indissoluble bond
of the universe." Philo and other Jews of Alexandria, spoke
Greek, and his ideas as to the Logos, or Word of God, are often
said to have been Platonic. It were hard to find them in Plato.
But they are in the Targums. When the Jew of his day read the
opening of St. John's Gospel, he read of truths not unknown to
him, until he came to this,—" The Word was made flesh and dwelt
among us, and we beheld his glory as of the only begotten of the
Father." The bearing of this on what is said, 247, line 3, will be
clear to all, and also on the organic unity of the Bible, which is
one of the many proofs that the Spirit presided in and over its
formation.

THE END.

The Wise Men:

WHO THEY WERE, AND HOW THEY CAME TO JERUSALEM.

By FRANCIS W. UPHAM, LL.D.

WE place at the head of our notice of this book, by the request of the writer, this opinion of his late brother,

Prof. THOMAS C. UPHAM,

the eminent metaphysician, well known to the Christian world :

" This book throws much and satisfactory light upon a hitherto obscure and unsettled subject. The title, however, fails to give an adequate idea of the richness and extent of its contents. Its careful reader, especially one who takes an interest in the origins of human thought and belief, will not fail to find himself rewarded with instruction of a very rare kind."

We also call attention to these words of

ABEL STEVENS, D.D., LL.D., the Historian of Methodism.

" It shows thorough historical knowledge of the period and localities of its theme, and extraordinary critical power, with equal candor in the treatment of the difficulties of the subject. None of these are evaded. This unusually interesting and important book, though suited to the highest critical demands, is well adapted to the popular mind, and should be in our Sunday-school libraries and families. It proves that the faith of the Church is as intelligent as it is, to the unbeliever, mysterious ; "

1

"The author has exhausted the historical and scientific learning upon his subject. His book establishes the historical reality of what many regard as only a poetic legend;"

And to this frankly honorable and noteworthy statement of Dr. DEEMS, in his admirable "LIFE OF JESUS:"

"This book is the first successful attempt that I have seen to clear up this pilgrimage; after reading it I canceled what I had before written on the subject."—*Note on page* 46.

A Readable Book for All.

The Publishers believe that learned books need not, necessarily, be dull or obscure. It is true that common readers generally turn from such books; but it is because so many of them are written as if they were meant only for scholars. We think the time has come when the historical and doctrinal questions touching Christianity ought to be, and can be, so treated that the people can pass upon them intelligently; and that it would help the truth, and make scholars more thoughtful and more wise in their thinking, if they more felt they were addressing the sober sense of the people. The writer of this book has steadily kept in view "the silent yet ever inquiring common mind;" and has tried to put all his readers in a position to judge of what he says. Any person of ordinary intelligence can understand his book; and if our ministers will give the assurance that it is not beyond the common capacity, they will find that it will be read, and read with interest and with profit. The way to shut out bad books is to encourage the reading of those that are good.

Difficulties as to the Second Chapter of St. Matthew.

How did the Magi know the star was the star of the King of the Jews? A great astronomer opened the way to answer this question more than two hundred years ago, and at last the answer has been clearly drawn out. How came the tyrant to give such honor to strangers asking a question so provoking his wrath? By pointing to the adjacent Parthian Power, by briefly proving that under its rule in Persia the Magi held on to their old rank, and by laying his finger on a fact in the youth of Herod before unnoted in this connection, Dr. Upham

2

gives a well-proven answer to this difficulty. So also to the caviling of Strauss and others of this chapter, as countenancing astrology or divination by the stars. But while these and other questions were not fully ànd clearly answered, many came to regard this chapter as the first Legend of Christianity; and the venerable Dr. Tholuck well said, of " The Wise Men : " " This book ought long since to have been written." The Duke of Somerset, in a recent book published in this country, which professes to give "the opinions now prevalent among the cultivated classes " in England, says, they " feel themselves justified in discarding this portion of the Gospel from authentic history." Stanley, Dean of Westminster, in a paper read before an association of clergymen, gives it as his opinion " that the truth of the Gospel History is now more widely doubted in Europe than at any time since the conversion of Constantine." In view of such facts, the clearing up of this chapter is more important than the finding of the Moabite stone.

Dr. Norton's Rejection of this Chapter from the Gospel.

In the Unitarian controversy, by the side of Dr. Channing stood Dr. Norton, Professor of Sacred Literature in Harvard University, a man whose rare scholarship was acknowledged by the critics of both hemispheres. Dr. Norton, though of a school of criticism then regarded by its Orthodox opponents as destructive, was of a reverential spirit, and his opposition to the Transcendental Infidelity is to be held in remembrance. Yet in his work on the Genuineness of the Gospels Dr. Norton spoke of this chapter as a "strange mixure of astrology and miracle:" and in his Translation of the Gospels, published in two octavos at Boston, 1862, he degraded this chapter from its place in the Gospel into an Appendix to the Notes in the second volume. This was Dr. Norton's dying challenge to the Orthodox. Translating its twenty-first verse, his pen stopped forever; the other two verses were translated by another. To this challenge the theological schools of Princeton, Yale, and Andover, with whom much of his life was a conflict, ventured no reply. England and Germany gave them no real help, and they answered not a word.

During that long controversy we, as a Church, had no trouble with that Rationalism, or spirit of unbelief, which is now very common ; nor have we ever suffered from it at any time hitherto, nor do we suffer now ; and yet we are firmly persuaded that in the future we can only be secure from it by great earnestness in Christian work. While some Christians crowd on the walls to gaze on the new engines brought for the destruction of Zion with an eagerness of curiosity that looks, to her assailants, like applause, and tends neither to quench their conceit nor cool their zeal, it the more becomes our Church to welcome every thing that defends the Bible and opens more of the wisdom of the Word of God. In this spirit we have acceded to the wish of some of our ministers and laymen, that we should bring out an edition of this book, together with another by the same writer, and we earnestly commend them to all Christians.

PHILLIPS & HUNT,
805 Broadway, New York.

4

DR. TAYLER LEWIS,

AUTHOR OF "THE SIX DAYS OF CREATION."

I have no hesitation in saying, of "The Wise Men," it is a remarkable production—of remarkable excellence, I mean. It is learned, original, instructive, and most suggestive. The dissertation on the East and the Far East is important, clear, and, I think, accurate. The chapter on the Persians must have the highest interest for readers of every class; and the application of it at the end, in the argument respecting the worship the Magi paid to Christ, is to my mind triumphant and conclusive. The chapters on the connection between the Magi and the Chaldeans, and the Magi and Daniel, open evidence for the inspiration of the Scriptures which is in a great measure new. . . . The book exhibits not only learning and talent, but that higher thing, genius. *There is hardly a page on which we are not startled by something strikingly original, while at the same time leaving upon the mind an impression of its profound truth.* Scriptural ideas are set in a new light. Passages in the Gospels, which have been passed over as having little interest, as well as many similar parts of the Old Testament, are presented in such a way, and in such connections, *as to give them a power and a freshness unperceived before. Whoever reads this book must acquire a new interest in the study of Scripture.*

The subject discussed presents a field on which few have ventured, and to a certain class of minds there may be suggested the question: How is the essential Christian truth concerned with our knowing who the Wise Men were? The reading of the book at once supplies the answer. There is a deep interest in connecting the Messianic idea with nations other than the Jewish; in showing that primitive revelation, though specially preserved in the religious history of one people, sent its early rays far beyond their narrow bounds, and that *the advent of a redeeming Messiah, was in fact a world idea.* It is this especially that gives to the third chapter, in connection with that on the relation of the Persian to the Jewish religion, *a transcending importance* for all who believed in a true historical kingdom of God on earth.

REV. CYRUS HAMLIN, D.D., LL.D.,

THIRTY YEARS A MISSIONARY RESIDENT IN ASIA MINOR; PRESIDENT OF ROBERT COLLEGE, CONSTANTINOPLE.

MESSRS. EDITORS: Will you allow me to call attention to a little book entitled "The Wise Men," by Dr. F. W. Upham. *Not only is the subject oriental, but the book is also, to a singular degree, in its substance, breadth, and spirit, an oriental product. I know not that Dr. Upham has ever even traveled in the East, but his book leaves the impression of its having been written by one who has resided there.* This Magian aroma doubtless results from his thorough study of the subject, and from a consequent nice and delicate apprehension of things very remote in time and place from all our common spheres of thought. The subject itself, in its relations to Christ in history, is interesting and important. Who were the Magi? If we consider them as belonging to the class so strongly condemned by Philo and by Roman writers, the whole scene, as narrated by Matthew, is incomprehensible. If, on the other hand, as Dr. Upham endeavors to show, they were Persians, then the scene is harmonious, credible, and beautiful. It shows that in those distant regions and ancient times, and outside of Israel, Christ was the true light that lighteth every man that cometh into the world. The sixth chapter gives a new interest to the remarkable life and history of the Prophet Daniel. . . . It is a work of *biblical literature* in its true and best sense; and every minister, or intelligent layman, who loves the study of the Scriptures, will find a rich reward in its careful perusal.— *N. Y. Observer.*

REV. HOWARD CROSBY, D.D., LL.D.,

CHANCELLOR OF THE UNIVERSITY OF THE CITY OF NEW YORK.

We wish to express our sense of refreshment at the appearance of a little book written by a scholar and profound thinker. It is modest and condensed in style, but full of information and suggestion. . . . The author reduces the expressions (in the narrative of Matthew) for the "East" from a vague to a specific import. In a very masterly and convincing manner he shows that the plural and singular ἀναταλῶν and ἀνατολῆ are not used in an indiscriminate way, but conform to the Hebrew Mizrach and Kedem, and are the Far East and the East, and that these were to the Jews of Matthew's day geographical designations, the Far East representing the Medo-Persian country beyond the Zagros mountains, and the East, Babylonia. . . . Apart from the main argument, we prize the volume for its healthy tone, its common sense, its true manliness as it deals incidentally with the questions of inspiration and interpretation. There has been such a confined atmosphere of pseudo-philosophy around us of late on these matters, the carbonic acid of diseased breathings and sulphuretted hydrogen of undigested learning, that it is a great relief to reach the oxygen again.

We commend Professor Upham's chapter, on "The Relation of the Persian and Hebrew Religions," to that profound historian, Agassiz. It may lead him to be a little more modest in his statements as to Jewish traditions.*—*N. Y. Evangelist*, Jan. 20, 1872.

---

* Undoubtedly the Chancellor refers to words in the oration, a few weeks before, at the Humboldt Centennial at Boston. This was widely read, the eulogist being as well known as him he eulogized. After stating what Humboldt did for science, he tried to shield his friend from the charge of Atheism. Pressed by the difficulty of this, he seems to have forgotten the many learned clergy who were there to show their appreciation of science, and did not expect such stuff as this: Humboldt " had too much regard for truth, and knew to well the Arian origin of the traditions collected by the Jews, to give his countenance to any creed based on them."

6

MRS. MARY S. ROBINSON.

Among religious American works we can recall but few which, while preserving the severity of their scholarship and the solidity of their thought, are adapted to the intelligent reading public; such, for example, as "The Interior Life," by Professor Thomas C. Upham, a book which obtained a wide circulation in our own denomination some years ago, and still finds place between the Bible and the à Kempis of many a devout Methodist.

A monograph from the pen of Dr. Francis W. Upham, a younger brother of the above-mentioned venerable scholar, deserves to take rank among the very best of the class of books to which we have just alluded. Its topic is religious; the inquiry evinces protracted study and profound learning; yet it is so far a popular book that no intelligently religious person can fail to read it with delight. We know of a young lady, claiming no more than an average capacity for reflection, who affirms that, to her surprise, her attention did not flag through the earlier chapters—in which the argument is developed—and that she fairly held her breath for interest as she read the concluding pages. On account of this rare adaptation, and of other combinations of merit, some of them equally rare, this treatise deserves a place in our standard religious literature; and as the works of the senior Upham were widely read by our Church people, we could wish that this production of his brother may also receive a welcome proportioned to its excellence. The latter possesses the simplicity, the luminousness of the former, and an endowment of genius distinctively his own. His book, though by no means voluminous, evinces a freshness and wealth of thought suggestive of a well-nigh exhaustless mental reservoir, and a tendency of its thought-currents to flow out in self-discovered channels. . . .

Throughout this inquiry we are conscious of being led by a guide endowed with rare spiritual illumination, discernment into the Scripture, and a skill of collation and interpretation of its texts such as no writer has possessed—none that we can now recall—since Robertson of Brighton left us his wonderful sermons. . . . Thoroughly evangelical, it is thus mentioned in a Review by Professor Brigham, one of the most learned of Unitarian scholars : "Even to those whose faith is different, the reading of a treatise so reverent, so wise, and so gentle in its spirit, cannot be without profit."—*Christian Advocate.*

REV. C. H. BRIGHAM, (Unitarian.)
PROFESSOR OF ECCLESIASTICAL HISTORY.

. . . The union of the critical faculty with a devout imagination is not common in our time. Yet occasionally we meet with writers in whom the critical faculty is aided rather than hindered by the imagination, and whose sight is made insight by the soaring of their thought. This possible union of devout imagination with scientific analysis, without injury to critical candor, is proved very strikingly in a small book just published on "The Wise Men of the East."

7

. . . The legal training of the author shows itself in the clearness of statement, the arrangement of the argument, the steady logical progress, the accurate references which gave chapter and verse for every citation, and the judicial calmness with which the work goes on. In this respect the book resembles the famous book of Dupin, on " The Trial of Christ." Every thing here is well considered. There is not a rash or random word. With a wealth of research, with notes as full and as rich in variety as the text is close to the subject, the impression is always of sincere work ; that all is for the illustration of the subject, and nothing from the vanity of authorship.

The second chapter of the volume is an exceedingly close and ingenious discussion of the meaning of the word ἀνατολῶν, by which Matthew characterizes the place from which the Magi came. . . . If patient pleading and the collation of historic and archæological facts can establish so nice a proposition, an excellent *prima facie* case has certainly been made out. The argument, too, is justified by the use of language in prophecies of the Hebrew Bible. . . .

The orthodoxy of the writer does not, that we can see, prevent his impartial examination of the story, his appreciation of its difficulties, or his admission of the objections against it. He could not treat a classic myth more fairly. . . .

This volume will be, to all who read it in sympathy with its faith, most interesting and fascinating. It belongs to a class of which we have too few specimens in our life of sensation and intellectual conceit. —*Christian Examiner*, No. cclxxvi, pp. 259-270.

From an Editorial in " Zion's Herald."

THE WISE MEN : WHO THEY WERE ; AND HOW THEY CAME TO JERUSALEM.

Under this title, Professor Francis W. Upham, LL.D., of New York, has recently issued a little volume of more than ordinary fascination. Its key-note is struck in its opening sentence: " There is a spirit that believes, and yet inquires." It is devoted to an investigation of the visit of the Wise Men to Jerusalem in search of the King of the Jews. The author well says that this wonderful pilgrimage will be none the less instructive for being better understood. Even the most elaborate Life of Christ, or most extended commentary, can scarcely more than hint at the varied proofs of the historical character of the Magian story. Only in the special monograph, like the present, can the event be considered in all its bearings, and the ages, and languages, and literatures be made to give in their strangely confluent testimonies.

Professor Upham is the youngest brother of Dr. Thomas C. Upham, so well known as the author of a system of Mental Philosophy, and other works. His father was for several years a member of Congress from New Hampshire. A brother, of note as a judge in the same State, died last year. He was himself educated for the legal profession. His legal training has admirably fitted him for the task of weighing evidence, harmonizing discrepancies, and summing up opposing arguments. . .

8

From a Critique in the Christian Intelligencer.

Ancient tradition makes the wise men Arabs. And Dr. Lange, in his great Commentary—the most recent exegesis of the Bible—says: " The particular part of the East from which they came cannot be determined." Dr. Upham has satisfactorily demonstrated their nationality, and the geographical region from which they came. . . .

As a whole, the work in style, method, and interest, ranks among the finest productions of English classical literature. It is a model for investigations of the kind. No one can read it without feeling a new interest in the Bible and the Saviour it reveals.

The Watchman and Reflector.

The first question, of course, is that which the title indicates, Who were these men ? The answer is decisive, emphatic, and proven : Magi from Persia. The reasons for the answer are drawn out with wonderful clearness. So far the simple words lead the way. But in order that such a visit from Persian Magi should seem credible, it was necessary to go farther yet. Accordingly, the character and religion of the Persians are briefly but graphically portrayed. Here the author shows a research and power of analysis unsurpassed by any of the scholars of the Old World. . . . No one who takes it up will willingly lay it down till he has seen the end.   Z.

The Evening Post.

It exhibits a scholarship elegant, searching, profound. It evinces the rare quality of an acute analytic power allied with the imagination. Its style is flowing, elegant, musical. The subject is treated from a position of " orthodoxy ; " but mild, gracious, not forbidding, characterized by the spirit of untrammeled inquiry, and the enthusiasm of belief; by power and freshness of thought, and by adoration.

The Hartford Post.

If a pot of old coin is dug up in the ruins of some forsaken city, the telegraphic wires quiver round the world, announcing the great discovery. But here is a discovery of quite another kind !—the solution of a historical and religious mystery. It is announced so quietly that we do not realize what a great fact this is. . . . This book meets the enemy in the gate. We recall our childish impressions of this Pilgrimage— our more mature ideas were not much better. We recall our very picture of the Magi ; of the bowed forms of three giant-like old men ; men of little account ; a sort of Fakirs or fortune-tellers wandering from a very great but indefinite distance, lonely, humble, tattered, and forlorn, in their long, dusty, graceless and travel-stained gowns, turbaned and sandaled ; wandering, they know not whither, to find the King of the Jews. Who were they ? Whence came they ? How could they learn of the King of the Jews by a star? and what was the King of the Jews to them ? What the book seeks to prove comes out point by point, till nothing is left to ask for. This old story of the Magi is made alive again, as with felicitous touch, and in brilliant coloring, Dr. Upham paints for us picture after picture, till we feel that these grand old Persians stand before us, and that the manners, religion, and history of the East are in harmony with this pilgrimage. . . . *It is seldom that learned people take the trouble to bring things within the comprehension of the common people, but this is a book for the people, and they feel it magnetically.* Its sentences are like new coins, just struck from the mint, the lines well cut, clear, and distinct. Any one can see the thought, yet it is often so deep that the longer it is looked into the deeper it seems—as this, "Christianity is often said to be a system of truths, *but even its most mysterious truths are facts.*" A third or fourth reading yet brings out something new. As with the flight of a Parthian arrow, it takes us into the East. The interest deepens from chapter to chapter, and the last, " On the Hebrew Religion," is the best of all. The style has passages of wonderful eloquence. It flows like a swift river, deep and full, yet clear as crystal. . . .

In the light of this unique book we read the thrilling story of the coming of the Wise Men as we never read it before; and in the still night we look with new wonder and awe into the blue depths above, and wish we knew which of all these glittering orbs was the one created to " herald through all worlds, and date through all time," the advent of Him who was the Maker of all the worlds.

The Catholic World.

A book written with sound and solid learning, and originality of thought.

Congregational Quarterly.

The book is a model of its kind. While it explains a mystery, it does so in so pleasing a manner as to captivate the reader.

Methodist Quarterly Review.

Professor Upham has been singularly felicitous in concentrating a large amount of new knowledge and fresh criticism upon a very old and difficult question. This little monograph is not only an original contribution to Biblical literature, but a fascinating book for the inquiring reader.

The Examiner.

The book holds the reader with a wonder that so much solid and varied information can be gathered about a single fact of the record. *Its conclusive answer of one difficulty shows how a great number of objections now urged against the sacred narrative may, by deeper study, become strong defenses.*

10

LETTER to the Author from the late

Professor Morse.

MY DEAR SIR:

I cannot refrain from expressing to you my great gratification in the perusal of your profound, yet clear, investigation of that most interesting event in Scripture history, the visit of the Wise Men of the East to the infant Saviour. The narrative by the Evangelist Matthew doubtless suggests to many minds certain difficulties, perplexing especially to astronomers, in regard to the new and peculiar star; but those difficulties, I have no doubt, are perfectly solvable; and certainly in regard to the country whence the Magi came, and why they were directed to come to Jerusalem, and how they came, your masterly research on these points leaves nothing further to be desired. Accept my warmest congratulations.

With sincere respect,
Your obed't serv't,
SAM. F. B. MORSE.

———◆———

LETTER from a mother in Israel to a lady-relative who had sent her "The Wise Men," and with whose permission it is published. It seems to have been jotted down from day to day. Some paragraphs are omitted, but no word changed. As a life-picture of Christian old age, of a type that is passing away, it is worth preserving.

DEAR L.: When I took up my pencil to write, came this thought—the bush burning but not consumed may illustrate the afflictions of the Church in the world, and of individual Christians. I am now past seventy. How have I been cheered and sustained in my varied life by events explained by Providence! So my soul was joyful in her King.

I have read "The Wise Men" once. I am now reading it again with the notes. *This book will live.* I have just closed the chapter—Kepler's Discovery. My soul is full of wonder, is oppressed with emotions I cannot utter! Ah, I have a poor head! The Wise Men, I had thought of them with *pain*, that such characters—sort of wizards—should come to worship; now these Magi have become brethren to my soul, like Simeon and Anna.

Surely if I understand the times, loving Bible-Christians are few compared with the numbers who are Church-members. They have forsaken the fountain of living waters. The Bible is a dusty book in parlor and hovel. I find myself often saying, Christ *has* a Church, and will keep it to the end. The chapter on Inspiration is so comforting. I take true

11

delight in the thoughts of that book. Truly " the Scripture is a fount-ain, not a reservoir." Each reading I find something new ; a few pages day by day. I want to see that book in every family. I am going to send for six copies. I have a few poor friends I would like to send it to. I keep it here with Bible on my table. *I never saw the care God has taken of his Church, nor felt the ages that have passed, as in reading this book.*

I enjoy much the quiet of my own room, toward the rising sun ; Boston's book on Providence, with Doddrige, Baxter, and Bunyan ; so you see I am not alone. May you be greatly blessed on every side, and at peace, waiting the call of Christ our Lord !

Yours lovingly,   C. M.

12

Publications of Phillips & Hunt,

805 Broadway, New York.

Dr. Porter, says Dr. Wentworth, is a well-known author and authority in Methodist history and polity. The first part embraces British Methodism in 248 pages; the second part contains over 350 pages, and brings American Methodism down to the present time. Bangs's History is too old, and Stevens's too bulky for general circulation, so Dr. Porter steps in and supplies the want with a volume of moderate size, which will be cheap at $2, yet is offered to the public at $1 75, in consideration of a confident expectation of a large demand. Dr. Porter was prominent in the early abolition movements of New England; participated in the General Conference of 1844; made a stout fight against lay delegation; and was cognizant of all the facts and phases of the Book-room troubles, and gives his own views, in a most catholic spirit, on all those questions and usages. Dr. Porter has succeeded in introducing a most excellent volume. It ought to be in every library in the land.—*Christian Standard and Home Journal.*

Rev. J. L. Peck says: The book covers more ground than any other book of its size relating to Methodism. It gives the facts and philosophy of its development down to the present time. . . . The volume contains a large number of *statistical tables*, by which the facts of the growth of the Church in all her departments are of easy access. We advise each preacher and speaker to secure this *treasury of statistics*. By its aid you can *save* a vast amount of time and labor.

The *Congregationalist* says: Dr. Porter's "Comprehensive History of Methodism," in a single 12mo volume of 601 pages, is an extremely convenient, and will be an undeniably useful, one. The story is told for the old country as well as our own, with clear compactness. It is modestly styled by the editor "a convenient manual for facts and dates;" but it is more than this, in that it not only has friendly answers for the frequent questions which almost any student has occasion to ask in regard to a denomination of Christians which rightly holds so large and useful a place in the Christian history of the times, but that it can give a very fair idea of the spirit which pervades and animates the Methodist body. We wish we had so good an equivalent volume upon Congregationalism.

Dr. Fuller, of the *Atlanta Christian Advocate*, says: Dr. Porter has the happy faculty of condensation. But few writers are able to crowd so much matter so satisfactorily into the same space as he. Here we have, in a 12mo volume of 601 pages, a history of Methodism in Europe and America, from its rise to the General Conference of 1876. But few would have ventured upon the task of performing such a work, and still less the number who would have succeeded as well as Dr. Porter has done. The amount of matter crowded into its pages is surprising, and though brevity is necessarily studied at every point, it is not a mere dictionary of dates or historic fragments, but connected, readable, entertaining history.

Dr. Porter is the first to attempt to write the history of Methodism in the dark days of 1844–48, including the abolition controversy in the Church; and, for the space occupied, he has done well, giving the clearest and most correct view of those times with which we are acquainted. It is worthy of the Church, and especially adapted to our southern field. Our people will find in this volume much to aid them in forming a correct opinion of the controversies between the North and the South upon slavery and kindred topics.

The *Pittsburgh Commercial* kindly avows: This handsome volume is appropriately named "A Comprehensive History of Methodism," as it gives in a compact manner information to the general reader which no other work of this character contains. Dr. Porter has the elements of character eminently to fit him for this work. The work is concise, synoptical, statistical, and racy. It is *worthy of a place* in any library, and people of all denominations will find valuable statistical tables, etc., suitable for all classes

Israel in Egypt; or, Egypt's Place among the Ancient Monarchies. With Two Hundred Illustrations. Heavy tinted paper. By Edward L. Clark. 8vo. $5.

From Bethlehem to Calvary. By Faith Latimer. Illustrated. 16mo. 90 cents.

Rivers and Lakes of Scripture. By W. K. Tweedie, D.D. Illustrated. 16mo. $1 25.

Domestic Life in Palestine. By Mary E. Rogers. 12mo. $1 75.

Geography and History of Palestine. By F. G. Hibbard, D.D. 12mo. $1 75.

Our Country : Its Trial and Triumph. By Geo. Peck, D.D. 12mo. $1 50.

Land of Shadowing Wings; or, The Empire of the Sea. By Rev. H. Loomis. 12mo. $1 25.

Land of Promise. By John Kitto, D.D. 12mo. $1 25.

Glimpses of our Lake Region in 1863. By Mrs. H. C. Gardner. 16mo. $1 50.

Jamaica, Enslaved and Free. 18mo. 50 cents.

Rome and Italy at the Opening of the Œcumenical Council. Depicted in Twelve Letters written from Rome to a Gentleman in America. By Edmond De Pressensé, D.D. 12mo. $1 50.

Rome: Its Edifices and its People. 12mo. $1.

On Holy Ground. Travels in Palestine. By Edwin Hodder. 12mo. $1 50.

History of the World. By C. Barth, D.D. 12mo. $1.

History of the Hebrew People. By George Smith, F.S.A. 8vo. $3. Half calf, $4 50.

History of the Gentile Nations. By Rev. G. Smith, F.S.A. 8vo. Sheep, $3. Half calf, $4 50.

The Great Republic, from the Discovery of America to the Centennial, July 4, 1876. By Jesse T. Peck, D.D., LL.D., one of the Bishops of the M. E. Church. 8vo. With 34 Steel Engravings. Cloth, $4. Sheep, $4 50. Half morocco, $5.

Selections from British Poets. Illustrated. 12mo. $1 50.

Exiles in Babylon; or, The Children of Light. By A. L. O. E. Illustrated. 16mo. $1 25.

Heroines of History. By Mrs. O. F. Owen. 12mo. $1 25.

Summer Rambles in Europe. A Series of Sketches of Life and Travels in Great Britain and upon the Continent. By Alexander Clark. 12mo. $1 25.

Home Views of the Picturesque and Beautiful. Sixty-eight splendid "Home Views," engraved on steel by the best American artists. Imperial octavo, printed on beautifully tinted paper. Turkey morocco, gilt edged, and beveled boards. $15.

Illustrated Historical Sketches. By Annie Myrtle. Square 16mo. 61 Illustrations. $1 50.

Heroes of Methodism. By Rev. J. B. Wakeley. 12mo. $1 75.

Women of Methodism. By Rev. A. Stevens, LL.D. 12mo. $1 50. Gilt edge, $2.

Poems on Moral and Religious Subjects. By Anne Lutton. 12mo. 50 cents.

Quotations from the Poets, Moral and Religious. By Rev. William Rice. Sheep. 8vo, $2 50. Half calf, $4. Superfine, illustrated, tinted paper, morocco, gilt, $7 50. Morocco, antique, $9 50.

Sayings of Sages. 12mo. $1 50.

Thy Voyage; or, A Song of the Sea, and other Poems. By Rev. E. F. Burr, D.D. $3 50.

Life Among the Chinese. By Rev. R. S. Maclay. 12mo. $1 75.

Life Among the Indians. By Rev. J. B. Finley. 12mo. $1 75.

Child's Sabbath-Day Book. Square 16mo. 45 cents.

Arts of Intoxication. The Aim and the Results. By J. T. Crane, D.D. 16mo. $1 25.

Bridal Greetings. With Marriage Certificate. By Rev. D. Wise. 24mo. 50 cents. Silk, $1.

Publications of Phillips & Hunt,

805 BROADWAY, NEW YORK.

FIFTY YEARS A PRESIDING ELDER. By Rev. Peter Cartwright, D.D. Edited by Rev. W. S. Hooper. 12mo. Price, $1 50.

LIFE AND LETTERS OF BISHOP HAMLINE. 12mo. Price, $2 25.

LIFE AND TIMES OF BISHOP HEDDING. By D. W. Clark, D.D. Large 12mo. Price, $2 25.

MEMOIR OF MRS. SUSAN HOWARD. By William Chapin. 18mo. Price, 35 cents.

LIFE OF REV. BENJAMIN ABBOTT. By John Ffirth. 18mo. Price, 55 cents.

ASBURY AND HIS COLABORERS. By William C. Larrabee. Two volumes. 12mo. Price, $2 25.

LIFE AND TIMES OF ASBURY; or, The Pioneer Bishop. By W. P. Strickland, D.D. 12mo. Price, $1 75.

LIFE OF JOSEPH BENSON. By Rev. R. Treffry. 12mo. Price, 80 cents.

BOEHM'S REMINISCENCES. Historical and Biographical. By. J. B. Wakeley, D.D. 12mo. Revised edition. Price, $1 75.

BOLD FRONTIER PREACHER. A Portraiture of Rev. William Craven. By Rev. J. B. Wakeley, D.D. 18mo. Price, 50 cents.

AUTOBIGRAPHY OF PETER CARTWRIGHT. Edited by W. P. Strickland, D.D. 12mo. Price, $1 75.

LIFE OF WILLIAM CARVOSSO. 18mo. Price, 75 cents.

BIOGRAPHIES OF CELEBRATED WOMEN. With twenty-eight splendid engravings on steel, executed by the best American artists. Imperial octavo, printed on beautifully tinted paper. Turkish morocco., gilt edge and beveled boards. Price, $15.

Domestic Piety and Family Government.
By Rev. J. H. Power. 18mo. Price, 40 cents.

Episcopal Controversy and Defense.
By Bishop Emory. In one volume. 8vo. Price, $1 20.

Nature and Design of the Eucharist.
By Rev. Adam Clarke, LL.D. 18mo. Price, 35 cents

Annihilation of the Wicked,
Scripturally Considered. By Rev. W. M'Donald. 12mo. Price, 50 cents.

Apology for the Bible.
A Powerful Antidote to Infidelity. By Bishop Watson. 18mo. Price, 45 cents.

Bible and Modern Thought.
By Rev. T. R. Birks, M.A. 12mo. Price, $1 75.

The Chronology of Bible History,
And How to Remember it. By Rev. C. Munger. Paper. 12mo. Price, 50 cents.

Index and Dictionary of the Bible.
A Complete Index and Concise Dictionary of the Holy Bible. By Rev. John Barr. 12mo. Price, $1.

An Introduction to Christianity.
By Rev. J. Sutcliffe. 18mo. Price, 55 cents.

Central Idea of Christianity.
By Bishop J. T. Peck. Revised edition. 12mo. Price, $1 50.

Early Years of Christianity.
By E. De Pressensé, D.D. 12mo. Price, each, $1 75. The Apostolic Era. The Martyrs and Apologists. Heresy and Christian Doctrine. Christian Life and Practice in the Early Church,

Publications of Phillips & Hunt,

805 BROADWAY, NEW YORK.

Apostolic Era;
Or, The Early Years of Christianity. By E. de Pressensé,
D.D. 12mo. Price, $1 75.

Catacombs of Rome,
And their Testimony Relative to Primitive Christianity.
By W. H. Withrow, M.A. 134 Illustrations. 560 pages.
12mo. Price. $3.

Episcopal Controversy and Defense.
By Bishop Emory. In one volume. 8vo. Price, $1 20.

Episcopal Controversy Reviewed.
By Bishop Emory. 8vo. Price, 90 cents.

An Essay on Apostolic Succession.
By Thomas Powell. 12mo. Price, $1 10.

Right Way:
Lectures on the Decalogue. By J. T. Crane, D.D. 12mo.
Price, $1.

Campbellism Exposed.
By William Phillips. 18mo. Price, 70 cents.

Romanism:
Its Decline, and Its Present Condition and Prospects in the
United States. By Hiram Mattison, D.D. 8vo. Paper
Cover. Price, 50 cents.

Philosophy of Religion.
By T. Dick, LL.D. 18mo. Price, 55 cents.

Resurrection of the Dead.
By C. Kingsley, D.D. 18mo. Price, 40 cents.

Ecce Unitas;
Or, A Plea for Christian Unity, in which its true Principles
and Basis are considered. By Eureka. 12mo. Price, 80
cents.

Wesley's Sermons. 2 vols. 8vo. $5. Plain calf, $7. Calf extra, $8.

Wesley's Letters. Select Letters, chiefly on Personal Religion. 12mo. 80 cents.

The Wesleyan Demosthenes: Comprising Select Sermons of Rev. Joseph Beaumont. With a Sketch of his Character. By Rev. J. B. Wakeley, D.D. Large 16mo, $1 25.

Wesley's Journals. 2 vols. 8vo. $5.

Asbury's Journals. Three volumes. 12mo. $5.

Cookman's Speeches. Speeches Delivered on Various Occasions. By Rev. George G. Cookman. 18mo. 35 cents.

Short Sermons on Consecration, and Kindred Themes. By A. C. George, D.D. 12mo. $1 25.

Educational Essays. By E. Thomson, D.D. 12mo. $1 50.

Moral and Religious Essays. By E. Thomson, D.D. 12mo. $1 50.

Fletcher's Letters. 12mo. $1 25.

Lectures and Addresses. By John Dempster, D.D. 12mo. $1 75.

Select London Lectures. By D. W. Clark, D.D. 12mo. $1 75.

Lectures to Young Men. By Rev. D. Smith. 12mo. 75 cents.

Letters to Dr. Smith on Slavery. By John H. Power, D.D. 12mo. $1 75.

Lorraine's Sea Sermons. 16mo. 60 cents.

Formation of a Manly Character. A Series of Lectures to Young Men. By George Peck, D.D. 16mo. 75 cents.

Sermons of Rev. Robert Newton. 12mo. $1 75.

Olin on Youthful Piety. Discourse I. Early Piety the Basis of Elevated Character. Discourse II. Resources and Duties of Christian Young Men. 18mo. 35 cents.

Arthur in America. Addresses Delivered in New York by Rev. William Arthur, of London. 12mo. 70 cents.

www.ingramcontent.com/pod-product-compliance
Lightning Source LLC
Chambersburg PA
CBHW020900130726
47900CB00014B/1303